ON THE TIP EDGE OF A MIRACLE

A MIRACLE IS ABOUT TO HAPPEN!

(1988) "At the beginning of his experience, Dennison felt like someone was shining a bright light, like a large flashlight or car headlight in his eyes. It startled him and, as it did, a voice said to him, 'Don't be afraid, just relax and go with it....'"

(8-17-2001) "Things will continue to escalate in the Middle East. Acts of terrorism will increase a lot. They showed me a building where many Americans are inside, that is bombed and many die. This along with a few other happenings will be enough to draw the U.S. into a conflict."

(8-17-2001) "A major church that has a lot of influence in the world and a lot of political and financial power is not as strong as it used to be in the past.... The Pope dies and the Church falls apart. It loses its power. There's also a scandal that happens before this and that weakens it, something like a sex scandal."

(8-17-2001) "The weather is another thing that will be getting worse. I think because of global warming. The oceans are getting warmer and so is the upper atmosphere. In between where there is colder air, the two mixing creates a circular wind pattern that turns into huge hurricanes. It happens around the same time as the corporation failures."

(8-17-2001) "Something happens to our money. They were telling me something about money is being printed, but there isn't that much gold to back it up. It's like an economy that is built out of assets that aren't really there.... Wall Street goes down. Mortgage companies collapse. Banks collapse. Big, big companies like insurance companies fail, just go down one after another."

(12-22-2004) "I heard someone say, 'Tsunami!,' then I saw this big wall of water come crashing down on a coastal city and the whole area was completely demolished."

(11-17-2010) "They kept showing me the date 2020 and they said it's a date when the earth is natural again. It is when mankind will be living in harmony with the earth.... They told me, 'There will also be three world catastrophes before then that will bring the world to its knees.' They went on to say, 'There are two dimensions coming together now. It's in progress and about one quarter of the way along. It's a very delicate process, somewhat like merging two crystal glasses without shattering them. The year 2020 is when the whole process will be complete; then will come the Golden Age when man will live in harmony with Nature. The world you now know will be gone.'"

(10-20-2010) "The money movers, the big financial people on Wall Street are putting their money elsewhere; they aren't putting it back into our economy like they're supposed to. People won't be able to pay their debts, banks collapse, money is worthless. There is like a mafia, a secret government that wants to rule the world."

(10-20-2010) "There's going to be uprisings: people against people, people against their government. I think it's in another country and not here, but it's going to be pretty bad before they make peace and come together to create something stronger."

(10-31-2010) "They told me a cosmic spiritual awakening is about to happen. Mankind is going to be forced to awaken spiritually...."

(11-7-2010) "There is a growing hunger within mankind for true spirituality. It is there to help us grow. The way we live now, the way we think, is based on greed. So many are only out for themselves. When you give to help another who is in need, you are the one who receives the blessing.'"

(11-7-2010) "A miracle is happening! Only the thinnest of veils is separating you. LET GO OF FEAR, AND LOVE—LOVE YOURSELF, LOVE OTHERS!"

(11-18-2010) "They were telling me those which we call aliens are cosmic beings. They are energy, light beings. They aren't "out there"—they are in other dimensions. They work for the Source and oversee mankind. They manifest bodies when needed. They navigate in and out of our three-dimensional world by using electromagnetic energy."

(11-20-2010) "We are about to experience a miracle! A miracle is about to happen again! At least there is a great potential for a miracle, but first we are in for a rude awakening that will, in the end, bring forth spirituality."

(1-15-2011) "Next I saw a city being flooded, and water is just seeping up the streets and rising higher and higher. It's a huge flood that is carrying cars away right off the road and even houses are floating ... out to the ocean or something. There is a bunch of people huddled together on a hill just watching everything."

(3-10-2011) "... A friend called to say Japan had just suffered a huge earthquake, something like a 9.0 in magnitude! At the moment there was a huge tsunami seeping in on the land and carrying away everything in its path. We turned on the TV and watched horrified as the wave swept cars and people off the roadways and into the sea!"

(11-19-2012) "There will be changes both outside, in the form of earth changes, and inside ourselves, in part caused by the outside changes. There will be more natural disasters, failed governments, failed money systems, economic collapse, wars, food shortages, job losses, and so forth. These will continue to increase over the next seven years until 2020."

(11-19-2012) "Mankind is being brought to its knees. We are being pushed to make us grow. We are being faced with our fears and our wrong thinking. When enough minds change, we collectively will change."

(Epilogue, 2013) "We are told we need to be prepared on a spiritual level because the more spiritual we are, the easier the transformation will be. We're being pushed to evaluate our lives and our impact on the earth. We are urged to turn away from greed and materialism and reach out to each other with love and compassion. If enough of us can do this, the energies will change and the miracle will happen."

ON THE
TIP EDGE
OF A
MIRACLE

DREAMS, VISIONS AND PROPHECIES
FOR THE FUTURE
1996–2012

DENNISON & TEDDI TSOSIE

BLUE DOLPHIN PUBLISHING

Copyright © 2013 Dennison and Teddi Tsosie
All rights reserved.

Published by
Blue Dolphin Publishing, Inc.
P.O. Box 8, Nevada City, CA 95959
Orders: 1-800-643-0765
Web: www.bluedolphinpublishing.com

ISBN: 978-1-57733-277-0 paperback
ISBN: 978-1-57733-450-7 e-book

Library of Congress Control Number: 2013947305

First edition: August 2013

Cover and Text Art: Dennison Tsosie

Printed in the United States of America
5   4   3   2   1

Contents

FOREWORD: A TRIBUTE TO TEDDI TSOSIE	xiii
INTRODUCTION	xv

~ 1996 ~

CARETAKERS	3
TECHNOLOGY	5
BLUE STAR	7
AN INVITATION	8
FUTURE POSSIBILITIES	9
A 25-YEAR COURSE	9
ANOTHER SCHOOL DREAM	10
SPIRALS	11
SHAKE UP IN THE WHITE HOUSE?	13
DOLPHINS AGAIN	14
JAPAN	16
SNIPPETS OF FUTURE POSSIBILITIES	18
KNIGHTS	19
CYLINDERS IN A TOMB	20
LIBERTY BELL	21
THE WHITE HOUSE AGAIN	22
A DEPRESSION	23

~ 1997 ~

SWORD IN A STONE	27
INTERMISSION	28
THE WATCHERS	31
OUR DISTANT PAST?	32
COMETS	33
A STRANGE DREAM	34

~ On the Tip Edge of a Miracle ~

DISREGARD FOR THE EARTH	35
FOUR HIGH PRIESTS	37
MORE SNIPPETS	38
A TIME FOR SPIRITUALITY	39
SEVEN DOORS	39
GATHERING OF ELDERS	41
TEACHING IN AN EGG SHELL	42
BIRD IN A NEST	43

~ 1998 ~

TWINS	47

~ 1999 ~

THE CHAIN OF LIFE	53
DOVES	53
THE YEAR TWO THOUSAND	53
COWS	54
ALIEN DREAM	54
A NEW HOME	56

~ 2000 ~

THE NEW MILLENNIUM	61
CROSS OF LORRAINE	62
DOWNWARD SPIRAL	63

~ 2001 ~

ICEBERG	67
RUMOR OF WAR	67
TWINS HAVE BEEN BORN	67
TATTERED FLAG	68
A COMING WAR?	68
A CRYSTAL DREAM	72
THINGS TO COME	75
TROUBLE IN THE CHURCH	75

~ Contents ~

A DREAM ABOUT ELVES	76
THE MIDDLE EAST	77
SERPENTS FIGHTING	79
AN EXPLOSION IN NEW YORK	80
SOMETHING HAPPENING IN THE CHURCH	80
COBRA DREAM	81
ARAFAT AND ISRAEL	82
GLOBAL WARMING	83
MORE FUTURE PREDICTIONS	84
A FAST TRIP TO JAPAN	86
DEVASTATIONS	88
THE DAY AFTER	90
MORE ON 9/11	92
THE TERRORISTS	92
WHAT'S IN COLORADO?	94
MORE FEARFUL SCENARIOS	94
THE NUMBER 26	96
SCREAMING EAGLE	97
WHAT IT MEANS	97
HARD TIMES AHEAD	98
YEAR'S END	99

~ 2002 ~

WAR ON THE HORIZON?	103
A GAME OF HORSESHOES	104
LIBERTY BELL	105
RED STAR	105
A GAME OF CHESS	106
GOING TO WAR	106
LIBERTY WILL RING	107
THE STOCK MARKET WILL FALL	107
ANOTHER WAR IS COMING	108
JIHAD	108
KNIGHTS CLASH AGAIN	108
FIGHTING DRAGONS	109
YEAR'S END	109

~ On the Tip Edge of a Miracle ~

~ 2003 ~

BLACK AND WHITE	113
A WARNING	114
SCENES FROM A DISTANT LAND	115
DO NOT FEAR	115
NORTH KOREA	117
FUTURE POSSIBILITIES	117
BIRD IN A CAGE	118
THE WAR BEGINS	118
PALESTINIANS	118
DIAMOND DREAM	119
ID CARDS	121
STOCKPILING OIL	122
DIAMONDS AGAIN	122
MANDELBROT	123
TROUBLING DREAMS	123
OIL SHORTAGE	124
BLACK DRAGON	125
BUSH	125
THE EARTH'S GRID	125
COLISEUM COLLAPSE	127
MORE SCENARIOS	128

~ 2004 ~

A SERIES OF SCENES	133
WHAT WAS THAT?	133
BILL OF RIGHTS	135
MORE VISIONS	135
DREAMS	137
THE BUZZARD AND THE EAGLE	138
MORE DREAMS	138
NORTH KOREA AGAIN	139
CROP CIRCLE DREAM	140
BLACK LIMO EXPLOSION	142
MORE VISIONS OF FUTURE EVENTS	142

~ Contents ~

MORE IMAGES	143
IMPORTANCE OF NUTRITION	144
ENERGY	145
BLUE STAR AND FLOODING	146
TSUNAMI	147
HOPI AND UFOS	148
END OF THE YEAR REFLECTIONS	149

~ 2005 ~

WE ARE ALL CONNECTED	153
VIBRATIONS AND ENERGY	154
SOLAR FLARES?	154
THE BLUE PEARL	155
STOP WORRYING	156
WE ARE BEING PUSHED	156
MORE INFORMATION	157
BLUE STAR AGAIN	158
FEAR BLOCKS ENERGY	159
EMOTIONAL TIMES	160
PORTENT OF A DISASTER	161
A TEACHING ABOUT FEAR	161
WE ARE LIKE FLOWERS	162
A DREAM OF THE GRANDFATHERS	163
AN UNBELIEVABLE INVITATION	165
YOU'RE GOING WHERE?	167
I	167
II	170
III	173
IV	176
V	180
VI	184

~ 2006 ~

SHIFTING GEARS	189

~ On the Tip Edge of a Miracle ~

~ 2007 ~

TEACHING AND SELLING	193

~ 2008 ~

DARK DAYS	197
UFO	206
STRANGE DREAMS	209
ANOTHER STRANGE DREAM	212
YEAR-END MEDITATION	213

~ 2009 ~

DREAM OF MARTIN LUTHER KING	217
NEW BEGINNINGS	218

~ 2010 ~

A NEW HOME	229
MAYAN CONNECTION	230
HIDDEN KNOWLEDGE	232
OUT OF BALANCE	233
ANOTHER CROP CIRCLE	234
REPEATED IMAGES	236
2020	236
THREE CATASTROPHES	238
THE ECONOMY	238
PURIFICATION	239
SHORTAGES AND HIGH PRICES	241
THE PRESSURE INCREASES	241
A SPIRITUAL AWAKENING IS COMING	242
LET GO OF FEAR	243
GOD'S LIGHT	245
SOLAR FLARE?	246
THE END OF A CYCLE	247
ALIENS	247
A MIRACLE IS ABOUT TO HAPPEN!	248

~ Contents ~

NUMBERS HAVE POWER	250
FUTURE ENERGIES TO COME	250
POTENTIAL	251
MORE SCENES OF THE FUTURE	252
REBIRTH OF THE STARS	253
BIRTH	254
EARTHQUAKE	255
WAVES OF ENERGY	255
WATER	256
FORGIVE ONE ANOTHER	256
ANOTHER EARTHQUAKE	257
MORE EARTHQUAKES	258
SEE THROUGH THE ILLUSION	258

~ 2011 ~

RIOTS	263
REVOLUTION	263
MORE EARTHQUAKES	264
BLUE STAR AGAIN	265
JAPAN EARTHQUAKE	265
HARD TIMES ARE COMING	266

~ 2012 ~

DRAGONS FIGHTING AGAIN	271
KIM JONG UN	271
FINISH YOUR BOOK!	272
MELTING OF THE POLES	272
THE END OF THE CYCLE IS NEAR	273
EPILOGUE	275
ABOUT THE AUTHORS	277

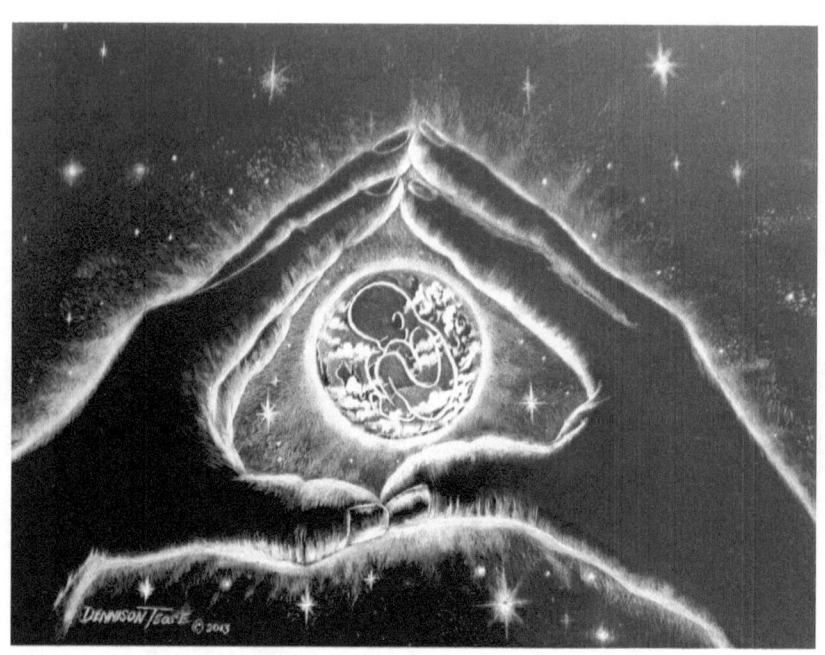

Foreword
A Tribute to Teddi Tsosie

Before this book was named *On the Tip Edge of a Miracle,* Paul and I were able to read it simply as "Teddi's Journal." As before, Teddi had scribed the dreams, visions and prophesies of her Navajo husband, Dennison Tsosie. Her first journal was published as *Spirit Visions: The Old Ones Speak* in 1997 by Blue Dolphin Publishing. *Spirit Visions* attracted worldwide attention, many long wondrous letters, and world travelers arriving at the Tsosie's door.

Teddi never intended this second journal for publication, due to a chronic illness that prevented them from offering hospitality to visitors. She and Dennison wanted these important messages to be shared worldwide, but Teddi's illness made them hesitate. This ambivalence finally evolved into a decision to allow Spirit's messages to be shared in a second book, despite their personal challenges.

These journal entries contain Dennison's dreams and visions of the future, but they also include historical and other research that Teddi did, which expands the meaning of much of the content. "The Watchers"—inner dimensional light beings who care for the Earth—claim to be directing this information to Dennison. They often made references to events in history, gave symbols of ancient origin, and detailed information about Earth changes, extreme weather events, and social/political/economic changes.

The information given goes way beyond the training and spiritual background of a Navajo healer, artist and silversmith. Dennison was often stymied by the images and information that he received. There are references to ancient civilizations on this Earth, "Star Nations," and predictions for the future.

As we continued to read Teddi's journal, we saw predictions that had already come to pass. By checking the dates of the journal entries with events that have already happened, we could see that Dennison had been shown, ahead of time, the New York twin towers tragedy, hurricane

~ On the Tip Edge of a Miracle ~

Katrina in New Orleans, the shock and awe of Baghdad, the wars in the Middle East, the terrifying tsunami in Malaysia, the Fukushima nuclear meltdown, and numerous other events. On spiritual and practical levels there are instructions for all of us. These are necessary changes that we need to make, both individually and collectively, to renew and sustain ourselves and the health of our planet.

Teddi has begun unraveling a complex mystery. People from around the world have and will add their own understandings to some of the ancient symbols, prophesies and teachings that appear in these journals. We are all being presented with an opportunity to participate in a worldwide treasure hunt, to expand truth and knowledge. More secrets will be unlocked as time passes, as readers add more pieces to this puzzle. The messages offer optimism and hope for our troubled world, and we are assured that our future can miraculously change. The doorway is being opened and instructions are being offered, by divine beings, to potentially manifest this miracle.

On the Tip Edge of a Miracle is an example of true synergy between Dennison and Teddi. Their love for each other, their love for our Mother Earth and all the beings that live upon her, birthed this gift into being.

As a true collaborator with her beloved husband, Teddi's research makes the visions and dreams more meaningful. Her smile, optimism and dedication to her spiritual path show us her most generous and selfless heart. We thank you, Teddi, for scribing these messages that may otherwise have been lost.

At the time of this writing, Teddi is in the hospital struggling for breath. COPD has compromised her lungs. Teddi, may the sacrifice of your long illness and your offering to the world bring you the miracle of healing. This is our prayer for you. In spite of your suffering, your spirit is radiant, inspiring, and filled with love.

Nancy and Paul Clemens, Publishers
August, 2013

Introduction

ONE APRIL NIGHT, shortly after we were married, my husband had an extraordinary thing happen. He had a vision or, as I told myself at the time, a waking dream.

The vision came unexpectedly after we had settled into bed for the evening. I sat in bed reading for a few minutes while he turned over to go to sleep. I had just turned off the light and snuggled down to sleep when he softly asked, "Babe, are you still awake?" I replied, "Uh huh..." He continued, "I saw the most beautiful city, it looked like it was made of glass or crystal, so beautiful and bright...." I was a little surprised that he was already asleep and dreaming and questioned, "You mean just now? Were you already asleep?" He replied, "I don't know, I think so." Then he fell silent for a short time and I'd just assumed he'd gone back to sleep when he said, "I'm still there...I can still see it and I'm not asleep! He proceeded then to describe in detail things he was seeing. If I asked questions he conversed with me, giving coherent answers.

The vision had no religious connotation, no obvious messages, and nothing of import to us as far as I could determine. It was mostly scenes of a crystal city, a hidden valley and an ancient calendar. What was remarkable was how he was able to see the dream and articulate what he was seeing and hearing in real time. Then there was his obvious enchanted wonder bordering on fear as the scenes unfolded. And there was a voice he heard of someone guiding him as the scenes unfolded.

A curious thing that he noted as we discussed it afterward was that at the beginning of his experience he saw or felt like someone was shining a bright light, like a large flashlight or car headlight in his eyes. It sort of startled him and as it did a voice said to him, "Don't be afraid, just relax and go with it...."

When it was all over and the scenes stopped, he took a deep breath, like a sigh, and said, "Man, that was really weird! What in the heck just happened?" I surely had no answers, though I did realize something highly unusual had just occurred and I was completely blown away. Curiously, after spending a few minutes discussing details and puzzling over it all, he simply turned over and fell into a deep sleep. I, on the other hand, couldn't sleep, so I got up and wrote down as much as I could remember. The next morning we discussed the events again over breakfast and he drew a few sketches to further illustrate what he saw.

One reason I was so blown away by the incident and didn't simply relegate it to the file of the unexplained in my life, was because of something I had done when I first got into bed that I speculated may have initiated the vision somehow. But I will get into that later.

The visions continued to happen sporadically after that night, and each time, because they were extraordinary and somewhat disturbing, I faithfully would get up and record as much as I could remember. Soon I bought a spiral notebook and began to keep a journal. Out of that first journal grew our book entitled *Spirit Visions, The Old Ones Speak*, which was published by Blue Dolphin Publishing Inc., in 1997. The book details how it all began, as well as Dennison's visions and teachings from 1988 through the end of 1995. This journal is a continuation of that work.

I realize having a vision is a very extraordinary claim, and one I myself would have scoffed at before this happened. So I ask you to please keep an open mind and save any judgments until later.

Perhaps I should begin by telling you a little about ourselves and how we got to the point of the first experience.

Dennison is a beautiful, humble Navajo man. His early years were spent living a traditional Navajo lifestyle on the Reservation. He lived in a Hogan, a traditional six- or eight-sided hut made of sticks, logs and mud with a dirt floor, along with his brothers and sisters.

His grandparents lived nearby and had a great influence on his life. All too often dad was working off the Reservation, trying to provide for his family, so they took up the slack left by his absence. Both were known for their medicine work. His grandmother was a hand trembler, and an herbalist. His grandfather, a crystal gazer. Dennison often went with his grandmother to gather herbs or attend to someone who was ill. He also followed his grandfather, helping and watching him as he went about his work. His grandmother and mother were both rug weavers and his grandfather was a silversmith. It was from him Dennison learned his trade.

~ Introduction ~

In school he was a victim of the mindsets and prejudices of the era and he ended up being "left behind" as the saying goes. It was of little wonder, when he graduated from high school, he was close to functionally illiterate.

I mention this because to me it adds validity to the information he receives...he didn't read it in a book. He seldom reads anything. I've attempted to read to him, but many of the words are not in his vocabulary and I have to stop and define them. He gets impatient then and simply wants a summary. Then he has questions that aren't answered in the summary and I have to go back and search them out. In the end it is a bit frustrating and I normally don't even try.

Our life together began in the late 1980's, in the mountains of northern Arizona, where we lived an ordinary rural lifestyle.

When we first met, he worked at a pulp mill in the caustics department. It was dangerous, hot, backbreaking work. This to me seemed a crime because he was also a very talented artist and silversmith. I wanted more than anything else to make it possible for him to quit his job and pursue his dream of making jewelry and art full time.

At that time I taught some art and sculpture classes at a local Junior College, so my focus was directed toward the arts. Days off from work often found us working on art projects or driving to Sedona or Flagstaff, where we both showed our work in galleries and sold jewelry in shops. Our main objective was to create enough of a market for our work that he could quit his pulp mill job.

We were both recently divorced, Dennison more recently than I. As so often happens with a divorce or the sudden death of a partner, Dennison was left feeling lost and without direction. The future he had envisioned for so many years suddenly ceased to be and a new direction had yet to fully unfold. We were newly married, but we hadn't yet built a long history together, nor had we built our dreams. This left him hanging somewhere in between letting go of the past and reaching for the future.

The emotional baggage of a broken marriage, continued stormy connections to his past life, coupled with financial woes, a hated job, and the insecurities of a new marriage, all served to create a nearly unbearable situation from which he could see no resolution. As he puts it, *"I hit bottom and I didn't know where to turn or what to do next."*

~ On the Tip Edge of a Miracle ~

Perhaps his feeling of hitting bottom was what opened the door for what he was now experiencing. As Dennison explains, *"When you reach bottom, you open up in a whole different way; it's like you die and are re-born. When I hit bottom, I knew I had to have something to hang on to, so I reached out to Creator. I didn't do this by going to church; I was never raised in a church. I did it by finding my way back to my Navajo spiritual foundation through finding a crystal in a store.*

"During my "emergency of the soul" Teddi and I were taking some artwork to a gallery in Sedona that showed our work. While we were driving, we talked about the possibility of make a living full time selling our art and my handmade jewelry. Navajo jewelry is common where we live, so I pointed out to her that I had lots of competition. She came up with the idea of making other types of jewelry rather than traditional Navajo style. Maybe something like the new crystal jewelry that she said was starting to come out in some of the shops there. I had no idea what she was talking about, so while we were in Sedona she took me to a shop that sold crystals, intending for me to look at some of the jewelry in there.

"When I entered the shop, the first thing I saw was a display case full of beautiful crystals. I was shocked because the only time I had ever seen crystals like this was when they were used for medicine work. My Grandfather was what we Navajos call a 'crystal gazer'. I remembered how, when I was small, I had watched him holding such a crystal and chanting over it until he saw pictures inside. This was often done for someone who was sick and they wanted to know what was wrong and what ceremony needed to be done. Using the crystal my Grandfather would divine answers to these questions and other questions people wanted to know.

"On this day I saw one crystal in particular that attracted me and I asked to see it. As soon as I held it, I knew I had to have it. At the time I don't think Teddi really knew what I was going through inside, but this was like someone throwing a lifeline to a drowning man. It represented something from my past that I once believed in, but somehow through the years I'd forgotten, or at least put out of my life. I knew this was a way of finding myself again, a way of re-connecting with who I was inside."

As Dennison was standing there at the counter I suddenly realized he was going to buy a large crystal. He completely ignored me when I

~ Introduction ~

began tugging on his belt loop so I discretely kicked his leg, hoping he would get the message and put it back. We were virtually broke and the crystal was quite expensive by my standards. To me it was just a pretty rock, and a frivolous expense. Instead of putting it back he continued to ignore me and paid for the crystal.

As soon as we left the shop, I jumped on him, demanding to know why he'd do such a foolish thing. He said simply, *"I've seen them used before by medicine men and I know they are powerful. I think I need it."* Sensing this was very important to him and his peace of mind, I backed off of my tirade and said nothing more. This simple purchase of the crystal led to a series of events, detailed in our book, *Spirit Visions: The Old Ones Speak*. It is an understatement to say it was life changing for both of us.

After purchasing the crystal Dennison became frustrated with trying to turn on the powers he was so sure it held. I "knew" the crystal didn't have any special power, but for the first time since our marriage he seemed to come alive after buying the crystal, so I was willing to go along with it. As the days went by, he became more and more obsessed with it, wanting to unlock its secrets.

We made a few trips to the Reservation, seeking crystal gazers who would be willing to teach him the proper songs and prayers that would open it up. When that didn't work out, we drove back to Sedona on his days off from work, seeking information about crystals.

I began reading various New Age books relating to crystals and their use, hoping to find information for him, but none seemed to address what he was looking for. During this time though, some of the claims in the books regarding a certain type of crystal called a "record keeper crystal" began to arouse my curiosity, and on one of our trips to Sedona I purchased a small one of my own that I found in a bargain box for three dollars.

The night of the vision, unbeknownst to Dennison, I placed this small crystal under my pillow as instructed in a book I had been reading. My intention was experimental and I felt a little foolish, so I didn't tell him what I was doing. Amazingly, as he was drifting into sleep, he began seeing the series of images, which he then related to me. I don't know if the crystal was the reason for his visions, but the possibility did enter my mind at the time.

I was at first confused, then a little puzzled as he described what he was seeing. I had never really believed people could have visions unless they were mentally unstable or on drugs. I did know neither was true of him, so I wasn't sure what to think was happening.

Thereafter he began to periodically receive more information and visions from an unknown source identifying themselves as "Watchers" or beings who were sent by the Source to watch over and interact with mankind from our beginning. It was all very frightening at first, especially for him. He even began to fear he was losing his mind, and quite frankly the thought did cross my mind too. But the information that came seemed worthy of consideration and the teachings full of wisdom. He was normal in every other respect, so I had to believe he was okay, and I had to believe in him.

The weeks and months that followed brought more and more of these visions and teachings and I began to record them in a journal. Later, much against his wishes, I shared some of them with friends and they shared them with their friends and so on, until out of it grew our first book.

I stopped the manuscript for our book at the end of 1995, however the dreams, visions and teachings continued, and for the most part I recorded them. Our journey continues....

Science has taken much of the mystery out of life and in doing so it has stolen much of the magic as well. It has taken away our faith and asked us to replace it with the wonders of technology. But what if science has missed something? What if some people can have prophetic visions, and dreams, see figures in crystals; heal with their hands and other wondrous things? What if there is a Divine Plan that we are all a part of? What if a few, like Dennison, have an ability to see a little farther ahead than the rest of us and thus shine a little light on this dark path we are treading?

Curiously a branch of science may now be building a bridge between the scientific and the metaphysical world. In the 1970's a small group of frontier scientists and quantum physicists began questioning the current worldview offered by classical physics. The implications of the results from repeated experiments forced them to pause and consider the metaphysical implications of what they were observing. It seems our "reality" may not be fixed, but actually viewed as pure potential, that is solidified

~ Introduction ~

only when it is observed, and that consciousness and the quantum worlds are interconnected in some way. It also seems that, as Native Peoples have declared for centuries, we are all interconnected with every other thing in the Universe. We are all a part of the Web of Life.

Since that time more and more scientists have come on board and a new worldview is being developed. I hope the skeptic and the believer alike will take time to explore some of the many books now being written on this exciting new field.

I would like to invite you now to join in our spiritual journey . . . May you find something within these pages that speaks to you. I also hope this journal will provide a stepping stone on your own path toward enlightenment.

Teddi Tsosie
May 2013

1996

Caretakers
MARCH 9, 1996

I FELT A NERVOUS SORT OF RELIEF as I bundled together my manuscript for *Spirit Visions: The Old Ones Speak*, getting it ready to send to the publisher. It represented our spiritual journey over the past eight years and I wondered if it was really any more remarkable than someone else's. Would it be meaningful to anyone but us? Could it possibly convey the wonder I felt each time some new experience happened or some new bit if information came to him? I sat down across from him as he sat at his workbench and asked if he would like to listen to a little of what I had written. I sought his re-assurance and his approval. He had not wanted me to share our journal in the beginning, and seemed indifferent as I continued to keep it and share it with others. I'm sure he would have been just as happy if I didn't record anything. I read the introduction and the first couple of chapters. He listened quietly, while he filed the rough edges of a piece of jewelry he'd been working on. At the end his only comment was, "Why do you keep saying Dennison, over and over?" I could see he was a little self conscious, the way we feel when we hear our own voice on a tape recorder. I asked if it sounded okay otherwise and he shrugged his shoulders and replied, "Yeah, I guess so."

Later that afternoon, as was his normal routine, he went out to pray and meditate before it got cold. I had supper waiting for him when he returned home. As we ate, he asked me,

"Were leprechauns and elves and beings like that ever thought of as angels?" I considered this for a time before I replied, "I'm not sure if they were ever thought of as angels exactly, but I suppose they could have been. I know some writers have drawn a comparison between angels and aliens."

He went on to explain, "When I started meditating, I was kind of thinking about what you were reading in your manuscript about when I first started having visions. I was wondering what the "Watchers" actually were. I was told they (the Watchers) were sometimes thought of as angels, and that they were here as caretakers of the earth and to oversee mankind. I had always thought elves were like caretakers of the earth, you know like nature spirits, so I wondered if they could be one in the same as the Watchers?

"They said we don't really have any idea what 'GOD' is. To put it in simple terms, 'God' is pure energy and pure thought in the form of light. God or The Source is totally conscious and thinks, feels, loves and creates. The way I understand it, when we die our soul rejoins The Source and becomes a part of it until we are born again into another body. When we do come back again, we go back into our same family group, over and over in different ways until we no longer feel a connection or a need to be in that group any more. Then we go on to a different experience. These are things our soul knows and understands, but our minds and beliefs block us from knowing.

"The Creator energies conceived the idea of man in thought before we became a reality. Then the earth was created and put here and designed to support us. For instance we were given a digestive system, which would work a certain way, so foods that we could digest and nourish from were also created. Everything was designed to work together with everything else. This was a slow process over millions of years, but there is no time as far as the Creator energies are concerned.

"In the beginning the Earth was just some particles of debris and ice. The ice was melted, the waters separated and land was brought forth.

"The Creator energies made the Watchers and gave them the ability to reason and think; gave them knowledge. Then they in turn began to create a form, which was to become mankind, using the available genetic material from the Earth to create this form. We all actually come from a common source, and share the same genetic material. Some became animals; some became fish, some insects, birds, etc., etc. We are all literally part of the same thing. Man was tried out in different forms and as time went by one thing or another would prove to be better while other things wouldn't be so good. So the Watchers would modify the genes and another form would develop, until man became pretty much what he is today. At first man was a doer, but not a thinker. He was a survivor, like your cat, but he didn't actually reason and invent things and ideas.

"Then there was a big leap and man began to think. I don't really quite understand everything they were trying to tell me, but somehow I think this wasn't supposed to happen. Some of the Watchers began to show man how to use tools, how to hunt with them, how to sew and make other things. They showed man how to use herbs, how to grow food and domesticate animals. They interacted with man a lot. Man began to look at them as Gods. Later these Watchers were taken away and others were brought in. Only now they didn't interact in such a direct way. Man was given different skin colors, different knowledge, different challenges, different skills and different lessons to learn. It became like an experiment and the Watchers or their workers would come back from time to time to check on things. They would check on the genes in man and the plants. They would take some things away and add others to change certain things in a particular direction. They even manipulated the weather and political situations to observe actions and reactions, in order to make people or things develop in certain ways. The Human form is unique and highly desirable, and now certain genes and genetic material is being taken to develop another better human form, maybe somewhere else, perhaps on another planet in another solar system.

"They told me, 'Man is being watched VERY closely now; they have discovered the secrets of the atom and are now unlocking the secrets of the human genes. They can clone animals and they can genetically manipulate food. What next?'"

Technology
MARCH 29, 1996

MY SON RECENTLY GAVE US his old computer. He spent several days teaching me the basics of it and finally convinced me that it could be a valuable tool. He wanted to get us up on the Internet, and build us a web site to give us another avenue to sell our jewelry. I wasn't sure how that would work and it made me a little nervous. I was willing to try though, because I was tired of having to first make the jewelry and then to sell it wholesale. When we sold wholesale, we made very little for the time and money we invested, and if having a web site would bring retail buyers, then I was all for it. On the other hand Dennison was very reluctant to have anything to do with the computer, and felt there was no need for it in our lives. Perhaps this was on his mind when he went to meditate, because he came home with the following information.

"If things continue in the present direction, there is going to be a separation of classes. A lot of people are being left behind as new technology becomes commonplace. Those who will bear the brunt of it will be the elderly, then the uneducated, and then the poor. There will be many in rural areas, like here, that won't want to change, and technology will leave them behind. In a way it's good to live simply, but what is going to happen is a gap will be created between those who understand and keep up with all that technology has to offer, and those who don't. It will eventually crate two distinct classes, the technologically elite, and those who aren't. Soon those who don't keep up won't be able to interact with the rest of the world, because they don't know how. There will be few jobs for them and most will end up living on welfare. The technologically elite will end up carrying them on their backs, and will resent it. They will make moves to cut back in welfare and social programs. At the same time health care costs, insurance costs, taxes and general cost of living will be dramatically increasing. Those without technological skills will not be able to make enough money to live on with their present jobs. There will be many, many more homeless or impoverished than there are now. A large majority of these people will be people of Color.

"Then there's the upcoming generation. Within the next five years there is going to be a lot of young people out there trying to get a start in life, and there won't be enough jobs. Technology will have eliminated a lot of them. Down-sizing will have cut out even more. Even now to rent an apartment is more than most kids can afford, and it will get even worse. Not to mention the cost of food, transportation, insurance, etc. There will be a lot of jobless, lost kids. It will lead to a lot more violence in the cities because of it.

"It will really be rough for the small businesses, especially the mom and pop operations, and those who have skills that don't fit into the new society. They won't be able to do a good job of selling their goods and services without being skilled in the new system.

"Major corporations will mass produce goods and market them for much less than the mom and pop operations can. Taxes will go up and they won't have the resources to pay with. Insurance and health care costs will go sky high and only those with good jobs that offer insurance coverage or those with lots of money will be able to get decent care.

"Our greed has created this along with our thinking and beliefs. Perhaps the only way to truly change things is if the earth changes come and break down our systems enough to force us to work together and re-evaluate where we are going."

Blue Star
APRIL 17, 1996

THIS MORNING AS WE WERE FINISHING BREAKFAST Dennison told me of a dream he had last night. I always marvel at the coherence and extreme detail some of his dreams have and recognize it as often being indicative it's more than a dream, and something to pay attention to.

"I dreamed of an eagle last night. I watched him flying around for a while, and as I watched, I noticed he looked as if he had something hanging around his neck. He landed on an old dead cedar tree that was gray and gnarled and lying over sideways. He just sat there on a branch that was sticking up.

"I studied him for a little while, until finally I felt like I should go over and take a closer look at the thing hanging from his neck; then I carefully crept over to him. Up close I could see it was a necklace. Slowly, slowly I reached over toward the eagle. He didn't move, so I took the necklace off of him and examined it closely. It was made of crude beads of different sizes, like turquoise, pipestone, jet and shell. Judging from its looks, it was very old. There was a pendant hanging from the beads, which was rectangular in shape with a scene inlayed inside. This scene was of a mountain with three peaks, reminding me of the San Francisco Peaks (a sacred mountain to both the Hopi and the Navajo). Beside the mountain was the figure of a Kachina. A Hopi Kachina with a mask and feathers. Up above the mountains was a blue star and a line or a beam going down to the Kachina. I went to replace the necklace around the eagle's neck, but he flew away when I tried to do it. That was the end of the dream… I feel like I should understand what it symbolizes, but I can't figure it out."

As I listened to Dennison's dream, it reminded me of something I had read a long time ago in *Book of the Hopi* by Frank Waters. I asked him if he knew anything about the Blue Star Kachina of the Hopi, but he said he didn't know much. Later I got my book and searched until I found the reference that seemed to pertain to his dream. It told of a war between the spiritual and material matters. The material world would be destroyed by spiritual beings and out of it one world would be created under the power of the Creator. It went on to say the time was near and would be heralded when the Blue Star Kachina dances in the plaza. The Kachina would represent an invisible blue star that would make its appearance at that time.

An Invitation

MAY 3, 1996

TODAY WE RECEIVED A FAX from the Buddhist priest and friend mentioned in our last book inviting us to Hiroshima in August, to join him in prayers for World Peace. We accepted the invitation, and this evening Dennison went out to meditate and ask what he needed to do, and find out why this was coming to us. As so often happens, his reply is something totally unrelated to his questioning.

"Tonight they were telling me that the oceans are heating up. Somehow this will affect the coastal areas with winds and big waves.

"The Earth is calling for moisture. In some places there will be lots of moisture, in others drought. There will be dry winds sucking moisture out of the Earth and the vegetation. Crops will be affected.

"There will be an earthquake in the San Diego area that will have devastating affects. I don't know when for sure, but I feel like it will be "soon"

"There is a war coming. The U.S. will be heavily involved. It will affect everyone."

~ 1996 • A 25-Year Course ~

Future Possibilities
MAY 30, 1996

MORE SNIPPETS OF FUTURE POSSIBILITIES came to him with this afternoon's meditation:

"They were telling me there would be a lot more tornadoes happening in the future. There will be a lot where none have been seen before. They are caused from cold air in some areas and very warm moist air in other areas both coming together. There is going to be a lot of weather extremes. The Earth is calling for moisture.

"Diseases will be appearing in animals, especially in the lower life forms like fish and frogs, also deformities. It will show up first in lakes and springs.

"There is also going to be a gas shortage. Something is going to happen to our oil supply and the prices will go sky high.

"I also sense our economy is going to take a dive. We should all watch our spending."

A 25-Year Course
JUNE 11, 1996

DENNISON SOMETIMES HAS VERY VIVID DREAMS, which he remembers later in great detail. They are quite unlike ordinary dreams. The following two dreams came on two different nights, but might be connected.

"Last night I dreamed about going to school. I think I was in high school. "They" told me I would be going to a special class, that I had been selected for this class along with a few others. I was also told it was to be a 25-year course; the funny thing was when I got there it was as if I'd already taken it before, but I'd forgotten most of it. I felt like a real dummy, as if I 'd been put back in first grade, yet I felt at the same time I needed to be taking it."

As I thought about Dennison's dream, the thing that seems somewhat significant is the "25-year course." In the beginning when he first began getting these visions and teachings it was just after the Harmonic Convergence in 1987. I recalled at that time he was given information about a book entitled *The Mayan Factor* by Jose Arguellos (See *Spirit*

Visions: The Old Ones Speak, pp. 29–35). The book contained a lot of information regarding the end of the Mayan calendar in the year 2012. I think the book was what the Harmonic Convergence had been based on. I noted at the time it was 25 years from the Harmonic Convergence until the year 2012. So, I wonder if "25-year course" in this dream began at that time…? If so, I wonder what he will be learning and what will he be doing with it when he's finished?

Another School Dream
JUNE 13, 1996

AGAIN, TWO DAYS LATER, Dennison recounted during breakfast,

"I had another school dream last night. I was sitting on what I thought at first was a low stone wall. I looked around and realized the stones were laid in tiered rows, like bleachers. There were some other people sitting around me, maybe ten or eleven others. They were of all different nationalities.

"Then four teachers came out and stood in front of us. One was wearing a brown robe with a hood like monks used to wear. He was wearing what looked to be a crystal and colored stone necklace. The other three were wearing grayish robes, and different colored pendants. All of them had hoods on their heads so you couldn't see their faces.

"The one in brown spoke and told us we were in this class together, and we would be learning a lot of things from them and from each other. He said we were already in touch with each other on another level, and some of us were already at least partly aware of it. He went on to say we would be meeting and working together in the future and we would recognize each other when we met. He told us we would each be receiving teachings, which we were to share, and we were working for the benefit of mankind as well as the Earth. He told us to remember where we were at now and what it looked like, because we would all meet here later on and we would recognize it.

"Then he and the other three just vanished into thin air. I looked around me to see who else was there, and what they thought about everything, but no one was there any more. Then I noticed I wasn't on a stone wall, instead I was on a stump in the forest."

Spirals
JUNE 26, 1996

When Dennison gets teaching meditations, they are always very interesting if not profound. They present a different way of seeing things and give us something to ponder. Some teachings seem relate to other teachings he has had in the past and when put together add even more insight. I don't know why they come this way, sometimes years apart. I suppose there's no such thing as time as we know it where this information comes from or else it's like radio stations, it's there just waiting until someone tunes in to it. This evening Dennison received the following.

"They gave me a teaching about spirals tonight. When they were giving it to me, it seemed so simple, I wondered why, oh why can't we see it and do it, then everything would be okay.

"The spiral is the most powerful force in the universe. It is the most powerful symbol, and it is the key to the universe. The universe itself is in a spiral; great storms such as hurricanes and tornadoes move in a spiral. Even our fingertips form spirals. The way they illustrated this to me was with a snake. When it's stretched out straight it poses no threat, and is has no power. But when it coils up, it forms a spiral, and then it is very powerful because it's ready to strike.

"Our ancestors understood the importance of the spiral and left its symbol everywhere. The spiral design itself creates a powerful energy, and so does a spiral that forms a triangle. This is a very powerful symbol and a piece of jewelry using any stone along with this symbol is very healing.

"There is spiraling energy that comes from our hands, and our feet. When we sit with the palms of our hands and the soles of our feet together, we create a powerful energy field around ourselves.

"The Earth spins and creates a spiral of magnetic energy at its poles, one negative, and one positive. They were telling me this magnetic energy is going to reverse, as it has several times before.

"They compared mankind to a coiled basket. The center is where Creator is. It is also our heart center. To find Creator, the Source, you must go inward to the center. Instead mankind is searching farther and farther outward. As he gets to the rim, it off-balances the basket. Man is searching outward, sending vehicles into space, building tall buildings to house his technology, tall temples to house his religions, always looking upward and outside himself for God. He searches the past for keys to understand himself, and he searches the future for answers to his problems, but he doesn't stay in the present, and look within. Creator isn't "out there" it is *within*. Man is on the edge of the basket, searching because he feels a longing pulling at him. This leads to dissatisfaction, and confusion, which leads to anger, greed, and war. That's where we are now, at the edge of the basket, and we are off balance. If we don't go back inward we will destroy ourselves. It has happened before four times. Each time man was created he was something different, with different lessons to learn. This time he is a combination of the others, animal, earth child and technologic, to see if he can find a balance between them. If he can, he will find Creator, and this will lead to the fifth creation."

Then, I suppose to illustrate some ways we can get back to a better way of living he received this at the end of his meditation.

"There was something else they were telling me about, I can't remember…It was something about meat…you know the fibers in some meat…anyway when wild animals like deer and elk graze, they eat a balanced diet of herbs and plants. Then when we eat them, we get some of the benefits of this. Their meat is nourishing, and in a sense medicinal. Domestic animals that are raised on man-made feeds don't have the same nourishing value, and is now harmful because of how they are raised and fed.

"People need to learn more about herbs, and healing plants. This will help them to get back to the Earth. For instance there's a certain tree bark, that when it's ground up and mixed with water it can heal some cancers. It was used in the distant past, but now it has been forgotten. If more people got back into learning together, and preparing herbs, this knowledge would come back.

"Water is the most precious thing on Earth. It is our most valuable resource. All living things must have water to live. Yet it's the very thing we have the least regard for. If you take food and water away from a wild animal what will happen? It will become tame. It will become loving and gentle toward you because you have what it needs. If it's necessary, this is what's going to happen to man. Take what he nourishes from away for a time, so he will learn to work together in order to survive.

He will have to go inside to find answers, and return to a more spiritual way of being."

Shake Up in the White House?
JUNE 29, 1996

WE HAD UNEXPECTED GUESTS drop in this evening while Dennison was out meditating. They were still here when Dennison returned, and we all visited until quite late. It was after we had gone to bed before I thought to ask if he had received anything while he was out.

He replied, "Yeah, I got a little...." He paused for a while, trying to recall everything. He has told me in the past it is a lot like dreaming, in that quite a bit of what he sees or hears begins to fade away after a little while, leaving half-remembered bits and pieces.

"I think I have gotten some of this before. I was strongly sensing a major earthquake that will happen in San Diego that will be devastating. I don't know when it will happen, but it seems like it's late summer, like the end of July or something, but I don't know which July.

"There's something happening out in the ocean too. I think it's heating up and it will affect the air currents and the weather patterns. Lack of water will be a serious problem, especially in the desert areas. There's going to be a lot of tornadoes too, a lot in areas that almost never have them. There's something happening in the atmosphere or the upper atmosphere that has something to do with this.

"I still sense an oil shortage or some sort of problem over our oil supply. The prices will go up a lot because of it.

"There's something going on in the White House that is going to come out soon. It will cause a real shake up. I was getting something about some kind of leader like the President, something about losing power or respect...when the President is forced to resign what is it called? Impeached?"

(The above was received before the Clinton scandal came to light.)

~ On the Tip Edge of a Miracle ~

Dolphins Again
JUNE 30, 1996

Last year Dennison had a dolphin dream. In this dream a dolphin came up out of a well (a wishing well?) and told him to squeeze its nose and make a wish. The next week, Blue Dolphin Publishing sent us a letter, saying they had been trying to reach us (at our previous address) and wondered if someone had published our manuscript yet. I had sent them our manuscript in 1992, on the recommendation of a bookstore owner. After not hearing from them in four years, I had assumed they weren't interested. Of course the rest of the story is that in the end we published our book, *Spirit Visions: The Old Ones Speak,* with them. Since that time the Dolphin has taken on a special meaning to us. When they come up in a dream or meditation, we pay close attention.

During his meditations today Dennison saw Dolphins. I don't really understand the symbolism, but we should pay attention.

"I saw four Dolphins in my meditation tonight. I felt like I was out in the water, and they were swimming side-by-side straight at me. When they got up to where I was, they began swimming in a circle around me. They were making that cry that they make, like they were trying to talk to me. Pretty soon this rainbow appeared in the sky and the end was in the water close by. Then one of the dolphins broke away from the others and swam to where the end of the rainbow was, and then it leaped up in the air and followed the rainbow until it disappeared. I looked back around for the others, but they had disappeared also.

"Next I saw this huge door in front of me. I walked up to it, and was just going to open it, when it slid upward like it was on pulleys or something. I was real surprised because I had expected it to open like a normal door.

"Inside I could see a hazy blue light far, far in the distance. I decided to go on in. Suddenly I found myself flying down the hallway really fast. As I began to get near the light I could see a bunch of ragged people milling around me. It was at night. As I looked closer, it looked like a war was going on. People were running around confused, and dead bodies were laying everywhere. In the distance was a gray wall and balls of light or fire were coming from the other side, and falling and exploding among the people. I looked around me and saw U.S. soldiers there watching.

"That scene passed and I saw a shoreline, like a beach. All along it, as far as I could see were birds. Many had long necks, like swans have, all different kinds of colors, white, gray, black and even orange, exotic birds like you would see in the tropics. They were all dead and some were pretty badly battered and broken. Off in the distance I saw a bunch of trees broken and lying helter-skelter, parts of houses and buildings and debris, there was devastation everywhere. There were dead bodies in the wreckage and people walking around dazed and lost. It was a horrible thing to see.

"The next scene was of a lava flow. I could see it as it engulfed trees, and they would burn. I could see rivers of red lava moving down the side of a mountain. There was a town and already most of it was blackened as the lava covered it.

"That passed, and I saw a bunch of soldiers marching in uniform. There were several hundred, and they looked like U.S. troops. A lot of them seemed to be carrying riot gear or something, because several had those plastic shields they use in riots. They were marching down the streets of a city. What was strange was there were parked cars along the sides of the street, but there wasn't anyone around anywhere.

"Next there was like a sea in front of me, and in the distance were a string of lights. As I got closer I could see It was a large ship, like a cruise ship and it was sinking. There were lots of lifeboats full of lots of people.

"After that I saw what looked like an open pit mine. When I got closer I could see this brownish or reddish-green liquid coming up out of the ground and covering up everything. There were pieces of mining equipment floating in this muck, but I didn't see any people.

"That scene passed and I saw a body of water filled with hundreds and hundreds of logs, thousands of logs. Then I saw the surrounding hills were clear-cut.

"I saw four large boats going along and an oil platform on fire in the distance. All of a sudden the water began turning blue-black and I knew there was an oil spill. It covered a huge area, miles and miles long.

"I saw a bunch of tunnels with trains in them. It was underground and there were lots of lights, lighting everything, like a subway maybe. There were thousands of people waiting to get on or off the trains. I didn't see any reason to be shown this. Everything looked pretty normal."

~ On the Tip Edge of a Miracle ~

Japan
AUGUST 2, 1996

We're once again in Japan. It still seems a little unbelievable to be here. We were invited a couple of months ago by our friend, the Buddhist Priest, to participate in the annual prayers for world peace held in Hiroshima on the anniversary of the dropping of the atomic bomb.

When we arrived at the airport in Osaka we were met by a friend and taken to his home to spend the night. After giving us a day to recover from our trip, our friend drove us to Hiroshima. We arrived exhausted and were very grateful when he got us settled into our hotel for the evening. Early the next morning he returned to take us on a tour of the city. The day was already hot and humid as we walked from the hotel to the center of town. He wanted us to view the skeleton of a building that was left standing as a grim reminder of the horror that encompassed the city a few short decades ago. From there we visited the museum to look at drawings and sculptures created by survivors. The drawings depicted the individual experiences and feelings during and after the bombing. There are no words to describe the impact this had on me. It is said a picture is worth a thousand words, these pictures reached into my very soul and spoke of their terror and grief. I couldn't erase the images from my mind as we traveled later that afternoon to meet with our friend and some of the people who worked with him. I now knew on a deeper level why it was so important to be here praying for peace.

Over the next few days we participated in a series of ceremonies with our friend and his group of priests. One ceremony involved laying out a huge mandala on the floor of his temple. It was made of crystals of various sizes, most being small crystals approximately 1" long. The end result was breath taking. Later a large group of people gathered around the mandala and our friend talked about the need of finding peace in our hearts before there could be peace on earth. Dennison explained that normally Navajo's didn't carry the pipe but he had been honored with a pipe in a Cree ceremony several years ago. He then told the story of the Peace Pipe and how it was given to the Sioux by a divine being, White Buffalo Calf Woman, to be used to pray for all life. Later our friend prayed for peace and Dennison did a pipe ceremony, blowing smoke from his pipe on to the crystals. In the end everyone in attendance was invited to dismantle the mandala and gather up as many of the small crystals as we wanted. We were asked take them and spread them everywhere we went. We were told to share them with others, because they were seeds of peace, carrying the energy of our prayers for peace.

The final ceremony was a play enacted by our friend and his Priests. It took place outdoors on top of a hill overlooking Hiroshima. A huge pyre was built of logs and huge green cedar branches. Later it was ignited and clouds of thick fragrant smoke billowed up into the air and spread over all in attendance. A symbolic play was enacted where enemies meet, threaten each other, but finally in the end make peace. It reminded Dennison of a Navajo ceremony known as the Enemy Way, which is done as a healing ceremony for someone who has been in battle. We all wrote our prayers on prayer sticks and our friend took them and offered them to the fire. At the end food and sake were given as an offering. In the gathering darkness we all walked back to the temple where a feast awaited us.

In the days that followed we accompanied our friend and some of his priests to the rural village of Kumano. While there they took us on some of the trails they travel when they do their austerities. One particular day we hiked along a narrow jungle path to a waterfall falling from a high cliff into a shallow pool. We removed our everyday clothing and put on white garments and one by one waded out into the pool and stood under the waterfall and prayed while it cascaded down on our head and shoulders. They said normally this was done by the priests in the middle of winter, and they would stay under it praying for as long as they could endure, as an austerity. We each in turn waded into the pool and offered a prayer. When my turn came it was all I could do to stand under it long enough to recite "The Lord's Prayer." Even on this hot humid summer day the water seemed incredibly cold.

In the evenings we would gather together and talk. Again Dennison shared his visions. Our friend in turn confided in him his concerns for his own religion. He felt that most Japanese people were losing their faith; what they displayed now was little more than lip service. He felt that since the bomb was dropped that technology had become the thing they worshiped. It left them with great mental and emotional stress, with nothing to nourish them inside. He wondered if Dennison could offer anything in the way of advice. He expressed how he thought of Native American spirituality as an active thing that drew the people into it and nourished them. He wondered how some essence of that could be infused into Japanese Buddhism. They talked of a time, such as Dennison had been shown, where a group of people from different cultures and spiritual ideals would come together, bringing aspects of their various teachings, to create a new way of thinking. Our friend said he understood the ideal and knew it would be a good thing if it could ever come about, however he didn't see himself as a part of it...his current duties were simply too demanding.

Snippets of Future Possibilities
OCTOBER 3, 1996

During Dennison's meditations this evening he was shown a series of events, without explanation. This has happened several times before. Some of the events seem to be repeats from past visions and some are new visions. I don't know if they are "markers" of significant events to watch for, or simply future events he's able to "tune" into, much as one surfing channels on the TV.

"I saw a ship again lying on its side in the water. I don't know what it means. Maybe it's not a ship really, but represents something else like the U.S. or the Government or something. (The ship of State?)

"I also saw a flag with a six-pointed star in the middle. It was flapping in a strong breeze and the ends of it were tattered and ragged.

"I saw a big building like maybe a large bank. There was a crowd of people gathered in front of it. The doors seemed like they were locked and the people were real angry, upset and afraid. It was almost like a riot was about to begin. I sensed it had something to do with the economy.

"I saw a star or meteor; like a comet maybe. It was red hot and moving fast with a tail streaking behind it, moving toward the earth.

"There was something weird that I saw next, it was a cartoon of an elephant wearing tennis shoes. He was dragging something...pulling something like a big bag with his trunk. The bag kept falling over a cliff and he was pulling on it, trying to keep it from going over. Maybe it has something to do with our economy and the Republicans.

"I saw a bunch of women gathered. Not just ordinary women, but high classed, well-dressed women. They were carrying signs, as if they were protesting or picketing for something. There weren't any men there, only women.

"The last thing I saw was a field filled with cows. Hundreds and hundreds of cows penned up. Then I saw bulldozers coming over a hill towards the cattle. I think they were going to slaughter and bury the cows for some reason.

Knights
OCTOBER 14, 1996

LAST NIGHT OUR DOG WOKE US UP wanting to go outside. Dennison was elected to get up and do it. When he came back to bed he said

"I was just dreaming of two knights having a battle. One was black and one was white.

"The black night was on a black horse. Everything on both the rider and the horse was black. He was wearing black chain mail and a black cloak, and on his shoulder was an emblem that looked like a dragon. A black cross was hanging from his saddle. The funny thing was he wasn't wearing a helmet; instead he had a black cloth over his head and wound around so only his eyes were showing. Kind of like a Ninja or an Arab or something. He was fighting with a chain that had a spiked ball on the end of it.

"The white knight was on a white horse and he was wearing a golden breastplate with stones set in it. He wore a white cloak and had a white cloth wound around his head and face, the same as the knight in black. A golden rope hung from his saddle and a vine was wound around the rope. At the bottom of the rope was tied a cup. A chalice, I think they called it. He was fighting with a sword.

"The two of them were really fighting with all their might, and for a while it looked as if the black knight might win. All of a sudden the white horse went down on his knees and the white knight fell off sideways. As he fell, he lost his sword. The black knight, seeing this, came swooping down on him swinging his mace. The white knight grabbed the chalice on the rope because it was beside him and he raised it to stop the blow of the mace. The chain of the mace wrapped around his wrist and the black knight started to grab the chalice from his grasp. As soon as he touched it, he disappeared.

"One other thing I noticed was they were fighting in a desert somewhere, with sand all around. Going through my mind were the words, "No one wants to know the truth...."

I lay thinking about his vivid dream wondering what it could symbolize. I also observed as I have several times in the past, how the dog or some other thing will occur to wake Dennison up after having a significant dream that we should pay attention to. I decided I'd better get up and write everything down before we both went back to sleep and the details faded from memory.

Cylinders in a Tomb
OCTOBER 24, 1996

DENNISON NORMALLY GOES OUT TO MEDITATE in the late afternoon or early evening, before it gets cold. My routine is to have dinner waiting for him when he returns. As we sat eating this evening, I asked my usual question, "Did you receive anything?" He was silent as he continued eating. Minutes ticked by without an answer to my question. At last he said,

"They were telling me that a tomb is about to be discovered. I don't know where for sure it is, but I felt it was somewhere in the Middle East. When they open it up, they will find some amazing things inside. I saw some cylinders with writing on them. They contain a lot of information about an ancient civilization and how they lived and how life as we know it evolved from that. There's a lot of other important information in them that relates to us now also, as well as some ancient teachings and knowledge. They will find some instruments that were used in building ancient buildings, like temples and I think even the pyramids. These instruments were very sophisticated; technologically advanced. There is also a liquid in there that looks sort of like mercury. It was used to dissolve certain hard substances. I asked them if it was like an acid and they told me "No, it comes from some place other than here." There are also two bodies in the tomb and they aren't exactly human.

"Next they showed me a road made of huge blocks of stones. They were so closely fitted together they looked smooth. This led into a huge cavern and I could see it curving downward into the depths of the earth. 'They' said this once connected to other tunnels, which came out at various places all over the earth.

"Next I saw a room containing shelves of what looked like golden records stacked on edge. In the center of the room was a stand with a glass looking dome. There was a large spindle in the center with a stack of these golden discs on it. It reminded me of some sort of old time record player. There was no arm or anything to play them, but there was a blue light beaming on one of them.

"I saw a tall square sided pillar with a pointed top (obelisk) there was strange writing coming down the sides.

"Then I saw something I couldn't figure out. There was a cylinder like thing, a huge thing with a large support block. Through this thing were several large wire-like things, reminding me of telephone wires. Along these wires were balls of light, which moved up and down them. These lights somehow lit up the whole wire, which glowed with light.

"Way off in the distance there was a light coming down. It reminded me of a jet landing, except there were seven beams of light coming down toward the ground. Where it touched the ground, it created like a swirling light. Above the thing in the air was these rotating lights going around. I really couldn't make out what it was.

"The whole thing was strange. At the very end of this vision there was an old curtain. It was like on a stage, and it slowly closed. The curtain seemed sort of dusty and old and worn, a thing of the past. Was this supposed to symbolize what I was seeing was something from the past?"

Liberty Bell
NOVEMBER 18, 1996

COULD THIS VISION BE A PORTENT of the loss of some of our freedoms?

"What does the Liberty Bell actually mean? Tonight as I was meditating, I saw a bell in a wooden tower and I knew it was the Liberty Bell.

Suddenly the tower began collapsing and falling apart. The bell fell to the ground and broke apart. I watched as the clapper went rolling down the hill."

The White House Again
NOVEMBER 24, 1996

ONCE AGAIN A SERIES OF SCENES appeared without explanation as Dennison meditated this evening.

"I got a lot of different things tonight. First of all there was something about UFO's. There's going to be a lot of sightings in the future. Lots and lots of people will see them and film them.

"There's something happening at the White House. Something going on within the Government...I sensed dissension, scattered energies and confusion...the falling apart of the system...the President resigns or something close to it.

"I saw a large city in a riot. I think I've seen this before. There were people actually shooting other people, cars on fire, and small bombs exploding. It was really, really bad, much worse than ones in the past. I think it was race related. There was US soldiers in there and there was lots of damage and death.

"I saw either a bridge, you know like those old arched stone bridges, or maybe it was a stone wall, anyway it was crumbling. I was thinking to myself, 'it might be the Great Wall of China.' I also saw a stone castle crumbling apart. All the stones were rolling down a hill, and piling up at the bottom. It was just falling apart as far as I could see in the distance too.

"I saw a large factory or plant with white buildings and some blue buildings. There was a very high fence around it and rolled razor wire along the top of the fence. There were warning signs and danger signs everywhere. The gate was locked with a large padlock and chain, the lock and chain were corroded. I saw some liquid seeping out from under a large door. It was grayish-green and toxic looking. I felt strongly that it must not be allowed to get into the ground water.

"I saw stacks and stacks of large barrels on a dock, and they were on fire. Thick black smoke was rising and some of the barrels were exploding. There were people watching, but no one was trying to stop it. I think it was barrels of oil.

"I saw the space shuttle explode, and break up. Did I see that before too?

I saw two flags crossed over each other like X. One was red with a symbol like crescent on it and going across the crescent was a knife or something. The other flag was yellow or orange and it had a crescent moon and a star on it. I felt like they were joining forces. In the background behind the flags I saw a sunset and standing out against the sunset was blackened rubble, and pieces of trees and things.

"I felt strongly there would be a lot more tornadoes next year. I saw twin tornadoes "walking" side by side across a flat area.

"I saw lots and lots of small animals lying dead. A bunch of rabbits were scattered all over. There were lots of small deer, like desert deer lying dead too.

"I saw a hallway full of young kids. It looked like it was in a hospital or some sort of institution. I felt like they were in quarantine or something.

"As I think about everything maybe a lot of this was in symbols. Like the rock wall and castle crumbling could symbolize the disintegration of a great power. The castle represents a ruler or leader maybe. The children in quarantine could symbolize an unknown virus that affects mostly the young. Or biological warfare."

A Depression
DECEMBER 29, 1996

DENNISON WENT OUT TO MEDITATE this evening; a short time later I was startled when the door opened. He had returned after what seemed only a few minutes.

"I saw a couple of things tonight, but it got so cold I couldn't concentrate any more so I just finished my prayers and came back in.

"First thing I saw was the symbol of hands joined in brotherhood. It was on a large door of a factory or large building. I sensed it represented a union or something to do with unions. Then I saw people leaving the building, carrying boxes of stuff out. A bunch of people was gathered outside. They looked like they were angry, yelling and waving their fists in the air. I heard a voice saying, 'Chicago, New York, Detroit…' I felt strongly something is going to happen that will lead to a depression.

"The next thing, I heard a voice saying, 'There's a big Government investigation going on right now. You will be hearing a lot of things coming out in the coming year. People are getting fed up with Government corruption. America's moral values will be tested."

1997

Sword in a Stone
JANUARY 19, 1997

As usual Dennison got up first and went downstairs to build a fire in the wood stove, then came back to bed to wait for the house to warm up a little before starting the day. He snuggled down under the covers and we lay there a few minutes relaxing, not wanting to get up. Sleepily Dennison said,

"Last night I was dreaming about walking down a path in a forest. While I was walking along, I came to a large rock with a sword stuck in it. The sword was all tarnished and rusted, but the handle had these jewels mounted in it. I thought about trying to pull it out, but it was right beside the path, so I said to myself, 'Maybe we aren't supposed to mess with it. It must have some great power or something because it's right here where anyone can get it and nobody took it.' So I started walking on, when suddenly it appeared right in front of me! It sort of scared me and I wondered what I should do. I thought maybe I was supposed to try and pull it out, like in the movies, so I reached to try it. The rock was about as high as my waist and the handle stuck up almost to my shoulders. I figured it would be hard to pull out because it was so rusty, and I wouldn't be able to get a good leverage on it with it being so high up. But as I started to pull it, it began moving up ever so smoothly. I kept pulling it up, but it was really long and finally I couldn't raise my arms any more, however, it wasn't all the way out. The newly exposed blade was shiny and seemed very sharp, so I was worried about grabbing it with my bare hands. Finally I took out my handkerchief and wrapped it around the blade and pulled it the rest of the way out. I was surprised at how heavy and long it was as I carefully laid it on the ground in front of me. Then I picked it up by its handle and moved it through the air. It made a whistling sound, sort of like those old long saws used to make when you flexed them.

"A voice spoke saying, 'The sword represents your path and your destiny. You've only begun.' After this the sword began to vibrate and whip back and forth, so I let it go and it flew end over end through the air, turning into a bright light, and then disappeared."

It was a curious dream so I wrote it down, hoping to discover what it might symbolize in the future.

Intermission
FEBRUARY 1, 1997

I SAT WATCHING TV and waiting for Dennison to return from his prayer and meditation. A few minutes later he came in and sat down, then got up and went to the bookcase and began looking through the books. At last he asked, "Do we have a book called, 'INTERMISSION'?" I had to stop and think about it for a minute, because it somehow seemed familiar. Finally I was certain we didn't, and asked, "Could you mean 'TRANSFORMATION?' He insisted, "No, I'm positive that's not it. Are you sure we don't have it? For some reason I thought we did. I thought I'd seen it in here somewhere." I again told him we didn't have it, and now in fact I was sure I had never heard of it. He returned to the sofa and sat down, so I asked why he was looking for it.

"They were telling me about this book called 'INTERMISSION'. They said it was written, or is going to be written, by a guy who is in touch with inter-dimensional beings. It's about his experiences and what they told him." I was thoughtful as I asked, "Could the title maybe be Inner Mission, like a pun on Intermission? Because you see, Intermission really doesn't make much sense for a title. Intermission means a break or pause between parts of an event, like an intermission at a movie." However he insisted this indeed was the title. He went on to explain, "The way I understand it, the Spiritual and Physical planes are going to come together. It's like negative and positive coming together, they both sort of cancel each other out, and this creates something like a pause, a moment of non-time.

"They showed me a funnel and explained the energies were like that, the top is the beginning and as we get down toward the bottom or end, the energies gradually increase or speed up. At the very end it is like a black hole, and we all have to go through it. It's what religions call the "Second Coming" or the time of judgment, but it is really passing into another vibration. It's coming out into the light! Not everyone will make it though. Some people just block the energies and won't try to become more spiritual. There are hard times ahead. Those who are spiritual and open will be guided, those who aren't will be lost."

Dennison was silent for a while, watching TV. I waited for him to continue and, when he didn't, I gently prodded, "Did you get anything else?"

"Yeah...they made me real comfortable. It was like I was enclosed in a bubble of light...surrounded by this mist...a misty bluish light. All my frustrations, my fears, my angers and cares were squeezed out of me and I felt calm, peaceful and happy, even excited, but I didn't know why.

"Then they told me we're going to be involved in a war. It begins with an attack on a major city in the US like New York. Then we strike back. It begins in the Middle East, then something in Africa, and so on. Eventually we'll be fighting three different wars and at least one is against the Arabs. In time they will become one war. At the same time there will be problems at home. Virtually everyone and every family will be affected in some way. They said the U.S. is weak because we are no longer united and we have no common goal for the future. We've lost faith in our leaders and in where the U.S. is headed. We are divided about everything. When our President gets us involved in the foreign wars, the division between people will become even greater and public opinion will be split.

"Others will see our weakness and take advantage of it. Subversives, terrorists from other countries, like the Arabs will come into our country. They will also infiltrate the gangs and people like the Skin-Heads and will whip up racial hate. One of the largest cities in the U.S will erupt into a major riot. These subversives will manipulate the homeless, the jobless and the uneducated people. They in turn will join in the violence. After that, it will spread to other cities. Terrorists will spread fear in the U.S. with attacks on power plants, railroads, oil refineries, etc. trying to cripple our economy. Our military will already be spread out in foreign wars or peacekeeping missions and martial law will be needed all over the U.S. In a way our Government asked for it, because it hasn't really addressed the problems of the homeless, and the poor, and it will build on that. Then someone sets off a bomb; it will be set off in a major city like New York I think, and Washington DC. Our country will be thrown into chaos. We will be at full war. Brother will fight with brother and father will fight with son. All will be affected. "They were saying something about satellites being able to track everyone's movements. The armies will not be able to surprise each other. I think, somehow, though the satellites have the ability to watch, they won't be as effective as we think they will be. It will end up being a ground war, fought hand to hand so to speak.

"They also said the U.S. has alien technology no one knows about, mind technologies as well as weapons technology. I saw this blue beam coming out of some sort of aircraft and everything it touched was vaporized. They don't even know how they will use it yet, or what applications it has to a war situation. But this is part of everything. Energies are about to change and as it changes, so will we. In fact it's already happening in a lot of ways. It comes in waves, where people everywhere begin to get certain things…ideas, dreams, feelings and attitudes, and things change a little. Then there is another wave of energy.

"They said all our thoughts, all our feelings are intercepted by other energies, and that we are all part of the Source.

"At the end they gave me a kind of quiz. They asked me, 'Who do you (humans) look up to the most, your governments or your religions?' At first I thought our governments, but as I thought about it, both have a lot of power over humanity and in a lot of ways they are the same.

"Next they asked, 'If you are all of the same light, what separates you?' I replied, 'Our beliefs and our fear.'

"Then they asked, 'If you are all from the same Source, why are there so many religions?' Again I said, 'Beliefs and fear.'

"Finally they asked, 'What do you value most, humanity or nature?' I said, 'Nature, because without it humans can't survive, but Nature can survive without humans.'

"After that it was like the light lifted and everything was back to normal. I then realized there was a murmur or a sort of a hummmmm sound just at the edge of my consciousness. It was only after it stopped that I realized it was there."

After some time of discussing everything, Dennison gave an ironic laugh and said, "I hope I'm not the guy who's going to write "INTERMISSION."

"Oh, yeah, they also said we are of one light, one flame, one tree, one blade of grass. We are the feathers of the same wing; we are of one seed and all come from a single root."

The Watchers
MARCH 10, 1997

Dennison came home tonight saying, "They were telling me about an ancient race of people who lived in a time prior to mankind now. You see the earth has had terrible cataclysms that nearly destroyed all life, two or three times before this current time of man. Each time man has existed in some form. These particular people built exquisite stone works, buildings or temples, places of worship, cities, and great stone designs. They were highly advanced, highly evolved. They were scholars with many writings in stone. They had doctors, artisans, agriculture, etc. Many of their stone tablets were buried and still exist, undiscovered.

"There were beings known as Watchers who lived there too and interacted with the people. They were looked up to as Gods. The Watchers manipulated them, took their genes; took their sperm and eggs. They also taught and guided them.

"The Watchers were beings created by the Creator Source and could manifest a physical-like form, with no soul because they were directly connected to the Source.

"When the earth was destroyed in a natural cataclysm, genetic material was gathered from the people and saved by the Watchers to insure the survival of the human race. Mankind was begun again, only with some changes. Even now sometimes genetic changes are made to fetuses and are implanted in people. Desirable traits, physical and mental are taken from some and implanted in others to create better, and better, beings. In this way humans have advanced to what we are now.

"We are nearing a possible time of great destruction again. The Watchers are gathering genetic material from desirable people, as well as plants and animals, to insure the human form continues. They will help save some of mankind, as well as animals, insects, plants, trees, etc., to insure a balanced environment can be rebuilt."

Our Distant Past?
MARCH 13, 1997

INFORMATION ABOUT THE PAST continued to come to Dennison as he meditated this evening. It was unclear whether these were the same people he received information about a couple of nights ago, or if these were other peoples.

"They were showing me a tribe or race of people who were quite advanced, but not in a technological direction. We haven't yet discovered records of them. They were very tall, maybe seven feet or more, and dark skinned.

"I was first shown a large underground room or cavern and large stone tubs all around within the room. There was a stream of water coming out of one wall forming a shallow pool at the bottom. There were a lot of people bathing or soaking in the tubs and sitting around the edges and visiting. I felt like the water was hot, like mineral baths. There were some other people with clay pots who came to fill them from the stream. I was told these people had the concept of the wheel, a written language, agriculture and domesticated animals.

"I was taken to another room, which also seemed underground, with lamps or something to light it. I was told they used oil for lights. In this room were several stone slabs, forming low tables. There were small fires under the tables and people adding little pieces of wood to the fires. Other people came in carrying bags over their shoulders and from these bags they poured something the texture and look of wet cement, sort of grayish tan in color, on to the tables. Someone else spread this stuff all over the table in a thin layer. I noticed other tables where they were rolling this stuff, after it was cooked or dried up, into rolls and stacking it. It sort of reminded me of the Piki bread the Hopi make; only this was thicker and much, much larger. When it was dry it looked like some kind of paper. I don't know, maybe it was.

"I was shown another room where they were making rope. There were long thin, reeds or grass that was split and twisted on this wheel or spool looking thing. It made a very nice thin rope.

"In another room women were weaving baskets of all sorts. I got the impression I was in some sort of factory or something. Everyone seemed to be working.

"I was then shown what could have been a classroom. There were three men standing in front of several seated people, several were children, but there were several adults too. The men standing had their hair in a bowl cut, but everyone else had long hair. They all wore rough woven clothing, long robes with the waist tied or shorter tunics. Some had shawls or blankets over their shoulders and wore sandals. I didn't see anyone wearing skins.

"Their hair was black and mostly straight. Several of the men wore a lot of braids, or braids and straight combined.

"Their dwellings seemed mostly carved out of the rock or cliff; perhaps they were natural caves or depressions in the cliff. There were a few buildings outside and most of the cooking seemed to be done outside.

"I don't really know why I was shown this."

Comets
MARCH 19, 1997

THE COMET HALE BOPP is making its appearance in the night skies lately. This evening after his meditation Dennison asked,

"Have you ever read anything about a Mayan legend of a serpent with two heads, one is red and one is blue? It symbolizes a comet with two tails. There is also a legend about two brothers or two priests who were taken away, but will return after a comet appears, to act as Spiritual teachers. There are lots of other prophecies too, like a chariot drawn by two white horses and the Egyptians talked about a snake with two heads, one black and one white. There's another about a bull or steer born with two heads. They all refer to a comet with two tails that will come again. It will bring in a new consciousness, as it did when it came in the past. The comet will be followed by a bright star that will come out afterward. I think it actually could be an alignment of planets that come together in a way to look like one big star.

"This sign will cause several Native tribes or peoples to come together with their prophecies. For instance there is some tribe in Africa that has a long stone cylinder with writing all over it, and the Hopi have their tablet pieces. There are others who have other things too. 'They' also said something about a tablet that will be returned to earth to be put back together with another tablet. This will be the foundation of a new religion, a new consciousness. There will be five elders who will be guided to come together. They all have certain teachings they will share with each other. They will become the Spiritual teachers and guides for the people in the times ahead, and they will receive guidance and direction.

"They showed me a stone or crystal inside the earth and a beam of light or energy going into the earth at one pole and going through the earth, through this rock or crystal and out the other pole. It will create certain energies and vibrations to help raise our consciousness. I'm not clear on what it really does, but I saw ice at the poles melting. A huge piece breaks off. There will be lots and lots of rain, horrible winds that blow in a spiral around and around the earth, spiraling down, picking up speed, rising, and touching down again. I saw whirlpools in spirals in the ocean, sucking boats and debris down into them. I saw bits of red-hot meteors or fireballs raining down from the sky. I don't know if they hit the earth or not, but there were lots and lots of them.

"Before this happens, we'll notice people becoming emotionally agitated, as if they feel some impending danger and many will panic, running all over the place in fear. We'll also see wild animals in large numbers coming to where humans are. They won't be afraid of man. They will come seeking comfort and protection because they sense something is about to happen. Just before the shift there will be a beautiful double rainbow in the night sky."

A Strange Dream
MAY 10, 1997

WE WERE DRIVING TO ALBUQUERQUE this morning when Dennison remarked: "I had a weird dream last night. I don't know if it means anything or not, it might just be a stupid dream or it might be symbolic of something else, but I can't begin to guess what.

"I came upon this village and the people there had been building a tower that went way, way, way up. There was a lot of commotion and people were gathering near this tower. I asked someone what was going on and they told me, 'There's an old man up there, and we don't know where he came from. He just seemed to materialize out of nowhere.' I looked up and could see an old man in a long white robe, with long white hair and a beard. I thought of that old movie with Charlton Hesston when he was that Bible character with the stone tablets...who was he? Moses! Anyway he looked like Moses or maybe how people think God looks. Someone was saying, 'He's thirsty. They're trying to get some water up to him, but no one can get all the way up to him.' Someone else asked, 'Where is the Government when you need them? They're always poking around when you don't want them to, but when you can use them, they're never there. Then someone else said, 'You spoke too soon, there they are!' Sure enough, way up the road came a convoy of military vehicles, bringing someone to get the old man down. Others began to remark, 'People depend on the Government to do everything nowadays.'

"About this time a woman came up to me and gave me something like statues out of an old church. It was like a set. There was a statue about twelve inches high, that looked like those priests that wear red robes and those tall funny looking hats, like the Pope or something. There was also a golden dagger in a red and gold sheath, and a gold cup, which looked old and tarnished. Inside this cup was a statue of the Virgin Mary. The woman said, 'My daughter stole these out of a church, could you please take them back?'

"Then suddenly there was a loud male voice clearly saying, 'Man must begin anew'"

Disregard for the Earth
JUNE 21, 1997

WE HAD BEEN GOING AT A HECTIC PACE since launching our book in May. We drove to our publishers in California and spent two weeks getting our feet wet with book signing, being guests on a radio talk show and holding a workshop at our publisher's home. Since returning home we've had almost nonstop company. Tonight was the first time in several weeks that Dennison felt like going out and meditating. He came home this evening saying he was glad he went, even though he was tired, because he got a good teaching.

"As I was meditating I heard a voice clearly saying, 'Mankind is steeped in his own waste; mired in his own defecation. As you sow, so shall you reap, the time of harvest is at hand.'

"As we grow more technologically, we become in danger of losing our humanness. We are molded and regulated by the machines we have created and in a sense are slaves to our technology. Observe our children and how so many have such little regard for others, even to the point of killing with little feeling. This stems from losing our connection with nature and with the Earth. We feel removed from all life. We don't experience our connectedness with all things. There is no connection with the food we eat, because we have not cultivated it or sacrificed a part of ourselves to obtain it. We simply buy it from the market. The meat we eat was once a living animal, who desired life the same as we do. It involuntarily gave up its life so we could nourish ourselves, but we give no thanks or thought to its sacrifice. We don't even stop to consider where it comes from.

"We pollute our waters and our soil because we don't feel our connection to it anymore. This is especially true in the cities because there is little opportunity to experience one's connectedness to the Earth there. People there nourish off the outlying rural areas, where the food is grown. Even the water comes to them bottled from mountain springs and streams because theirs is too polluted to drink.

"As the population increases, there is becoming less and less farmland because it's being bought up by developers for housing and factories, thus becoming part of the cities. Where will our food come from when there is no more farmland? Already our soil is depleted of nutrition, it is poisoned by chemicals and pesticides, and the water that nourishes our crops is foul.

"We had to set up national forests to protect our forests and wilderness; perhaps we need to set up something like that to protect our farmlands.

"There is so much demand for food that we create ways to grow more, faster, and tamper with the very genetic make-up of the plant to produce it. We are killing ourselves in the process.

"We are like a pen full of cattle. The food and water to keep them comes from the surrounding area. As the cattle breed and the herd grows, the pen is expanded and expanded until there is nothing left to sustain them. In the meantime their waste has fouled everything around them.

"The earth is like a rock. It's slowly beginning to heat up. A hot rock radiates heat into the air around it, and the same goes for the earth. This heat is affecting the atmosphere and the oceans and this in turn is changing the weather. Global Warming."

Four High Priests
JUNE 28, 1997

This evening after his prayers and meditation Dennison asked me, "Do you know anything about four high priests who will come down from the mountain?" I asked, "What mountain?" He replied, "I don't really know what mountain. Have you read or heard anything like a prophecy about that?" I told him I hadn't, at least not that I could recall." He went on to say, "They were telling me there are four high priests, very high priests who will soon come down from the mountain and bring knowledge and some teachings to the people. They will be traveling to some power spots to activate certain energies. They are going to be carrying three stones. One is a crystal, one is like a meteorite, and one is a certain mineral like copper or something. One stone is from outer space. (I asked him at this point if the meteorite was the stone from outer space or if this was a fourth stone, but he wasn't sure which.) They will be wearing blue-gray robes and one of them is a woman, to represent the feminine energies.

"Have you ever heard of something called "Yaw-way"? Is it something Mayan?" (I replied that Yahweh or Jehovah is the Hebrew word for the name of God; could that be the word he was trying to say?) He nodded, "That's probably it, because this energy is like God energy, except they call it Yahweh energy. This will be a balance of masculine and feminine energy. Somehow these four priests have come here before, during the time of the Egyptians. Maybe they just manifest at certain times to bring in teachings…?"

More Snippets
JULY 2, 1997

Our non-stop company has continued through June. Along with entertaining company we have also been preparing for an art show over the 4th of July. This evening Dennison decided to go out and meditate while I finished the dishes, and our friends, who had been visiting for the past few days, packed to leave the following morning. The fast pace of the past two months suddenly seemed to catch up with me and I felt exhausted. With an apology to our friends I said an early good night and went to bed.

Dennison woke me later when he got home and asked if I was okay. I assured him that I was just tired, though I felt like I was getting the flu. I gave him a hug and asked my usual question, "Did you get anything new?" He shrugged and replied,

"I wish I knew why I keep seeing certain scenes over and over in my meditations. I saw a ship sinking again. I also saw lava flowing down the side of a mountain.

"There was a large bridge collapsing, and another scene where there's lots of people standing with bundles of belongings, like refugees.

"There was what I thought might be an oil refinery with huge flames shooting up from it, like an explosion or something. There were clouds of thick black smoke all around. Then I saw a dolphin swimming toward me. The dolphin kept swimming back and forth and standing up in the water as if to make sure I noticed him.

"Next I saw a bunch of trees. They looked like fruit trees with lots of pink and white blossoms all over them. There were kids sitting under the trees of every race and culture, and they looked like they were studying a book. I could see a book with pages turning. I tried to see what was on the pages and it looked like pictures with calligraphy along the side. I thought maybe it was stories and poems and things.

"I don't really understand any of it; it doesn't seem to mean anything."

A Time for Spirituality
SEPTEMBER 3, 1997

DENNISON HAS STOPPED GOING OUT TO MEDITATE as faithfully as he used to, always seeming to be too busy or too tired. I think from time to time we all feel like we're in a rut and going nowhere. I also sense Dennison is getting a little burned out, trying to juggle his spiritual work with the demands of our business. He has been having such feelings for a while. My health has also continued to be a problem since early July and I'm sure that is wearing on him too. When he returned from his meditation and prayers, he told me,

"Tonight I asked, what do I need to change in my life? Where are we going and what do we need to be doing? I didn't really understand what they were saying; it was like in poetry or something. It went sort of like this:

"There's a time when things have to change, a time for spirituality to take root.

"There's a time when seeds have to be exchanged for different seeds and planted for spiritual growth, like the changing of the seasons.

"There's a time when a new light will be shown and hearts will be opened with inner thoughts. Eyes will be opened with deeper connection. Hands will reach far and wide and gather love and warmth among friends in a circle.

"In a world of mixed emotions, different cultures will join together to bring in a new spirituality. Like an iceberg breaking, hungry minds will join with others of like minds. These are the keys to open the future... collective minds changing...bringing in deeper spiritual awareness."

Seven Doors
SEPTEMBER 5, 1997

A WOMAN WHO HAD READ OUR BOOK wrote to Dennison saying she felt so isolated and lonely because she had no one to share her spiritual beliefs with. She went on to say her husband was a fundamentalist Christian and not at all understanding of her beliefs, and it created a large gulf between them. She was thinking of leaving him. She asked Dennison to please meditate and see if he could get some answers for her. He did so this evening and got the following.

"Tonight they were telling me there are seven "doors" which are being opened. So far three of them have been opened.

"The first door is for people who are involved in a religion. They will be tested how much faith they have in their religion. They will be forced to examine what parts of the religion they believe in and how their soul is nourished by it, what truth it holds that speaks inside of them. The whole family will be tested, especially the relationship between mates. Usually the female is more in touch with spirituality and what holds truth. If there is no bond between the couple, one may be pulled away to search for another faith, or completely dissolve their belief in religion.

"The second door tests a person's foundation, such as their jobs or their relationships with family, friends, and relatives. Each will be tested with the other. If this person doesn't fit in the job circle or family circle or social group, they will either leave voluntarily or be pushed out, often leaving all material things in their life. They are given a choice to stay in their job or their relationship or to let go, to simplify and to go in search of a stronger foundation or another spiritual path. In doing so they are actually being guided toward a direction.

"Through this journey they will find other spiritual people, mates, friends and teachers. They will find true family and they will find something familiar to their soul or spirit. They will find themselves and their identity through the people and teachers they meet along the way. By doing this they will also find where they need to be and the work they need to do. People are being guided to different areas, different energy spots.

"The third door is now being opened. The energies will be strongest in October. People who have been searching are now at a place where they are being nourished, and finding groups of like-minded people. These people will also be their support and their power.

"There will be more people opening up to the new energy. This energy will ground people who are floating and are unstable and not connected. By making connections with these groups they will have a greater sense of self and why they have chosen to search for these stronger connections. By learning from others they meet, and by finding teachers, they will find what is really needed on their spiritual path.

"Some will find the place where they should be when these changes come. They will still be tested again, and through it they will find what their true identity is, and in finding this truth will gain inner strength. They will then become teachers and strong leaders, strongly connected to others already there. Then as other spiritual seekers come to this point, another foundation will be built, thus creating stronger ideas and stronger spirituality for those coming behind to build on.

"The fourth door will be opened the first part of next year. Communities and groups will be tested to see how strong they are…see how well they can work together. They will be tested with the changes coming."

Gathering of Elders
OCTOBER 18, 1997

LAST WEEK WE ATTENDED a "Gathering of Native Elders" held by someone we had been introduced to in Sedona. It was by invitation only, and Elders from several Native tribes, some as far away as Canada and South America, came to discuss their tribal prophecies.

We were excited to be invited and looked forward to hearing what they had to say. Housing was arranged for some of the older guests, but the rest of us camped on our host's acreage. The weather turned unusually cold and bitter for the time of year and my lingering health problems grew worse from being continually out in it. But we were both excited to be there and decided to stay in spite of the uncomfortable conditions.

Maybe it was because of the cold weather and very poor planning, but by the end of the second day various people began to feel slighted or neglected and several started complaining and grouching. Soon people began to separate into different factions, each accusing others of various slights and wrongs. To add to this, outside people began drifting in uninvited as news spread of the gathering. Tempers flared and the tension rose with each day that went by. Soon it became too much for Dennison and me and we slipped away quietly and went home.

Dennison felt somewhat let down and disappointed as we drove back home. He had hoped this was the beginning of the coming together of the various people he had been told about in past meditations. The reality that some of the people who should be spiritual teachers and leaders had ended up acting like spoiled children was a rude awakening. He fell into a sort of funk over the next few days. Finally this evening he went out to meditate and seek answers. I can't say that he found any, but he felt much better when he returned home.

I had hot tea and a snack waiting for him when returned. As he relaxed and warmed himself, he asked,

"What does a palm tree represent? I saw three palm trees side by side and a man in a white robe standing in front of them. A strong wind like a hurricane began to blow the trees until they were bending over. The wind kept blowing the man in the robe over until he finally grabbed the middle palm tree. I could see he was barely able to hang on. Then the first palm tree was uprooted and blew over. After that the third tree blew over leaving the one in the middle where the man was hanging on. Suddenly the wind stopped blowing and the man sat down under the palm tree; then all the fronds fell off the tree in a pile around him. After this the wind began to blow again and the man curled up, and as the wind blew, he turned into sand. Then water washed up and covered the sand and the trees. Something told me the three trees represented three words or three letters.

"Is it a Christian symbol? Maybe the three letters are GOD.

"After this I saw a flag with a hole burned through the center. It was blue and red or red-orange in color with a red star in the middle. The hole was in the middle of the star.

"I also saw an eagle with a ball and chain shackled to its leg. The eagle kept trying to fly, but each time he was jerked back to earth. There was one feather lying on the ground by itself. I wonder if the eagle represents America, or maybe freedom?

"I know there must be a message in all those symbols, but they just don't make any sense to me."

Teaching in an Egg Shell
OCTOBER 28, 1997

"I GOT A KIND OF LITTLE TEACHING TONIGHT. When we're small, we're in like an eggshell. We're surrounded by all the comforts, everything we need to nourish from, like the white of an egg nourishes the chick.

We are protected by a shell, our family. We feel secure and happy until something happens...like we lose a loved one or a job or something else, and we don't feel nourished any more. When this happens, we eventually seek something more and we peck out of our protective shell. Then we find we're in a nest with pieces of our shell around us. We've grown beyond our shell, but we're still in a nest, surrounded by a protective barrier of sticks and feathers. We begin then to seek things to make us once again feel secure, comfortable and nourished, like before, so we begin to acquire things like cars, clothing, gadgets, a home, money, etc. always something more.

"Pretty soon our nest becomes full of stuff and we feel empty. Nothing we have really means anything, and we say, 'is that all there is?' This finally makes us climb out of our nest, seeking meaning. We let go of material things to seek spiritual. We try to get back to the Earth, to find our beginnings. We fly a little, but find we have to keep coming back to the nest for our material comforts."

Bird in a Nest
NOVEMBER 9, 1997

DENNISON GOT ANOTHER TEACHING TONIGHT. I think it may be a continuation to the one he received a week or so ago.

"In the beginning, when Man was created, there weren't any teachers, any schools, or anyone to tell us how to survive. So we had to look around us, we had to study Nature and imitate the things around us. Our entire culture was built on the study of Nature and we survived for thousands of years by living that way. Now we have forgotten how to do this, and we turn to other ways of living and thinking, and we are in danger of destroying ourselves because of it.

"Have you ever watched a bird build a nest? They look for just the right twig, the right piece of grass or fluff, and they know just where to place it so the nest will be strong. They don't just build the nest any old place either; they look for a place where the eggs will be safe and they have food available. Like an eagle for instance, you will see them build a nest on the side of a cliff or in the top of an old snag, with almost no branches, so nothing will be able to climb up. Up there they can see far into the distance and spot any danger as well as any food nearby. Often they will build near a lake, where there is a supply of food and water.

"As the young hatch, they use the food they bring to teach them as well as nourish them. At first the babies have to stretch their necks up to reach for the food and this makes them use their muscles until they grow stronger. Later they have to tug at the meat in the parents' beak; they have to struggle to get it. As they grow, the meat will simply be dropped in the nest for them to fight over. They learn at a very early age how to struggle and survive. The parents know they must teach this or their offspring will die.

"All of Nature is that way, everything works together. Nature takes care of itself. Bears know when to hibernate, birds know when to fly South, salmon migrate to the right places, trees bloom and fruit at the right time, wolves kill only what they need, rabbits pull the fur off their bellies to line their nest just before their babies are born. They never make a mistake; they still live as they were created. All of Creation still follows its instructions of life and survival, except for Mankind.

"Especially now, we have forgotten the importance of struggling to survive and take for granted all the things we have for our comfort and nourishment. In doing so we have lost our appreciation and our respect; we don't even attempt to live in harmony with the rest of Nature. We are soft, and if these things were taken away from us, how many would be able to survive? What would happen if the whole world were without electricity for one week? It's incredible…just something so simple, something that we all lived without a hundred years ago…could cause a worldwide disaster.

"When we first learned from Nature, we followed Natural Laws, we organized the way we lived, the way we governed ourselves, and created our religions from these laws. We lived by these understood laws for thousands of years, without prisons, without mental institutions, without homeless people and children murdering for the sake of murdering. Maybe it's time for us to re-learn from Nature, even if it's forced on us."

1998

Twins
DECEMBER 31, 1998

Early in the summer of 1997 I came down with what seemed to be the flu that progressed into a bronchial condition and unremitting asthma. The illness left me tired and breathless with the slightest exertion, and I coughed continually. Soon it became evident I could no longer fully hold up my end of the work load. Besides losing me as his helper while making jewelry, Dennison had to assume more and more of the household chores. Added to this were my increasingly frequent trips to a lung specialist some four hours' drive away, and he insisted I shouldn't go alone. His jewelry output slowed, and our already stressed finances took a dive to a new low.

Dennison's prayers and meditation times became shortened and more and more sporadic as he tried to cope with all the added demands on his time. Finally he stopped going out altogether, saying first that it was too cold, and then that the energies had changed and he didn't feel the pull to go. There were a few dreams but I didn't keep up with my journal, and the information slipped away.

As the days flew by, my health slowly improved and by this year's end our life had finally returned to normal. Somewhere along the way though, Dennison began to grow more and more focused on money and less focused on the spiritual.

He would work long hours every day, seven days a week, driven by the pile of medical bills and assorted others that accumulated over the year. When he finished work, he would watch TV and go to bed. He never felt drawn to go out and meditate like he used to. It concerned me more than I liked to admit, and from time to time I'd nudge him, suggesting it might be nice to go out and meditate and pray, or simply go out in the forest and relax. He'd say he was too tired or that he didn't have time to break away from his work. He still continued doing some healing work, but he seemed changed a little, more focused on the material world and less on spiritual matters. I realized we had been through a lot and maybe he was just a little burned out, so I didn't press the subject. I just hoped he would at some point return to his regular meditation and prayers. I missed that aspect of our lives.

Tonight, as the year drew to a close, we had a long heart to heart talk. He explained to me how very helpless he had felt during my illness. He felt the healing he did for me didn't work and his prayers for help went unanswered. The more worried he became, the less he could focus, and the more he began to feel abandoned by Creator. He thought maybe he had failed a test somehow, that he had proven unworthy of the work he had been given to do, and now it had been taken away from him.

I suggested perhaps his faith in the Divine Wisdom of Creator was the test, and giving up what he had been doing was failing it. I asked if perhaps he had shut himself down, closed the door on Spirit because he had felt abandoned.

As the evening drew to a close and the New Year waited on the horizon, Dennison lit a smudge and we prayed.

Maybe it was because he unburdened himself and was able to relax a little or perhaps it was simply time for a change, but for the first time in a long time Dennison had an unusual dream.

The dog wanted to go out early this morning, so Dennison got up to let him out. When he returned to bed he said,

"I was just dreaming something about the Grail. It started out when I was listening to a sound that at first I thought was a horse trotting on pavement. Then I noticed a big old grandfather clock was making the sound…tic-tock-tic-tock-tic-tock tic-tock… As I listened, it seemed to make me drift into another state of consciousness. All of a sudden I felt like I was in a meeting. A man in a white robe was speaking, "Out of two stones an energy was manifested. From this energy twins were born of an unwed woman. One (twin) is as the morning dew; the other is as a mountain. This woman is in the Middle East. The twins will bring in the Grail, which will change mankind. They will cause an upheaval between two peoples (two nations or possibly two religions?). Something will be found that all nations will desire and will fight to possess. There will be major upheavals. The grandmother will weep. Eventually one (twin) will be a sacrifice and will lead the way to peace. It will carry the energy of peace and love, and will unite all religions into one energy through love. This has been told in prophecies and is now being prophesied.

"I think the "morning dew" represents freshness and purity of spirit, Spiritual. The "mountain" represents the earth or the solid material world, a battle between Spiritual and Material. Maybe the dream is a symbol or metaphor in some way."

I lay there pondering the dream, trying to make sense of it, somehow the description of the unwed Middle Eastern woman and one twin being a sacrifice and leading the way to peace and love, etc. reminded me of the Biblical Mary and Jesus. Suddenly I recalled reading somewhere that Jesus was said to have a twin brother. Could this somehow be related?

1999

The Chain of Life
JANUARY 8, 1999

WE HAD JUST FINISHED OUR BREAKFAST and were lingering over a last cup of coffee when Dennison said,

"I forgot to tell you, I was dreaming about a huge chain last night. It had big heavy links like a logging chain, even bigger. The chain was being stretched to the point of breaking and the big heavy links were pulled out long. Someone was saying, 'The chain which holds life together is about to be broken....'"

We both pondered what it could mean, trying to guess at the symbolism. I gently proposed that he might want to meditate and see if he could get clarification, but he didn't seem interested in doing so.

Doves
MARCH 9, 1999

This morning Dennison remarked,

"Last night I was dreaming of a bunch of doves being slaughtered for no reason."

I knew birds sometimes symbolized death or departing souls and I wondered if this has anything to do with the killing in Kosovo. I made note of the dream in case it meant something later.

The Year Two Thousand
MARCH 30, 1999

I THINK THIS DREAM may be connected to the dream on the 9th.

Dennison woke up this morning saying,

"I dreamed of a bunch of people dying for no good reason. I almost felt it was maybe related to a religious ideal. I was wondering why they would do such a thing over something so unimportant.

"I also saw numbers like two, then zeros. Maybe it was the year 2000. I was being told about some sort of energy that's coming, universal energy. It happens every so many thousands of years, and it is coming again. It's like the fingers of two hands inter-meshing with each other, our existing energy on Earth and this energy that's coming. Some people feel it will bring in a transformation of mankind, maybe bring in a new religion or spirituality; a spiritual awakening. Others think it will bring in changes like a major world war or natural disasters. But it actually can be what we want it to be. What it does is amplify the existing energy. If we are open spiritually, it can enhance that spirituality and bring a mass transformation, but if we are still stuck in our materialistic and greedy way of thinking, it will amplify that, and the moment will pass and the opportunity will be gone for several more thousands of years."

Cows
APRIL 6, 1999

D<small>ENNISON HAD ANOTHER DREAM LAST NIGHT</small> that seemed significant. Since he no longer meditates like he used to, I wonder if the information is now coming in his dreams.

"I dreamed of cows in a pen, lots of cows. Some men in white uniforms were getting ready to shoot them all and there were bulldozers coming to bury them. I felt like some bad thing was happening, like an epidemic or something."

Alien Dream
JULY 8, 1999

A <small>LITTLE AFTER</small> 3:00 <small>AM</small> Dennison suddenly sat up in bed, making a sort of cry as he did. I was lying there half-awake, needing to go to the bathroom, but not wanting to wake up and do it. I assumed he was having a bad dream and reached over and touched his back to bring him back to reality. I asked, "Are you okay?" No answer. I waited a moment, rubbing his back. He sniffed and said his nose felt stuffy; then he tried to blow it. I asked, "Did you have a bad dream?" He shrugged my hand off and said, "Naw, I'm okay." He lay back and I assumed he was going to sleep again, so I made my trip down to the bathroom. When I returned, Dennison was more awake. He said,

"I was dreaming of aliens...they looked a lot like humans, except they had a third eye in the middle of their foreheads." I was hoping for something prophetic or wise, but this sounded like a typical bad dream, so I said, "Hmmm, scary huh?" He ignored me and continued. "Maybe it was a symbol for being psychic because they could tell what anyone was thinking, and they would answer whatever you wondered about. I was wondering what was going to be happening in the near future... you see I was in this room that was oval or round and I thought I must be in a UFO. The being was there with me. I couldn't tell if it was a man or a woman, but it felt like it was a man. There was a large crystal-looking device beside him, and when he waved his hand over it, a light beam came through it and scenes appeared on these screens that were on the wall. It was like something out of a science fiction movie. So I was wondering what would happen in the near future and this scene appeared on the screen.

"It was of a war going on. I couldn't tell who was fighting whom, but somehow I felt like Americans were involved.

"They also showed me a battery with the negative and positive posts. They said the negative and positive poles of the earth were going to change soon...switch. The negative pole will become positive and the positive will become negative. When that happens, everything will stop for a little while; then when it starts again, it will be in the opposite direction and everything will be opposite. Everything electrical will be affected; cars won't run, satellites will fall out of the sky, electromagnetic energy will be changed, asteroids and meteors will be attracted to the earth. We will know when it's about to happen by watching nature. Animals will act differently, birds and fish will be confused, streams and rivers will reverse their flow, and there will be terrible electrical storms. A blue or purple haze will be seen around the earth at the moment everything stops, and then reverses.

"They said water would become polluted with human waste and chemicals, because sewer lines and storage tanks would rupture under the stress. We'll have to collect and purify rain and snow for a while. Water will be very scarce.

"They also told me some other things like, 'Remember, zero's mean change.' I thought, 'The year 2000 has lots of zeros.' They also said a great leader would die. For some reason I thought of Abraham Lincoln. Maybe it means the leader will be assassinated. And by 'great' I think it means more like someone powerful, not necessarily great as in wonderful."

A New Home
SEPTEMBER 25, 1999

OUR LANDLORD INFORMED US earlier this year that he has put our house up for sale. The past several months have been filled with looking for another place to live. We have been blessed with very reasonable rent for the past several years, and it has been a reality check to find what homes were currently renting for. We had grown discouraged when we found suitable homes were very scarce, and quite out of reach of our present financial means. By summer we began to feel a little desperate knowing we needed to find a suitable place to move to, while realizing we had no means to do so, when quite unexpectedly a friend offered to invest in a house, if we could find something suitable in her price range, and then rent it to us for the same rent we were presently paying!! It was an unbelievable offer, and we felt strange about accepting it. However she insisted she wanted to do it, to the point of finding potential homes herself and calling us to go look at them.

After looking all summer we finally found a perfect home, with a garage that could be converted into a workshop for Dennison. Our friend agreed with our choice, and made an offer on the home. The offer was just accepted. It should be final by the end of October and we will be able to move in shortly thereafter. Spirit has a strange way of working. We are awed and very, very grateful!

~ 1999 • A New Home ~

DECEMBER 1999

WE MOVED INTO OUR NEW HOME in November of 1999. Moving is always much more involved than one anticipates, and we worked until we were exhausted. As we unpacked and got settled in, we felt a great satisfaction and pride in our new home, as well as awe at how things worked out.

2000

The New Millennium
JANUARY 2, 2000

THE NEW MILLENNIUM started like any other New Year. After all the apprehension over the potential problems of Y2K, it's nice to know the world goes on as usual. We are finally getting settled into our new home, and find that even though it's much smaller, it suits our needs very well. It seems the following dream is already being fulfilled as far as changes in our own lives, and I wonder what the New Millennium has in store for us.

Dennison started the year off with a dream about the significance of the number 2000.

"Last night they were telling me zeros symbolize change. The number 2000 has a lot of meaning. The "2" represents a place where there is a fork in the road. One path is material, and the other is spiritual. Beginning this year people will be tested to see what path they will choose. Each "0" represents "doors" of energy for certain changes; these changes are what will test us.

"One '0' represents changes in relationships. Our relationships with family, mates, friends, people we work with, other countries, and so on. For example a couple reaches a point of divorce…there are certain things they both value: children, home, money in the bank, etc. How will they deal with it? Can they work together to make it as easy as possible or will they try to destroy each other with it? The same is true with international affairs; we can find ways of creating compromise or we can choose to go to war.

"One '0' is a door for economic changes, both personal, and national or worldwide. Energy problems, personal financial problems, business financial problems, stock market problems, a recession, these will be coming to test us to see where our values lie.

"One '0' is a door for changes in the earth itself. We will begin to realize the consequences of the way we treat the Earth. Global warming will begin to show its effects. There will be devastating tornados, hurricanes, floods, great storms that will damage homes, crops and businesses. There will be earthquakes, volcanoes and tidal waves, all on a grand scale that will devastate lives. How will we react?

"Each '0' is separate, and yet each affects the other. Some people will deal with things in a spiritual way, and some will take advantage of the situation to make money or other material gain. Those who seek material gain will continue to be tested again, and again. Their lives just won't seem to work until they finally choose a spiritual solution. Those who seek the spiritual path to begin with will find suddenly opportunities will come, and they will be guided. They then will need to reach out to those who are still having problems, and help them to understand how a spiritual way of thinking and acting will open things up for them. These problems will just keep happening, and getting worse until more and more people start acting in a spiritual way. With each new spiritual person reaching back to those who are still living in a material way, the energies begin to change."

Cross of Lorraine
OCTOBER 27, 2000

RECENTLY A FRIEND IN JAPAN contacted us to say he had been reading our book, *Spirit Visions*. He referred me to pages 167 & 168 of that book where in March of 1992 Dennison had gotten some information about a coming Holy War in the Middle East. He noted on page 168 there was an emblem that looked like a cross with two arms. He wanted to tell us this emblem was known as "The Cross of Lorraine" and he had come across it while reading a book about Qumran and the Dead Sea Scrolls. He said the book said it was an ancient symbol of Brotherhood and Unity.

I had forgotten about the symbol and looked up the pages he had indicated. After looking at the cross I decided to look for more about it on the web. I came across a very interesting and informative site that had lots of information about the Holy Grail, the Merovingian Kings of France and the Knights Templar. The site also has a very interesting article on the Cross of Lorraine. This article said this had been the first and most important symbol for the Knights Templar.

It was a hermetic symbol for transformation and a vehicle for the reconciliation or union of opposites. It symbolized the intersection of creative forces and destructive forces. It also symbolized the Union of male and female principles.

It was also a symbol of "as above, so below," and the trinity or union of two opposite forces to create a third force. It represented the balance of creative and destructive forces.

The Cross of Lorraine was alleged to have been introduced by Hermes, who taught mankind the secrets of the time before the flood. This was secret knowledge taught to man by a race of Gods or fallen Angels-Watchers. It said the Cross of Lorraine was a sigil of the "Doctrine of the Forgotten Ones." I was unable to find out any more on what the Doctrine of the Forgotten Ones might be.

Downward Spiral
DECEMBER 31, 2000

THE YEAR WENT BY much like the past few years, in that after Dennison's dream at the beginning of the year, we slipped back into our old routine of work and worry. His desire to pray or meditate just wasn't there. He seemed to want to avoid any discussion of spiritual matters in any respect. Perhaps because he was so focused on material matters, he had very few dreams of a prophetic nature.

~ On the Tip Edge of a Miracle ~

Soon after moving a major problem developed with the septic system of our house, it ended with the hiring of an engineer to essentially remove the soil from our yard and rebuild a new septic and leach system. It took eight months of heavy equipment noise, mud and dust to complete. All the while we had no toilet and ended up installing a composting one. But soon after installing it we discovered my medication killed the action of the compost. And so it went, one by one problems followed in endless succession: problems with the home, problems with the car, financial problems, and problems within our families. They came so often we could only sit and laugh for fear of crying.

As the year drew to a close, it seemed we were in a downward spiral. We were still "out of the groove" and I knew it was time to re-assess where we were going and why. His dream last January seemed to apply very much to us now. On this eve of 2001 I talked at length to Dennison about my feelings.

When had money and material things become so important to us? How had we fallen into the material trap and why? Our spiritual life had diminished to almost nothing and I missed it very much. He agreed, but maintained the energies had changed. He explained that there is a time for teachings and then a time to put them into practice or to absorb the truth of them. There is a time for predictions and a time for them to come to pass. He said energy came in waves like the ocean, coming in and then retreating. He said we too had lessons and trials to get through like everyone else, and that we were now going through such trials. He then remarked that he had been having strange dreams lately, but they didn't make much sense so he hadn't mentioned them.

He also said he thought he had somehow gotten burned out on doing his spiritual work but now he was beginning to feel more open to it again.

We decided to burn a little sage and meditate and pray before going to bed this evening. It felt so good and we promised ourselves we would begin doing it more often. It was too easy to let life slide by without taking time to connect with Creator.

2001

Iceberg
JANUARY 12, 2001

WE WERE HAVING BREAKFAST when Dennison said,

"Oh, I meant to tell you: I had a weird dream last night that this huge, huge chunk of ice had broken off at the South Pole, and was floating in the ocean. It was causing some problems they said."

It wasn't long afterward that we heard in the news about a very large iceberg, measuring some thirty miles across that had broken off the ice at the South Pole, and was causing problems for some penguins that were trying to migrate, because they couldn't get around it.

It had been more than a year since Dennison had any dreams or messages, and I wondered if the energies he had spoken about in December were once again coming back to him.

Rumor of War
JANUARY 30, 2001

DENNISON WOKE ME UP THIS MORNING and told me he was hearing a voice as he woke up saying,

"Your President is going to start a war with Saddam Hussein."

Twins Have Been Born
FEBRUARY 22, 2001

DENNISON WOKE ME UP THIS MORNING just before our normal time to get up saying,

"I heard a voice talking to me as I woke up. They were telling me 'Twins have been born. They are highly evolved spiritually and are here as teachers. One is a male and the other is a female.' I think they are born in Israel. They will bring peace to two peoples or two religions that have been fighting for a long time."

His dream rang a bell with me. It seemed sometime in the past he had gotten information about twins being born in the Middle East. I went back to our book *Spirit Visions* and found a couple of references that might be about the same thing. Then I went to journal notes of Dennison's visions, which lay buried in a box in the closet, and found indeed he had gotten something in Dec. of 1998. The meaning though remains unclear.

Tattered Flag
MARCH 8, 2001

Dennison mentioned over breakfast this morning that he had dreamed of a flag with an elephant on it.

"The flag was a U.S. flag, but it was faded until you could barely see the stars and stripes. Over the background of stars and stripes was an elephant. The flag itself was torn almost in two, with a large rip down the middle, right through the middle of the elephant and the edges were tattered and frayed. It was hanging from a weather-worn wooden pole flapping in a strong wind."

I wondered out loud if there is going to be something happening in regard to the Republican Party that would divide the nation.

A Coming War?
MARCH 19, 2001

Last night something woke up the dogs, and they in turn woke us up with their barking. After things settled back down again and I was almost asleep, Dennison suddenly asked,

"What do two buffalo calves mean?" I asked if it was a dream and he replied, "Yeah, I was dreaming about them when the dogs woke us up. There were two buffalo calves exactly alike running and playing." I asked him if there was any more to it, but he couldn't remember anything. My first thought was the "twin" theme again; then I recalled that in some

Native American traditions, buffalo symbolized spiritual nourishment and wisdom.

I wondered aloud if the dream might be a metaphor for that when Dennison interrupted me, "I almost forgot, before the buffalo dream I was dreaming about a Holy War. I was dreaming about some people fighting and someone was telling me a Holy War was about to happen. The only thing is, there's like Roman soldiers fighting…you know, like gladiators." I asked, "Can you remember who they were fighting…was there anything about anyone in the dream that could identify who they were fighting?" I figured if this was a dream with some sort of message, there might be a clue in who they were fighting with.

He was silent for a long time before he replied, perhaps trying to recall details of the dream before it faded. "There's a shield with something that looks like a "C" with an axe or hammer crossing it on one of them… (I made a mental note that it sounded like the USSR symbol of a hammer and cycle.)… There's another shield with a black lion and a yellow flag. It's not a lion exactly, more like a black panther with red eyes. The shield is a dark color. There's one shield that has a red cross that's like those crosses people wore on their chests (Crusaders?)."

Seconds passed then he continued, "There is a man standing, holding a staff in one hand and a big book in the other. There's a ribbon hanging out of the book like a Bible would have. Maybe it represents a Holy War? He's wearing a red cloak and he has a crown on his head, like a king or a leader. It's funny, on top of his staff there's a snake…a cobra head with the hood open. I thought at first he was wearing white gloves, but I can see now it's like bandages around them. There's an old fashioned watch like they used to have where a cover opens up, like a pocket watch. It's on a chain and this king is holding the chain in his hand with the book and the watch is hanging down.

"There's rubble all around, broken things like pieces of pottery, balls and chains, and broken swords and all kinds of stuff. The man has one foot resting on a pile of rubble. It's strange…instead of armor on his legs, he's wearing black leather boots, those tall skinny boots kind of like Nazi boots (jack boots?). I'm standing there watching them fight. I can hear people shouting and the sounds of fighting and a rumble in the distance, the sounds of battle. Another strange thing is there are also cannons, and soldiers like the revolutionary war, and Vikings! Maybe it's like all the wars blending together or something. It's like a living painting and I'm looking at it. Under the soldiers are two dogs fighting and two kids scuffling and someone is telling me a Holy War is about to start."

I later asked Dennison to draw a sketch of the man holding the book, since he seemed to be the central figure. I had envisioned his crown like a European king, and was surprised at how it looked in the sketch. I remarked about it to him and he told me it had at first looked to him like the crown of thorns depicted in paintings of Christ on the cross, but later he saw it wasn't. That made me wonder if this was supposed to represent the Christian "Antichrist" and the war of all wars, Armageddon?

Maybe the two boys fighting and the two dogs fighting meant "everybody and their dog" are fighting (see sketch on facing page).

I felt at the time he received this it was very significant, but I wasn't really sure in what way. I shared the dream and the picture with a couple of friends to get their thoughts.

One suggested the different figures fighting symbolized different countries. Another felt the figure could be the Antichrist talked about in the Bible and the war Armageddon. No one though took it too seriously.

As I transcribe the journal into the computer I realize since 9/11 and the subsequent wars I have come to see more meaning in the dream.

Perhaps the cobra on the staff with an open hood symbolizes "ready to strike."

The bandaged hands on the central figure may symbolize, "blood on his hands."

The Arab style head covering symbolizes "a connection with the Saudis."

The Bible symbolizes "a Holy War."

The watch may symbolize "it's time or the time is near."

The Roman style kilt could symbolize "a conqueror."

I also found the Black Panther symbolizes the archetypal struggle between forces of light and darkness. And in early medieval symbology it was often depicted as a symbol of Christ.

~ 2001 • A Coming War? ~

A Crystal Dream
MAY 1, 2001

WE WERE JUST FINISHING SUPPER when Dennison suddenly said,

"Oh, I forgot to tell you, I dreamed about our friend, the Buddhist priest last night. I dreamed we were in Japan and he was taking a group of us up to a cave in the mountains where there was supposed to be a large crystal that was imbedded in a piece of rock. There were several people there, and some of the priests too. Our friend was telling everyone that we were going to be going up on this mountain and we'd be there a long time, possibly most of the night, so we should bring a blanket or something to sit on. I had on a heavy jacket so I figured that would work well enough to sit on if I had to. He also told us if anyone wished to stay it was okay, because it was a long trip. He went on to say, even though it was dark, there would be lighted torches along the way so we could see the path.

"Everyone was supposed to bring a crystal to use to help activate this big crystal in the cave. I was carrying that large smoky citrine in a backpack and you had a round crystal ball that you were carrying. There was one monk, who was carrying a long slender green crystal. It was really large and he had a rope tied around it to form a handle so he could sling it over his shoulder. Our friend had his shoulder bag slung over his shoulder and he admonished the monk saying, "Why on earth are you bringing that big thing?" But the monk just ignored him and was just sort of dancing around being silly the way he did when we were with them in Kumano. There was another man I didn't recognize, who was going with us too.

"We started along this path that was overgrown with jungle, and as we climbed, we came across several small temples where we stopped to pray. As we continued our climb, the other man we didn't know was explaining that we would be coming to four waterfalls, and we would be stopping for a while at each one to meditate. He said 'the first waterfall is for your Spirit. The second is for connecting you to your Spirit. The third is to recognize who you really are. The fourth is for illumination.'

"After we passed the waterfalls, we came to where there were these large, perfectly smooth round rocks spaced every so often along the trail. The same man said, "Don't step on the rocks, but stay in the spaces between them as you walk along. The stones are the lessons set for you along your life journey. The monk ran and danced ahead, making jokes as we followed, laughing at his antics. Then he came to this one stone, stood on top of it and called ahead to our friend, 'Hey, do you recognize this stone? This is the stone from Canyon De Chelly. Remember when we stayed there, and you found it, and said it was a heart stone?' I noticed this stone was red, like the red rocks around here. Our friend returned and glanced at the stone and replied, 'Hurry up, we don't have time for that; it's getting late, and we have a lot we still have to do.' But the monk insisted saying, 'Don't you remember finding it while we were there?' Our friend however ignored him and walked on ahead. A little while later the monk came upon another stone, and called our friend again, 'Hey, this here's a stone from that cave we were in when we went to in the Grand Canyon.' Our friend, annoyed, replied, 'You're crazy, we were never in the Grand Canyon. I don't know what you're talking about.' But the monk insisted, reminding him, 'Sure we were, don't you remember when we did a ceremony in that cave? Remember I left that necklace on that statue in there?' Our friend remained adamant that they had never been there, and remembered nothing about a cave, or a statue. He waved him off as to dismiss his ridiculous assertion, then turned away and ignored him, continuing to climb on up the mountain.

"We came to some steps cut out of stone going steeply up and curving around the mountain. As we began to climb them, the stranger told us to be thinking about our path in life, and where we were going as we were walking up these steps. After a while we came upon a large temple or building with lots of light coming out of it. It reminded me of the "court house" I saw in that first vision I had a long time ago. The doorway was kind of funny shaped, like an arch, except the top came to a point instead of being a curve. When I entered inside, it took my breath away, it was so magnificent! The whole room was filled with crystals and light. In the center was this large crystal, and then thousands of smaller crystals were laid out in a spiral all around it. There were tiny lights that blinked from crystal to crystal going all around, and around, until they got to the big crystal, and made it light up into this brilliant light. The whole room was dazzling with its light.

"I slowly became aware of a very tall person standing in a corner off to one side, although I never could really see him, just sort of his outline.

He was really tall, and thin, and wearing this white robe. He spoke and said, 'This crystal is the center of the earth. You will notice lots of small beads around it; they are seeds to be used for the earth's needs. Take them with you to help replenish the earth.' He went on to say, 'When the birds no longer fly and the animals are dying out, you will know the time has come. I know there are a lot of people waiting for this to happen….' Then he chuckled, and it made us laugh with him, like it was funny. He continued saying, 'People will come together, but there is still time to laugh.' Then our friend said to him in reference to me, 'He's come a long way to get here.' The person spoke to me saying, 'I need you to come back; there is something left from the past in a temple. You are very connected to it.' Our friend spoke up then and said to me, 'This is the Keeper of the Crystal, thank him.'

"Inside this same room was a very large bell hanging from these big beams. In front of the bell was a great big log hanging down with a huge rope that was pulled to ring the bell. There were five or six monks who came forward and started pulling on the rope to get the log to swing. As it struck the bell, we couldn't hear anything at first, but then after a few seconds you could like feel this intense vibration that became a buzz, and this became a deep ringing vibration that actually moved us back from the sound waves. The sound just kept on and on, ringing. The man who was explaining things on the way to the cave spoke up and said, 'That is the sound of Mother Earth's heart beat.' Our friend then said, this place is not usually open to people; it's been closed up for thousands of years, but now it's time for it to open.' Once again the bell was struck and the sound wave was like a force as it hit me, nearly knocking me down as the sound of the ringing grew louder, and louder. As the last of the ringing echo died away, I woke up, and noticed it was growing light outside. For some reason I could still hear the after-echo of the ringing and I wondered if someone had rung the doorbell. I looked at the clock but it was only 4:30 AM."

Things to Come
MAY 20, 2001

THIS AFTERNOON I MENTIONED TO DENNISON, now that the weather is warmer, it might be nice if he started to meditate again. At first he seemed reluctant, but this evening after dinner he said, "You're right, I need to start again. I'm going to go out for a while, and see what happens."

When he returned from his meditation and prayer, he said, "They told me that there's going to be a separation of ideas that splits the political leaders in Washington D.C. It will affect all the people.

"This energy crisis in California is being "created" in order to put money in the pockets of top executives of big power companies.

"There's going to be some real weird storms coming soon. They will be unpredictable, with high winds and floods.

"I saw the oceans rising. There were large waves created, and winds along the coast. They were causing a lot of damage to coastal towns, really devastating. They said it happened before and it is going to happen again.

Trouble in the Church
MAY 30, 2001

WE WENT TO TOWN LATE THIS AFTERNOON to do some banking and buy groceries; it's a good two-hour drive each way and it was nearly 9:00 PM when we returned home.

I noted, as we unloaded groceries, how beautiful the night was. The air smelled a little like rain and was cool enough to need a jacket, but the sky was incredible with a million stars seeming to be almost within reach. Dennison felt the pull of the night too, and said, "I think I'll go out for a while and pray."

When he returned, I made us some tea and toast for a very late supper. As we were eating, I asked if he had received anything. He replied, "It was pretty quiet out tonight," which I took to mean he received nothing. A little while later as we were finishing our snack, he said,

"They were telling me there is going to be a split in the government that involves both parties.

"There are some top religious leaders, three or four of them, who are going to resign their positions. It will create some real problems within the Church, maybe even leading to a collapse of sorts. I don't know what is going to cause it, maybe a disclosure about things they are covering up, maybe something else. But these are high profile leaders of a powerful church that I'm talking about.

"Is it the Mississippi that is the long river that runs up from North to South across the U.S.? It's going to change its course and split in two, creating a fork, because of heavy flooding. They said it has been prophesied in the past and it's going to happen soon. The split will symbolize a split in the people of the U.S. and their way of thinking.

"There's going to be more violent storms. They were showing me this huge, huge hail, like the size of softballs that fall from the sky, and burst apart when they hit the ground. They had a kind of bluish-pinkish cast to them. They said there's going to be lots of hail, most of it large… like this…that will cause lots and lots of damage. Lightning will be associated with these storms too, lots of it. Also there will be these mini-tornadoes or very violent whirlwinds that come up unexpectedly in places you don't usually have them. They will be very destructive too. These things are caused by problems in the atmosphere caused by our own disregard for the earth.

A Dream About Elves
MAY 31, 2001

AT DINNER THIS EVENING Dennison suddenly remembered to tell me about an odd dream last night. It turned out to be a very significant teaching.

"I was dreaming about midgets…not really midgets, what do they call those little people, you know, like Nature Spirits? ELVES. I was dreaming about these elves. They were dressed in sort of ragged clothes, and pointed shoes. Some of them had these sticks or staffs, and they were poking me with them, waking me up. One of them seemed to be the leader. I noticed his stick had a feather tied to it. He asked me as he was poking at me, "Am I scaring you? Are you afraid?" I told him, "No, I'm not afraid, you aren't scaring me." I noticed their ragged clothes, and wondered if he was asking me if I was afraid to be poor, and ragged. Then he tossed his staff down a small distance away. He asked me, "Can you jump over that staff?" I told him I probably could, but he insisted that I show him I could do it. So I jumped over the stick. Then he threw it a little farther away and again asked me, "Can you jump over that?" Again I jumped over it. This went on a couple of more times, and each time I jumped farther, and farther. After this he took three or four steps forward, and again threw the stick. This time it landed quite a ways away. He again asked, "Can you jump over that?" I looked at it, and analyzed in my mind whether I could do it or not, but I really in my mind knew there was no way I could make it.

"As I stood there several of the other elves started encouraging me saying things like, 'Go ahead, you can do it! I'm sure you can do it, just don't think about it, and you will do it.' I knew this was some sort of test, so I was determined to at least try.

"The leader said, 'If you think you can do it, then go ahead; but if you don't think you can, then don't try. I hesitated for a while, listening to the others encouraging me to go on and try. Finally the leader said, 'I believe you can do it. If you believe you can, then you'll be able to do it. Just concentrate on what you want.' So I closed my eyes, and thought about where I wanted to go, and really focused on being there, then suddenly I was on the other side of the stick, like I jumped farther than I could."

The Middle East
JUNE 2, 2001

WE PARTICIPATED IN A CRAFT FAIR in a nearby town today, and we were both tired when we finally got home, and unloaded all our stuff. I started cleaning up the left-over breakfast dishes and other chores left from our early departure. Dennison decided to go out and pray and meditate for a little while, and re-energize.

When he returned, I had a light supper waiting. After we ate, I asked, as usual, if he had received anything. He just looked at me strangely, and shook his head, then sighed. I took it to mean he hadn't gotten anything, but he soon followed with a question.

"What's going on in Jerusalem?" I told him that I'd just heard on CNN that a suicide bomber had blown himself up in a Disco, killing fourteen teenage Israelis when he did so. Now a lot of the Jews were calling for retaliation. In the meantime their Prime Minister was calling on Palestinian leader, Yasser Arafat, to enforce a ceasefire. Dennison then asked, "What's the problem? Why are they fighting in the first place? I replied it was really complicated, but it was actually over land. Both the Israeli, and the Palestinians wanted the same land, and neither wanted to tolerate the other being there. He wanted to know if the Palestinians were Arabs, and I told him they were. Then he asked, "Who is next door to Israel? Who are allies with the Palestinians? I thought a moment. I'm surely no expert on the Middle East, and actually try to ignore much of the news about that part of the world because it always seems as if they are fighting about something. I told him I thought Iraq was nearby, so was Iran, Syria, Egypt and Saudi Arabia, but felt Iraq might be the most likely to be an ally if called upon. By this time I was wondering what he had gotten that brought up all this interest in the Middle East.

Dennison next asked if I could get him a map of the area, so I got out our atlas, and coincidently opened it up right to a map of the Middle East.

Immediately his eyes went to Iraq, and he pointed to it, and said, "There's going to be a war breaking out between the Arabs and the U.S.. It's building up right now, the energy is moving that way. It will affect the oil supply.

"Would you say New York is the financial capitol? Do they call it the financial capitol? I was told something would happen in the financial capitol. I think a bomb or something will destroy it. I think that we will get involved in a war after that happens, but if we do, it will be disastrous!! I saw a huge army gathering. I saw lots and lots of military equipment. I saw a red sky, a black/red sky, a foggy red sky and devastation everywhere….

"Then they told me we will be involved in a Holy War by the end of this year. There's going to be a separation in the White House, a very drastic separation. I think it's all over us getting involved in a war. I don't know if it is the same war with Israel and the Palestinians that I saw or another war somewhere else, but I imagine it's the same one.

"I don't want to know this! Oh, I hope I'm wrong! I hope we don't get involved. If we do it will be a terrible, terrible thing."

After he finished talking, he just sat there, very visibly upset. I could feel a hollow in the pit of my stomach, and fear well up as the implications of what he said soaked in. Lately too, he's received a couple of dreams, one in particular regarding a Holy War about to begin in the Middle East. It now seems very real, and very near. That we, and the rest of the world, would be deeply affected by it, there is little doubt.

Serpents Fighting
JUNE 5, 2001

THIS EVENING WHEN DENNISON RETURNED from his prayer and meditation he said,

"I once again saw three serpents fighting. Remember, I've seen something like this in the past? Anyway these three huge serpents were fighting or playing with each other and raising a lot of dust. One was red, one was black, and one was yellowish-white. I don't really know what that symbolizes, but it came to me they represented different nations.

"I also saw a group of Mayans gathered in a circle doing a ceremony. There's going to be a large gathering soon, and they are going to be praying for the Earth, and the coming together of the Native peoples for peace. It has to do with a serpent."

(I recalled as he told me this, that there is a Mayan pyramid in Mexico where the steps of the pyramid look like a serpent (Quetzalcoatl) moving during the summer equinox. Mayan Priests and many other people gather there and pray at that time. The summer equinox is coming up soon.)

"I strongly sense we'll be involved in a war by the end of next year.

"I saw a bunch of students protesting something and a riot breaking out...but this didn't go any further because a camper pulled up close by."

~ On the Tip Edge of a Miracle ~

An Explosion in New York
JUNE 12, 2001

ONCE AGAIN DENNISON WENT OUT TO MEDITATE AND PRAY. The warm summer nights are seductive and I'm glad he again feels the pull to go out.

"There's going to be an explosion that devastates an area. I don't really know where or when. The name New York came to me, but maybe it's the one I saw happening in Jerusalem....

"I also saw a meteor shower of small pieces that will hit the earth and cause a lot of damage to a city. They said it will be a sign to watch for.

"There will be a rainbow that will appear in the west. No rain will cause it. I think I've gotten something like this a few times before too. I think it's associated with a polar shift or electrical energy shift of the earth.

"Three people will be coming from the East bringing spiritual teachings. There are two men and one woman.

"There are new energies coming. The old energy is coming to a close and the new energies come in, and boost things up. I don't know if it's a spiritual boost or exactly what that means.

Something Happening in the Church
JUNE 23, 2001

OUR JEWELRY BUSINESS HAS BEEN EXTREMELY SLOW THIS YEAR. I suppose it's due to the economic slow down, and people waiting to see what's going to happen to the economy. We had hoped by now things would be picking up, but we actually were doing more business in January than now. With many bills due, and no money coming in Dennison went to pray, to ask for guidance, and a direction to go in. When he returned home, he said,

"They said to be patient; we're going to be really busy in the very near future." I remarked sarcastically, "I'm patient; it's the people we owe that are impatient!"

Dennison went on to say, "Something is going to happen to the leader of a major religion very soon. Maybe it's the Pope, he's pretty frail, or maybe it's something else, but it will have a major impact. "

"I was also told there is going to be a lot of guerrilla wars happening. I don't know if they mean terrorists or what. I sense the U.S. is going to get involved in some way."

"That's all I got because a pickup came driving up where I was and parked. It seems like I can't go anywhere without people coming up while I'm meditating, to see what I'm doing. The woods are full of people camping and they don't seem to have any respect that someone might want to be left alone."

Cobra Dream
JULY 4, 2001

WE WERE SITTING ON OUR FRONT PORCH waiting to see the fireworks that were to be set off at the Country Club, which is just over the hill from the house. Dennison casually turned to me and remarked,

"Last night I was dreaming of a Cobra and a Lion fighting. The Cobra was much larger than life size, and what was unusual was the Cobra had a mark or a stone or a jewel in the middle of its head, right where the third eye would be. This stone was red and reminded me of a ruby or garnet or something."

It was such an unusual dream that I immediately suspected it had a deeper symbolic meaning. Later when we went back into the house, I began trying to research the symbols, but was unable to come up with much. Finally I got on the Internet and began looking for Lion symbolism, and Cobra symbolism. I came up with a lot of very interesting information, but what impacted me the most was finding the Lion had early Christian symbolism, in particular symbolizing Christ. In fact in some Gnostic writings he was referred to as the Righteous Lion. On the other hand the Cobra is associated with many Middle Eastern religions. Most interesting was finding out some serpents, including some Cobras, have a primitive or parietal eye or sensing organ in the center of their head where the third eye would be. A red bony structure or "stone" will grow in this spot. In Indian mythology the Cobra with a red gemstone such as a Ruby in place of the third eye represents Shiva who, in Indian Mythology, is the Lord of Destruction.

For some reason this made me think of the dream he had on March 18th of the Holy War about to begin. In discussing what I'd found with Dennison he expressed that he had felt at the time that the Lion and the Cobra had represented the Christians and the Arabs. Also the man in the robe in his dream of the Holy War had a Cobra on the head of his staff.

Arafat and Israel
JULY 15, 2001

Dennison went out to meditate, and pray this evening. When he returned home he asked,

"Is Arafat very strong – powerful?" I shrugged; I don't even pretend to know anything about such things. I said, "I suppose he's strong enough that the Israelis see him as a threat." Dennison continued, "I think Israel is planning to 'take him out' somehow. Either assassinate him or disable him in some way. Is the U.S. selling arms to Israel?" I told him I supposed so, that I thought we had been selling them weapons and fighter planes for a long time. He went on to say, "I mean like nuclear weapons. They told me the U.S. is supplying them with nuclear weapons. We are working with them somehow." I reminded him that we have been trying to negotiate a peace between Israel and the Palestinians for a long time. He replied, "That's just on the outside. Actually Israel is gearing up for a war with them. They are going to attack them and we're in on it in some way, backing them up.

"Remember the lion I saw in that dream fighting the cobra? I think the lion somehow also represents Christians—Christians who have big money interests in the U.S., who have political clout, and money enough to create pressure. They are behind the scenes. They have a personal interest in getting rid of the Palestinians in Jerusalem, so they have something to do with all of this too. They see Jerusalem as their Sacred Ground, and the place where Christ will return. The Palestinians somehow are in their way, so they will help the Jews against them. Our President is strongly influenced by them and is working with them.

"Then there is some Arab country that is working with Arafat in some way, backing him up. Maybe Iran, or someone like that. That's pretty much all I got."

Global Warming
JULY 30, 2001

DENNISON'S MEDITATION TONIGHT brought the following information:

"Tonight they gave me some more information on global warming. They were talking about the ocean heating up at the poles, and the ice cap melting. Somehow the water is moving in a circular motion because of the effects of the warming. It's eroding the ice underneath, and a large chunk or sheets will break, causing some problems. Somehow the warming is going to cause something to happen with algae, and in turn that will affect the marine life. There's also something about the salt balance in the oceans. Fishes will be getting diseases, especially the larger, more sensitive species like whales, and dolphins. This disease will cause their skin to look grayish-pinkish, and have sores. Fish will move to areas that aren't their normal habitat, trying to find a better place. Some of the larger species will get into water that's too shallow. There's going to be problems with lots of the fish, and this will really affect the food chain and food supply from the sea.

"There's a volcano in the Northwest that's going to be causing problems. Instead of the lava going to the top, causing it to blow, it will come out in other places, unexpected places, like the side. It will cause some major problems for the surrounding towns. This is also caused from the earth heating up and pushing magma from inside the earth up through old vent holes or weak places. I think it's winter when this happens because I saw snow all around.

"Another problem is a lot of trees will be getting diseases. There's a layer around the earth that helps filter out harmful rays from the sun and the cosmic rays. This layer is getting thin and depleted in some areas, allowing some of these rays to come through. Certain trees and plants are sensitive to the rays and have no protection, so they are damaged and weakened, and then disease sets in.

"There are insects, like mosquitoes that are carrying some diseases. You've probably heard something about it. It's more widespread than they think and it's going to cause more problems than expected. It will especially affect the animals. Now it's mostly small animals and birds, but soon larger animals will be affected, like elk, deer, cows and horses, etc. with lots of deaths from it. Humans will be affected too, but not as much.

"There's going to be a war that starts over two planes being shot down. I saw two planes coming down, and a large explosion happening right afterward. It's connected with the Middle East, but I don't know if it happens there or here. Somehow though, we are involved.

"I still see that bomb or explosion happening too; I think it's in the Middle East this all takes place.

"Countries other than the U.S. will have to work to resolve some of the problems that are causing global warming. The U.S. is still looking at greed over everything else. Other countries see the effects, and even are experiencing problems, and want to work to change things, but even though the U.S. sees the effects, we try to minimize it. Other countries, especially Japan and Germany, are leading the way.

They said mankind MUST change. We've reached our limits and are now destroying ourselves. We're at a transformation point. I don't really understand what they meant by that."

More Future Predictions

AUGUST 17, 2001

DENNISON FELT LIKE HE SHOULD GO OUT to pray and meditate this evening. When he returned he told me,

"I got so much information tonight that it was almost overwhelming, mostly because I don't really understand most of it. It has a lot to do with finance and politics and I don't know anything much about those things. There are a lot of things that will happen that are separate, but all weave together and will affect each other over the next two years to create our future.

"Things will continue to escalate in the Middle East. Acts of terrorism will increase a lot. They showed me a building where many Americans are inside, that is bombed and many die. This along with a few other happenings will be enough to draw the U.S. into a conflict. They told me 'Your President is 'gung-ho' and out to prove himself and is too ready to 'kick-ass.' He makes decisions too fast before he has all the facts, before he takes time to think things through. He is not capable of handling a war.' This will be a major influence on future events.

"He will pick a fight with Saddam Hussein or someone like that. The whole world will watch, but no one wants to back him up.

"Another thing they showed me is two major corporations, really big companies like a computer company, maybe Microsoft, and a power and gas company or a company that deals with energy resources (that kind of big), that have widespread influence and financial clout and have their fingers in a lot of other things, go down—collapse. They aren't really as sound as they appear. The effects are far-reaching and it seriously hurts the economy. There are thousands who become unemployed because of it. The existing businesses can't absorb all of them into their workforce, so thousands remain unemployed.

"A major church that has a lot of influence in the world and a lot of political and financial power is not as strong as it used to be in the past... its leader dies. I think it's the Catholic Church they were talking about. The Pope dies and the Church falls apart. It loses its power. There's also a scandal that happens before this and that weakens it, something like a sex scandal. The collapse of the two major corporations has something to do with the church problems too. Like maybe they invested in these companies or something and when they collapse, it seriously affects the church. They said there has been some sort of prophecies about the death of this Pope and his death will be a sign. It will be the other significant event that will affect what is to come in the future.

"There's going to be an invention that will change the balance of financial things in the world. It is another fuel that is environmentally friendly, cheap and can be manufactured. I think it is somehow made with oxygen and can be made into either a liquid or a gas and can be used in place of gasoline and natural gas. It will become a major competitor to the oil companies. They will try to stop it, but the people demand it and it becomes more and more popular because it's cheaper and cleaner and easy to get.

"Somehow food production is going to stop or slow down. Something happens to our food supply, and it becomes hard to get lots of things. Maybe it's a drought or some disease that affects the crops or maybe some sort of germ warfare.

"The weather is another thing that will be getting worse. I think because of global warming. The oceans are getting warmer and so is the upper atmosphere. In between where there is colder air, the two mixing creates a circular wind pattern that turns into huge hurricanes. I saw two tornadoes; huge tornadoes, walking side by side, and they devastate a city. I saw these tall buildings being hit with them. It happens around the same time as the corporation failures.

"Something happens to our money. They were telling me something about money is being printed, lots of it, but there isn't that much gold to back it up. It's like an economy that is built out of assets that aren't really there. It's all on paper, but nothing is there to back it up, or at least not enough to back it up. No hard assets. Wall Street goes down. Mortgage companies collapse. Banks collapse. Big, big companies like insurance companies fail, just go down one after another.

"They also showed me some large green bugs about four inches long. They looked like some kind of weird grasshoppers that aren't like our little grasshoppers. They devastate the green crops and are carrying some kind of disease too. I think maybe this is what happens to our food that creates the shortages I was telling you about earlier.

"All of these things are going to take place in a relative short period of time and will all play parts in the Holy War that is going to happen. The energies are already set into motion and will build as time goes by. We should all prepare ourselves on all levels."

A Fast Trip to Japan
AUGUST 26, 2001

EARLIER IN THE SUMMER we were again invited back to Japan to teach a three-day workshop. The same group of people has asked us back again because they have come to have a better understanding of what Dennison has tried to teach in the past and they now want to learn more about Native spirituality.

~ 2001 • A Fast Trip to Japan ~

It was nearly 8:00 PM when we arrived in Japan feeling tired and somewhat disoriented. As the crowd of people boarding and deplaning cleared out, we began to realize there was no one there to meet us. This was extremely unusual for the efficient Japanese, so after clearing customs and picking up our bag we sat in the main lobby waiting and wondering. Finally, after nearly two hours waiting, we at last saw a familiar face rushing toward us calling out, "Denny-san, Teddie-san, I'm sorry, traffic bad!" After the mandatory bows and warm hugs he scooped up our bag and rushed us out to his vehicle.

We drove another two hours to an Inn near Mt. Fuji where the rest of the group was setting things up for the next day. After warm greetings we sat down for a few rounds of hot tea and rice crackers with our hosts while we visited and caught up on what was expected of us during the weekend. Finally we were taken to a nearby restaurant for a very late supper, and whisked off to bed. By then it was nearly 3:00 AM Japanese time; who knew what time it was by our body clock.

The insistent beep, beep, beep of our alarm intruded on my dream and I struggled to figure out where we were and what that blasted sound was. Exhausted, I forced myself out of bed, turned off the alarm and headed for the bathroom. When I came out, Dennison was already dressed and making some tea. I sat on the edge of the bed, wishing I could crawl back in and sipped my cup of the steaming brew.

As we finished up and prepared to join the rest of the group, Dennison remarked, "Last night I dreamed of two Gorillas fighting. One was black and the other was a whitish color. The black gorilla was really going after the white one and attacking it over and over again, leaving it bloody around its head."

I wondered if the Gorillas symbolized some kind of guerilla warfare or terrorist attacks.

The weekend flew by and we soon were again navigating the Tokyo airport, dreading the long flight home, yet glad to be on our way nonetheless. As we settled into our crowded seats, we decide this would be the last trip to Japan, especially under such rushed circumstances. We're getting too dang old for life in the fast lane.

~ On the Tip Edge of a Miracle ~

Devastations
SEPTEMBER 4, 2001

The Labor Day weekend was now upon us and the whole area around our town was filled with people wanting to make the most of the last weekend of summer. There were also hunters everywhere, trying to bag an elk. Dennison decided to go out and meditate anyway, hoping he wouldn't be interrupted or mistaken for an elk. When he got home, he recounted the following series of visions.

"I saw a lot of things, some that I've seen before. They just came as scenes, like watching movie previews or the news with the sound off. You don't really know for sure what they mean. Maybe I'm just too tired to focus my mind to get all of it or something. I don't know why I sometimes get stuff this way.

"I saw what I think was a nuclear accident happening. The fallout devastates a large area. I didn't get a sense where it is or when. I think it's caused from a big earthquake.

"I saw a volcano and I saw the side of a large mountain sliding down in slow motion. Trees and stuff were sliding down, and lava was flowing down the side. There was a large city nearby that was being threatened by the lava. The sky was black, and there was ash all over, and people were trying to evacuate, but a lot of them were choking, blinded from all the ash. I sensed it was in the Northwest, but maybe I'm just using my logic to think that. I don't know where it was, maybe Mexico or even some place else.

"I saw bunches of fish coming into shallow water where they aren't usually seen. It's because of the oceans heating up and making them behave differently than normal. Their food sources are in trouble.

"I also saw a large ice burg floating in the ocean. Again it is from global warming.

"I saw this huge meteor or comet that is coming; it was a large glowing ball with a tail of light. No one expects it, and it's coming too close, and a lot of people are in a panic.

"There was bunches and bunches of birds that are acting funny. They are in large flocks, and they fly into windows and buildings, cars etc., like they have lost their direction or are out of balance.

"I saw large green fields of plants. I was thinking it was corn when I saw them. The plants were covered solid with insects, maybe grasshoppers.

"There was a beam of light coming down from the sky. I don't really know what it was coming from, but it was kind of strange. It reminded me of those UFO movies where this beam of light comes down from a flying saucer or something.

"There are going to be some huge sun flares in the near future. They will cause a lot of problems with communications and electrical devices.

"I saw those huge, huge tornadoes again.

"Something else I saw that I didn't understand was a very large building, like a warehouse, filled with large containers of what appeared to be water. The containers were clear like glass or plastic and filled with a clear liquid.

"I saw a computer chip and it was melting in one corner, slowly melting down. I don't know if it symbolized the computer companies getting into financial troubles or what.

"There were a bunch of planes flying in formation. They seemed to me to be war planes when I saw them. There were twenty or thirty of them, and I had the feeling they were going into battle.

"Israel is going to still try to take out Arafat. On the outside they seem like they want to negotiate a peace, but they plan to get rid of him, to break the Palestinians.

"I saw two bombs going off in a city. There is a great loss of life.

"I saw a black dragon in a small cave. It looked like it was just waking up. It was on its back and it was moving its tail, and kicking its legs, like it was trying to get right side up. It was really black and shiny, almost oily looking. The cave was covered with this black gooey, slimy stuff and that's why the dragon was having a hard time. It seemed to be getting angry and frustrated, getting very angry. I don't know for sure but I think it symbolizes the Arabs. I think that's all I got. At least it's all I can remember right now."

~ On the Tip Edge of a Miracle ~

The Day After
SEPTEMBER 12, 2001

OUR PHONE RANG YESTERDAY MORNING shortly after 6:00 AM, waking us. It was a friend of ours who said, "Do you have your television on?" I told her no, that we were still in bed. She said, well get up and go turn it on; something terrible is happening, a plane just crashed into the World Trade Center." Sleepily we got up and turned on the TV. I half listened to the excited comments being made by the newscasters as I made coffee. I was just bringing Dennison some coffee as I watched a second airplane crash into one of the buildings. I was confused and asked Dennison if that was another plane or were they re-running film of the first crash. He said he didn't really know, but he thought it was another plane. I said, "Oh my god, what ever on earth is happening??"

Later people began to call us, asking if we had heard what had happened, wanting to talk, wanting to know if Dennison had gotten anything about it in any of his visions. At first I thought he hadn't, but later I remembered a couple of things that sounded like it could be referring to this.

Once on 6-12-01 he said, "There's going to be an explosion that devastates an area. I don't really know where or when. The name New York came to me, but maybe it's the one I saw happening in Jerusalem." Another on 7-30-01: "There's going to be a war that starts over two planes being shot down. I saw two planes coming down and a large explosion happening right afterward. It's connected with the Middle East, but I don't know if it happens there or here. Somehow though, we are involved." And again on 8-11-01 he said, "They showed me a building where many Americans are inside, that is bombed and many die." I know there have been other hints in the past that didn't mean much at the time.

The same friend who called to tell us to watch the TV this morning called and said she really needed something to help her to cope with what happened. She asked if we could all get together and pray or something, so tonight we had a prayer circle in our home and several of our friends came over to pray with us, and to talk and seek comfort after the terrible attack on the World Trade Center and the Pentagon. We are all still in shock, and unable to comprehend all the implications of the attack. Tonight after the prayer circle Dennison went out to pray, and to see what he could get from the Grandfathers.

When he came back, I anxiously asked him what he found out, what's going to happen next. He replied, "I really didn't get much about that for some reason. Maybe my own energies are just too scattered, I don't know. The first thing I saw was a flock of doves flying back and forth in waves, landing briefly and then flying off again, like they were restless or confused or something. Then when they land again, a candle comes up in the center of the flock, and after a minute everything becomes very bright and I see a tree begins to grow up from the light.

"This tree becomes covered with fruits and flowers as it continues to keep growing up into the heavens. I kind of felt like the doves was the souls of all those people who were killed in the attack. They told me there are four beings coming; they are highly evolved and very spiritual. They will be here as helpers in the times to come.

"They told me to watch for the animals to begin coming closer to us humans. They are trying to communicate in a way, to make contact. They will be seeking comfort....

"I saw some sort of numbers on a chalkboard. Someone was there writing long, complicated formulas really fast, crossing out some numbers, and adding other numbers, line after line of numbers, like algebra or something. I tried real hard to understand what they were showing me, but I never understood algebra very well, and it just went over my head. I asked why they were showing it to me, because I didn't know what it meant. They just said it was the key to something, and I would recognize it again when I saw it.

"They showed me a sort of pyramid-shaped building, and there were these huge doors that opened outward from the center. They were just opening, and closing. I have no idea what that was supposed to mean.

"There's going to be an object that will be found in Egypt or some place in the Middle East. It is a box of sorts. They said it was an ancient communication device that was brought to earth in the past and given to the people.

"They were also telling me there's some sort of signals being sent in higher frequencies and we haven't been able to sense them yet.

More on 9/11
SEPTEMBER 14, 2001

"They were telling me that the plane that crashed in Pennsylvania was headed for the White House. There's still a bunch of the terrorists here in the U.S. that aren't through with what they set out to do. There's going to be some more things that happen here, and in other countries in the future.

"They also said that Americans are calling for revenge, but we should remember, "Violence begets violence." There are going to be more things that happen here, and other parts of the world. Our forces will be scattered. Other countries will have their own problems to deal with, and we'll have to take care of ourselves.

"There will be innocent victims who are killed for no good reason, and the world will cry out. Those who back us now will turn away, and also those within the Arab world. They will begin to see us as being as bad as the terrorists, and will withdraw their support from us, and some will even aid the terrorists, and support them.

"They told me to pray all the time for peace, and for our President to find wisdom, and moderation. There are other alternatives."

The Terrorists
SEPTEMBER 16, 2001

DENNISON HAS BEEN GOING OUT TO PRAY EVERY NIGHT since the attack. Tonight he came back to say, "The stock market is going to go to hell. Also what is going to be affected is our gold market. Once the money is gone, there is nothing to back it up, and that is going to bring up the price of gold, and its value. I don't really know how that works, that's all financial, and I never understood that sort of thing.

"These terrorists are backed by a religion; it's Islam, but a different type of Islam. It's a HUGE organization, a large religious group, more than Bin Laden and his group. It has followers all over the world. They are over here in this country too. If we strike any of them, these people here will retaliate. They have places already planned for strikes. They have been studying lots of different things, like the airlines, the where and how to strike where we're most vulnerable, and how, and when is best to strike.

"This organization has people who are training, and who have trained to go into different areas, pilots, and power plant workers, different companies like that. Their objective is to break down the financial market in this country. These strikes make our stock market go way down; it makes people afraid to go out and spend money. If people don't spend, businesses fail. It also puts a huge burden on the insurance companies. It puts another huge burden on helping clean up, and helping the victims' families, etc. Then we send the military here, and there, and that is another huge expense. That's what they want.

"The way I understand it, they study different areas to find which is the most powerful, and effective, then train to get into it. They even get into top-secret areas.

"The next thing that's going happen, I think, will be an attack on our power plants, like our nuclear power plants…do we have any big gas storage facility? A big company or something that stores fuel? I saw something like this that's underground. I don't know how that is, but they want to strike that. Then I saw like three large carriers, ships; they look like they are more for fuel or supplies. They are looking at those too.

"I think they are looking at some of the dams too. They want to cut off our power supplies. They are looking for ways to penetrate those too, to get someone working inside or get inside some way.

"There's some sort of a communication system that they have that they communicate with. I don't know if it's like a computer system or something. Maybe it's the Internet. Like maybe they have a code or just ordinary words they say that means something different, so if anyone sees it, they don't know what it really means.

"I don't know how this works…how would they shut down our communications? The phone company? Or the Internet? I saw some big cables in tunnels that serve to carry our communications. They are trying to shut down our communications.

"Was there another plane involved? I think they were going to hijack another plane but somehow that didn't work out. They were going to use it to hit the Pentagon too. They were going to hit it twice to try to completely destroy it, but they didn't accomplish it. They are still working on some airplane attacks. They still haven't finished with that.

"What is going to be affected too is our food sources...the transporting of it...when one part goes down, it affects another part...like the ships that bring food in or the trucks that deliver it, etc.

"What they're saying is that the terrorists are waiting for the Americans to settle down into a normal flow again, where they can get into the system after our security gets a little relaxed, get on the inside so they can be more effective."

What's in Colorado?
SEPTEMBER 20, 2001

DENNISON WOKE UP THIS MORNING saying, "Does Osama Bin Laden have a son?" I told him I'd never heard if he even is married or has a family. He went on to say, "I was dreaming something about his son, but I can't really remember what. It was like maybe he'll be important later on."

I don't know if this is of any significance, but I'm making note of it in case it proves to be later on.

We were on our way to Gallup to buy supplies when Dennison suddenly asks, "What's in Colorado that they would want to hit?" I thought a minute and then replied, "I think Cheyenne Mountain is there." So he asks, "What's Cheyenne Mountain?" I reply, "I'm a little vague on exactly what it is, but I think it is where NORAD is located, and it is pretty impregnable, and very secure." He thinks about this a little, then asks, "Is there anything else there? Colorado keeps coming up over, and over. I think they are going to try to hit something in Colorado." I try to think, but the more I think, the less certain I am that Cheyenne Mountain is even there, and can't think of anything.

More Fearful Scenarios
SEPTEMBER 25, 2001

IN SPITE OF OUR HAVING COMPANY, Dennison decided to go out this evening, and meditate, and pray. When he returned, I made him a cup of tea and a muffin. As he ate, I waited for him to tell us what he received, however he remained quiet about it until our guest went to bed.

"Our President is going to blame Iraq, saying they are hiding terrorists associated with Bin Laden. He will also say they have biological and chemical weapons that they will use against us. He will want to attack, and destroy Saddam, but there will be a real kick-back.

"The people will begin to demonstrate against the action, and turn against the President. I saw huge demonstrations. Cities come to a standstill because of it. Even congressmen and some senators change their support. Other countries like Japan, Germany, France and Switzerland, etc. will speak out against what he wants to do. He will depend on air support from some countries, but I think some of them don't come through.

"When the war starts, the terrorists will retaliate, and the first thing they will try to hit will be the oil and gas supplies.

"I saw a series of scenes of some of the things that are going to be happening in the future. I saw an underground explosion where that underground cable looking thing was, that I saw before.

"I still strongly sense Colorado. I saw a mountain explode from the inside. Not like a volcano, but an actual huge explosion from underground, inside the mountain. I felt strongly it was in Colorado.

"I saw something like a subway, an underground tunnel under a city. There was an explosion in it, and I sensed it had to do with chemicals or germ warfare.

"I saw a train that's going to be targeted. There was something on it like a bunch of bombs that they can't stop from blowing up. A bunch of people are killed.

"I saw a small plane flying with maybe four passengers. The plane is hijacked and someone is held hostage. I think this hostage must be someone very important because I saw a bunch of jets coming, and a helicopter flying right beside the plane. There is something like a bomb. I felt like this bomb was tied on the plane some way. I don't know, but maybe the bomb was nuclear and that's why there was so much attention given to the plane.

"There was a large group of people like at a stadium, and they were running, running for safety. There was lots of smoke all around, and a bunch of shooting. They were shooting the people as they were running for safety.

"I saw a refinery or a plant of some sort, and part of it was on fire. At first I thought it was a power plant, but then I saw a bunch of big white tanks on fire, and I thought they were filled with gas or something like that.

"I saw a large number of dead birds just lying around. A bunch of them scattered all over the place.

"I also saw all these cows dying. They were in large pens, maybe like feed lots or something, and some were lying down, and others were standing or going down. They were obviously dying.

"I saw the number 26. They showed it to me a couple of times so I would be sure and notice, but I didn't get any sense of if it was a date or what it symbolized.

"We will be going to war, but the world is against us doing it. Toward the last, one country will really support us. I don't really know who it is, maybe England, but they are there for us when others have turned away. People are going to have to stick together. It will be what makes us strong. It won't be the military or the police force that protects us; it will be the people sticking together that make us strong, and that's how we all come through this."

The Number 26
OCTOBER 2, 2001

IT RAINED OFF AND ON ALL DAY TODAY but by evening it seemed to be clearing up, so Dennison decided to go meditate with the full moon. It seemed he had only been gone a few minutes when he returned saying it was raining like crazy again.

After changing into his sweats he sat down and said, "I just got a little bit of information before the rain hit. They showed me the number 26 again. It must mean something important. I meditated on it a little bit to see if I could get anything more, but instead they just told me that our President is walking a thin line, and what he does will determine how things will go for the world in this war. Right now he's under a lot of pressure to retaliate. Everyone wants Bin Laden to pay for what happened, so he's the main focus right now. But we're not going to stop there because he's only one little part of it. They might not even get him. After they attack Afghanistan, they plan to attack some other countries, like Iraq. There's still a grudge there, and of course there's the oil. If the President will be patient and just keep doing what he's doing now, the Moslems will take care of Bin Laden themselves and maybe even Saddam. But if he gives into the demands for retaliation, and moves too soon or too much, the Arabs who are now partly supporting us will end up turning against us. Others, like Russia and China, will then begin joining in with them. We will end up finding out we've opened a can of worms."

Screaming Eagle
OCTOBER 7, 2001

WHEN WE WOKE UP THIS MORNING, Dennison asked, "Did you hear that Eagle screaming last night?" I looked at him like he was crazy and replied, "No, why on earth would an Eagle scream at night? Are you sure it was an Eagle? Maybe a coyote got a rabbit or something." He insisted, "It was an Eagle for sure. It woke me up out of a sound sleep, but I could tell it was an Eagle." I pondered this for a while. I knew he is seldom wrong about such things. It occurred to me he could have been dreaming, and asked if that could be what it was. He replied, "No, I'm sure I was dreaming of something else, because I sort of remembered my dream when I first woke up to the sound of the Eagle screaming. Maybe it was on another plane...?"

We let it go at that, but later this morning a friend called and said, "Turn on your TV if you don't have it on; we're bombing Afghanistan!" A little later in the day I thought of the Eagle scream again, and thought of how the Eagle is the symbol of America. Perhaps it was the "Grandfathers'" way of letting him know America was attacking.

What It Means
OCTOBER 8, 2001

LAST FRIDAY WE HAD LUNCH WITH A FRIEND. During the conversation she asked what Dennison had been getting in regard to the war lately. We told her a few of the things he had seen, and in doing so mentioned that he had seen the number "26", and felt it was significant, but didn't know if it was a date or what. This morning our friend called and asked, "Did you figure out what "26" meant?" I told her no, we hadn't. She laughed and said, "It was all over the news yesterday." We had bombed Afghanistan for the first time yesterday, but it was October 7th and I could see no connection with the number 26. She then explained she had been watching the reports of our attack on TV and the newscasters were saying that it was the 26th day since the terrorist attacks on the US.

Hard Times Ahead
OCTOBER 29, 2001

"I DON'T KNOW if this has anything to do with the same thing or not, but I saw real high barbed wire fences around what looked like schools. There were armed guards watching the outside while these kids played inside the fence.

"I also saw a bunch of fighting going on in a city, shooting and explosions and smoke and fire all over. Maybe it was a riot or something, but for some reason it looked more like a battle going on, an actual battle going on in a U.S. city.

"Then I saw those lines and lines of people again. People lined up in front of a building. Maybe they are unemployment lines, or immunization lines or something like that. Maybe even food lines....

"And I saw Red Cross tents set up in towns and cities. I saw that before too. I don't know if it's because of some disease or because of something else.

"I still feel like something is going to happen to our oil supply and there will be shortages.

"I saw an eagle flying, carrying an American flag. As he is flying, he drops the flag and it slowly falls to the ground. I don't know what that would symbolize.

"There's going to be a lot of mining going on in the near future, like for coal and gas. They are going to do it on protected lands and government lands and it will really be a bad thing for the environment. They will use the energy crisis to justify it, but it really isn't for that, it's just greed that's behind it.

"Our government is going to end up in deep financial difficulties because of the war, and natural disasters. We'll all end up having to pay for it all later.

"At the very end I saw a mist and a huge rainbow coming out of it and covering the sky horizon to horizon. No matter how bad things get, everything will be good in the end."

Year's End
DECEMBER 2001

THIS HAS BEEN QUITE AN EVENTFUL YEAR, and I'm glad to see it come to an end.

Health is once again becoming an issue in our lives. In November Dennison injured his back when he slipped and fell on some ice while carrying a large armload of wood. We found later he had sustained a compression fracture in the middle of his spine. This is in the very place where he bends to do his jewelry. He is in constant pain and the medication given to him by the doctor leaves him groggy, so he only takes it at night to help him sleep. Added to this in late September, I began having what seems to be a recurrence of the lung problem I had in 1997. So far it hasn't yielded to treatment and is growing worse. This is normally a busy season for us, however our jewelry production is slow at best and we've had to lose some business because of it. Despite the pain I know he is in, he keeps working with little complaint; the stress and concern over our health and financial issues two years ago is still fresh.

I look forward to the New Year—it's time for new beginnings!

2002

War on the Horizon?
JANUARY 1, 2002

TONIGHT WE RETURNED HOME EARLY from a New Year's party/Volunteer Fire Department benefit. Dennison remarked as we were changing out of our clothes, "I really feel like we should do a prayer, and meditate a little before we go to bed."

He brought out his smudge, and lit a candle. We each spoke our prayers, then settled back to meditate.

An hour passed in what seemed moments. Somewhere in the distance I could hear the sound of car horns honking, and a few firecrackers pop as 2002 arrived. Dennison took a deep breath and stretched as I opened my eyes and tried to bring my mind back to the moment. He lit another piece of sage, and offered me the bowl. We again smudged, and sat in silence for a few minutes.

Dennison spoke, "I saw a bunch of things related to war. I don't know if it's supposed to be what is going to happen in 2002 or what.... The first thing I saw was a bunch of military vehicles in a convoy. I strongly sense we'll be going to war with another country. I also saw an explosion, a very large explosion, like an atomic bomb.

"What would a red dragon represent? I saw a red dragon....

"I saw a bunch of people like news reporters and soldiers in a group looking down in a hole. People were shouting, 'They got him, they got him!!' I couldn't see who it was. I think maybe it was Bin Laden or someone else like that.

"I saw a large vulture, you know those big...Condors.... I saw a large Condor flying in a circle. There were lots of dead people lying all around."

~ On the Tip Edge of a Miracle ~

A Game of Horseshoes
JANUARY 17, 2002

FINANCIALLY THINGS CONTINUE TO BE DIFFICULT FOR US. Dennison's back pain is slowly diminishing but is still very painful after he works for a short time. At the same time my health continues to decline. It seems just as we are about to get on our feet again, something else comes along to knock us back down again. We wonder if we're going in the wrong direction with our lives. Are we being tested? Are we somehow creating it ourselves, and if so why? Or maybe, as my son says, "Shit just happens." Perhaps these feelings are what prompted the dream Dennison had last night.

A little after 2:00 AM this morning the dog began to bark and wanted to go outside. After things settled back down, as so often happens, Dennison related a dream he had just before being awakened.

"I was just dreaming about playing a horseshoe game when Sam (our dachshund) woke me up with his barking."

"I was still sleepy and wanted to go back to sleep. I wasn't really too interested in hearing his dream. Hoping to put him off until morning I simply sort of grunted and turned my back to him. This didn't discourage him though, and he continued,

"It was a little different than a regular game of horseshoes because there was only one stake, way, way in the distance. Also it had a sort of small box-like enclosure around it. You know, like a three-sided narrow box without a top, so if you didn't get the horseshoe to come down just perfectly it wouldn't go around the stake. Another thing is the whole area around it was dark, except for a blue spotlight, which was shining on the stake.

"Someone was telling me, 'you have four horseshoes and four tries. You have to believe in luck in order to do it.' I looked and could see the stake was a long, long way off, way farther than in a regular game. I thought, 'there's no way I can do it.' But I went ahead and threw the first horseshoe and it disappeared into the darkness, not even getting close to the stake. I tried throwing again, taking careful aim and giving it all I had, but it also just disappeared in the darkness. They spoke to me again and said, 'Try again, but this time visualize ahead of time how you are going to make it.' So I tried again and this time it went right in the box and on to the stake. They said, 'See how it works? Now throw the last one, but this time have faith. Believe it will go where you want it.' So I threw the last horseshoe and it went right on top of the stake ever so easy."

I lay in bed feeling encouraged and strengthened. Surely this was a message not to give up, just establish our goals and have faith. I also recalled another similar dream last year where elves were asking him to "jump farther than he could jump."

Liberty Bell
JANUARY 23, 2002

AROUND 4:00 AM Dennison woke up sneezing and congested. It was some time before we were able to settle back to sleep. When I was finally falling asleep, Dennison spoke saying he recalled a dream he had been having.

"Someone was telling me, 'The Liberty Bell has rung twice and it will ring again two more times.' They continued saying, 'The Flag has been waved, but then it should have been folded and put away in a drawer.' The last thing I remember is seeing an eagle silhouetted against a flag. He was carrying two arrows in his claws."

We lay there talking for a little while, trying to figure out the symbolism or message. I wondered if the two arrows had anything to do with the Liberty Bell ringing twice. I also wondered if it could mean WWI and WWII, or the two planes that crashed into the WTC, or even that we will be involved in two wars.

Red Star
JANUARY 27, 2002

WE WERE EATING LUNCH when Dennison suddenly recalled a dream from last night. "I was dreaming something about that red star again, like I've seen so many times in the past. I sensed they have nuclear weapons or nuclear material. I suppose it could be North Korea. Somehow we need to keep our eye on them.

A Game of Chess
MARCH 23, 2002

I LAY IN BED THIS MORNING trying to catch a couple more minutes of sleep when Dennison brought me back to reality by saying,

"It's funny but I was dreaming of a game of chess. I was looking at a chessboard, and someone was saying to me, 'They are going to kill the Black Knight. The Pawns are in place.' I wonder what that means."

He went on to remind me of another dream he had a long time ago of a black knight and a white knight fighting in the desert. He asked, "Did we ever figure out who they represented?" I told him, "No, but we wondered if it was Saddam and the U.S."

Going to War
APRIL 17, 2002

DENNISON SUGGESTED WE MEDITATE THIS EVENING. It had been a long time since we had meditated and it felt good to be doing so. Afterward he related the following:

"First I was being told something about salt mines or something like that. It didn't make much sense. They said, 'Someone is going to blow up some salt mines.'

"Next I saw a refinery on fire; huge tanks of oil were burning.

"I saw power lines cut – or maybe it was symbolizing our power is going to be cut off.

"I heard someone say, 'You don't know it yet, but at this moment your President is planning to go to war with Iraq. Other countries who support you now will be against it and won't support you when he decides to do it. One country will back you, but they don't really agree. The people within the country don't agree.' I strongly sensed that country was England."

"They also said, 'There will be an explosion during the early morning.' What I was shown looked like an atomic bomb or something big like that.

"I saw something else I couldn't figure out. It must be a symbolic thing, but I don't understand the symbols. Remember those old fashioned

Chinese boats that had bamboo sails? Anyway, I saw these boats filled with people. I felt they were refugees. We were shooting at them, like ducks in a row as they sailed by. I wondered why we would do such a thing because they were unarmed and made no resistance."

Liberty Will Ring
MAY 5, 2002

I WOKE UP ABOUT 1:00 AM WITH HEARTBURN. I got up and took something and when I got back into bed, Dennison woke up. As I lay there trying to go back to sleep, he said, "I was just dreaming someone was saying, 'The Liberty Bell will ring, and the sound will be heard around the world.' What do you think that could mean?"

It made me think about taking history in school, and learning about "the shot heard around the world" when one man fired his gun at Bunker Hill, and it started the Revolutionary War. Perhaps since the Liberty Bell symbolizes freedom, our freedom has been threatened with 9/11 or will be threatened in the future in some way, and whatever we do to retaliate will have an effect on the whole world.

As we once again settled down to sleep, Dennison suddenly recalled, "Oh, I almost forgot, they were also telling me 'Two Titans will soon clash.'"

The Stock Market Will Fall
JUNE 2, 2002

AS WE WERE FINISHING LUNCH, Dennison said, "Oh yeah, I was going to tell you that last night they were telling me something is going to happen to the stock market by the beginning of August. Remember last year I was told about those two big companies going down? Somehow that, plus a lot of other things will strongly affect the market and lots of people will lose their shirts. People who have invested everything in technology stocks will lose it all and have to start again."

~ On the Tip Edge of a Miracle ~

Another War Is Coming
JULY 15, 2002

WHILE EATING BREAKFAST THIS MORNING, Dennison said, "When I woke up, I was hearing a voice saying, 'You will be involved in another Gulf War after the elections.'"

I asked him if it was the Presidential elections or the elections coming up this year. He said he didn't know, but felt it was probably the coming elections this November.

"They also were telling me something about our two political parties. The Democrats and the Republicans will become like one party. At least they will both stand for the same things. Somehow this isn't for the good. It was like our two-party system won't stand for anything anymore."

Jihad
OCTOBER 7, 2002

THIS MORNING AS DENNISON WAS WAKING UP he said, "A weird thing happened last night. I woke up feeling like someone was standing beside the bed. I opened my eyes to see who it was, and as I opened my eyes I heard a man's voice saying, 'Jihad'. I know I've heard the word before. What does it mean exactly?"

I told him it was an Arab term meaning "Holy War."

Knights Clash Again
OCTOBER 8, 2002

WE WERE HAVING OUR MORNING COFFEE when Dennison said, "Remember once a long time ago I had a dream about a black knight and a white knight fighting in the desert? Last night I had another dream about them. In this dream the black knight was chasing the white knight. They were both on horseback and the black knight had a mace that he was swinging as he chased the white knight. The only thing was, instead of a spiked ball at the end of the chain, there was one of those balls Catholic Priests put incense in and swing...what do they call it? (a censer)...any way, smoke was coming out of it.

"I wonder what that means? Maybe because it's associated with a religious ceremony, it means a religious war?"

Fighting Dragons
NOVEMBER 28, 2002

DENNISON WOKE ME UP LAST NIGHT to say he was dreaming of dragons.

"There were two dragons fighting at the edge of a cliff. One was gray or off white, the other was black. They had their tails twisted together like each was trying to off-balance the other and make him fall over the cliff. At the bottom of the canyon was a black river. In my mind I felt like it was oil.

Off to one side was another dragon. This one was red. He was holding a chain, snapping it like a whip at the feet of the two fighting dragons, trying to make both of them fall over the cliff."

We lay there trying to figure what the symbolism meant. I felt the two fighting dragons could be the U.S. and Iraq, and we were on the brink of war (symbolized by the edge of the cliff); the black river at the bottom of the cliff was oil. I didn't know who the red dragon was, but I wondered if it could somehow be China or North Korea since he had seen a red star so often and associated with them or at least their flags.

Year's End
DECEMBER 2002

THIS HAS PROVEN TO BE yet another very difficult year for us. The lung problem I started getting in the fall of 2001 continued to grow increasingly worse, not yielding to any treatments given. The prescribed medications had many severe side affects, one being the wasting of my muscles, to the point that I am nearly unable to walk, and once I sit down I can't get up by myself; and now virtually all the things I used to do are now left to Dennison. But in many ways we were also so very blessed. The people in our little town have been very supportive, and friends have

~ On the Tip Edge of a Miracle ~

done so much for us it's impossible to count. Words are inadequate to express how grateful we are for each and every one, and how wonderful it is to know we aren't slugging things out by ourselves. During the fall I spent a couple of weeks at a lung research hospital and each day since I can feel myself improving.

Through all of this Dennison has been my hero, always there for me, encouraging me in my darkest moments, loving me, praying with me and for me. I know he must feel helpless, but he never lets me see it. I recall the dream where the elves wanted him to jump over a stick, always moving it farther until it seemed impossible to jump over it. Indeed he has "jumped farther than he ever thought he could."

This New Year is indeed a new beginning!

2003

Black and White
JANUARY 8, 2003

T̲ʜᴇ ᴘᴀsᴛ ᴄᴏᴜᴘʟᴇ ᴏғ ᴍᴏɴᴛʜs we've begun to fall into a habit of praying together almost nightly. With my first illness Dennison closed down inside because he felt abandoned. This time I think he has been more than a little frightened of losing me and of losing all that we've worked for all these years. It has opened him up to seek guidance and comfort from Creator. And of course these prayers and meditations have given me strength and comfort too.

Tonight the threat of a war with Iraq weighed heavily on our minds and hearts as we sat down to pray and meditate.

He stretched and sighed as he came out of meditation and this brought me back to the present. He added a little sage to the diminishing piece of charcoal and we each drew the fragrant smoke over ourselves in a benediction. We sat quietly and gathered our thoughts. At last Dennison spoke, "Did you get anything?" I related the few impressions I had received, then I waited for him to tell me what he received. He closed his eyes to bring back the images he had seen.

"I saw a large crowd of people gathered in front of a tall building with lots of windows in it. The sun was reflecting off the windows like silver. These people were standing in a circle, looking at something in the center. They were all yelling and waving their arms; some had money in their hands, like they were making bets. I noticed a lot of them were Blacks, Hispanics, etc., people of color. There were some white people too. What was strange was the people of color had white headbands and the white people had black headbands. As I got closer, I saw that in the center of the circle were two cats fighting, sort of like the cock-fights they used to have. One was black and the other was white or light tan. They were really going at it hard, howling and screeching like cats do. It looked like the white cat was getting the worst of it, his face was all bloody, his eyes swollen nearly shut and his ears were all ragged, and white tufts of hair were all over the place. The poor cat was on his back trying to defend himself, while the black cat was ripping at his belly with its back legs.

"The next scene I saw was a whole line of cars stopped. It looked like they were on a bridge. As I got closer, I could see it was a freeway with over-passes going in several directions. Cars were stopped in all directions like a giant traffic jam as far as the eye could see. Everything was at a standstill. Some people were getting out of their cars, looking to see what was going on, and others just sat in their cars, waiting.

"After that I saw a bunch of men in white robes and white coverings on their heads, with eye holes cut into them, like the Ku Klux Klan. There were red crosses on the front of their robes. I've seen them before in either a dream or a meditation.

"Then the last thing I saw was a bunch of white doves. There were hundreds of them."

Curiously tonight Dennison again saw the black and white symbolism he has been seeing of late. In the past he's seen black and white dragons fighting, black and white chess pieces, black and white knights fighting, and black and white dogs fighting to name a few.

We spent a few minutes trying to decipher the symbolism. I wondered aloud what the black and white represented...could it be two countries such as the U.S. and Iraq, or maybe good and evil? I also wondered if the building with all the windows represented the UN. Neither of us could understand the KKK symbolism, and speculated it could possibly symbolize racial profiling or racial problems. The White Doves we both agreed might be souls of the dead.

A Warning

JANUARY 12, 2003

WE TRIED TO MEDITATE THIS EVENING, but my meditation soon drifted into slumber. The sound of Dennison snoring woke me up. We were both too tired when we started. Dennison did get a little something though.

"I clearly heard a voice say, 'Your leader has a loud voice. He should be careful what he says; he can off-balance the whole world.' I also saw lots of small fires burning in the night."

~ 2003 • Do Not Fear ~

Scenes From a Distant Land
JANUARY 17, 2003

WE FINISHED OUR PRAYERS and decided to go ahead and meditate a little. It was still fairly early and the dogs were restless so I had a hard time getting relaxed. Dennison said he was able to get a little though, just small scenes he couldn't really understand.

"First I saw two men racing on horseback. One was on a white horse and the other was on a black one. Both men were dressed like Arabs. They were racing down this long road, both whipping their horses to make them go faster, their white robes flying in the wind.

"Next I saw a train filled with people. It was filled to overflowing with people hanging on the sides, out the windows, and on the roof, anywhere they could find a spot to hang on. There were others on the ground trying to find a way to get on. They all looked like ordinary people, not soldiers.

"I saw some mud brick huts, like in a village somewhere. There was an old man and two little kids, a little boy and a girl. The little boy was eating something out of a bowl. There was a skinny dog eating out of it with him. The girl just stood and watched them. The old man sat with his back against the wall of the hut. His shoulders were slumped over and his eyes looked empty, like he'd given up.

"I saw an American flag burning. It was hanging from a short pole and the stars and some of the stripes in the corner were all that was left of it.

"I saw it snowing…rain…raining. I don't know what it was really. There was just this white stuff coming out of the sky, big globs or big flakes of this white stuff falling like wet snow. It would stick in these big patches or spots all over everything. People were running all over screaming and trying to get out of it. I can't understand what it was."

Do Not Fear
JANUARY 30, 2003

WE AGAIN MEDITATED AFTER PRAYING THIS EVENING. Afterward Dennison related the following:

"They told me we need to reach out more. We've isolated ourselves while we've been dealing with your illness. Now it's time to start being there for others again. They said, 'When you help others, you will be helped. Doors will open for you that otherwise would remain closed.'

"They told me we must not fear in the times ahead, because fear blocks energy and guidance. The way not to fear is to pray and meditate. It keeps the energy moving and the channels open. The more we do it, the easier it becomes.

'Peoples' minds are purchased with fear. If something is created to make you fear, and then the person or persons who created the fear offer you security and protection, it's easy to accept and follow any rules and regulations they might impose on you. You then become a prisoner of your own fear. They can control you without you even knowing you are being controlled, and even if you are aware you are being controlled, you accept it because you feel secure under that control.'

"I saw a strange thing, and I'm not sure what it means. I saw a man standing on a hill. At first I thought he was an Indian wrapped in a blanket, but as I saw him closer, I realized it was a man wrapped in an American flag. The blue with the stars was at his feet, touching the ground. He wore the flag like a blanket pulled up pretty far over his head. One side of his face was painted with red stripes so it looked like part of the flag. He was looking away from me, over his right shoulder down on a city or town. I could see explosions in the distance, like there was fighting going on. Then I was shown the other side of the man's face... it was painted with gray camouflage.

"At the same time I could hear rain outside our house. I could hear it hitting the roof like it was really coming down. I thought to myself, 'We are finally getting some rain.' It didn't seem strange that there was no sign of rain or any storms coming. But as I came more out of the meditation, I realized it wasn't actually happening. It was part of the meditation. Maybe it means cleansing, or purification."

North Korea
FEBRUARY 18, 2003

AFTER PRAYING THIS EVENING we decided to meditate a little. We were deeply in to our meditation when the cat began to meow like she had lost her love. Instantly we both opened our eyes and the meditation was over. I asked Dennison if he was able to get anything at all because I surely didn't. He replied,

"Yeah, I got a little. I think it had something to do with North Korea. Remember those war dogs during WWII? They had jackets that were packs on their backs...anyway I saw a Doberman with a pack on its back. The pack had a red star on it. This dog was in a cage and the cage was surrounded by rolled barbed wire. The dog in the cage was barking and growling, lunging at everyone and everything—even throwing himself against the cage. He had white foam and saliva coming from his mouth like a mad dog." I speculated it could mean the leader of North Korea was like a mad dog.

Future Possibilities
FEBRUARY 26, 2003

TONIGHT WHEN WE MEDITATED Dennison saw a coliseum again. He said, "I saw that stadium again. It's in a large city and I saw it explode. There were some important people inside. I tried to get where it is, but I couldn't get anything.

"Then I saw a plane starting to land and it suddenly caught on fire. I don't know if it was a malfunction or if it was terrorists. On the side of the plane was the words "United States."

"Next I found myself looking up at the Statue of Liberty. I was at the bottom like a tourist. It was lit up by all these lights. Then I noticed it had a big crack running all the way up.

"Then I saw an elephant with a ball and chain around one leg. He was pulling a storage tank or a tank like you see on a tanker truck. An oil truck.

"Last thing I saw was a bunch of dead cows, like a whole field of dead cows.

Bird in a Cage
MARCH 14, 2003

THE WAR WITH IRAQ IS LOOMING and perhaps that is what brought the following dream. At breakfast Dennison said,
 "I was dreaming of a bird in a cage trying to get out. It was fluttering all around the cage, beating itself against the bars. I wonder what that could mean?" I speculated maybe it symbolized Saddam.

The War Begins
MARCH 19, 2003

AS I AM COPYING THE NOTES from my journal to my computer I suddenly realize on this exact date (March 19th) in 2001, Dennison had the dream where he was told a Holy War was coming. In that dream he saw a man in a cloak holding a book like a Bible in one hand and a staff in the other. The unique part was he had a crown of what looked at first to be thorns, but was actually part of a Saudi head dress. He was also wearing jackboots. Ironically, one year to the day we are now set to invade Iraq. So much has happened since that dream. Little could we imagine at that time that in six months, on 9-11-01, our world would be changed forever.
 Tonight we prayed for peace, and then meditated a little, until the phone rang and brought us out of it. Dennison said, "I didn't get much, before the phone rang, but I did see a bunch of bee hives. Swarms of bees were buzzing all around them, like something had them all stirred up. Maybe it means we've stirred up a hornets' nest."

Palestinians
MAY 15, 2003

THE SOUND OF THE WINDOW BLIND clattering against the window frame woke me up. It was warm when we went to bed and we had left the window open a little to let in the cool night air. Sometime in the night the wind had come up. I got up and closed the window and returned to bed.

Dennison woke up then and asked if I was okay. I told him I just closed the window. As I was drifting back into sleep, Dennison asked, "Who are the Palestinians with?" My sleepy mind had a hard time comprehending what he could mean. Finally I replied, "Their leader is Arafat if that's what you mean. I think they are supported by Iran and most other Arab groups." He absorbed that while I waited for him to explain. A few minutes went by and I began to wonder if he was asleep again, so I asked, "Why did you ask about the Palestinians?" He took a deep breath and said, "Someone was telling me the Palestinians are planning something big, something big is about to happen and they will be behind it...I don't know, maybe it was just a dream.

It seems the Palestinians are always doing something to the Jews and the Jews retaliate. Also the constant news coverage of the war has me a little too saturated with news of the Middle East so I simply replied, "It was probably just a dream; we hear so much like that now it's no wonder you would dream about it." I rolled over and was almost asleep again when Dennison said, "Before that I was dreaming about someone riding a beautiful black Arabian horse. The horse had a lot of silver on his bridal and on his chest, really fancy. The man was wearing silky robes that billowed behind him as he rode the horse. He had a turban with part of it hanging down and winding across his face, covering all but his eyes. He was carrying a long thin sword that was curved. I also noticed his boots were strange, pointed and kind of curled up at the toe. He looked like something out of the past, something out of a story. I watched him riding the horse, running full speed up a sandy hill, then stopping and turning the horse. It was obvious he was an expert horseman and it was neat to watch him. He raised his sword in the air, like a sign to attack. Then a voice said, 'The war isn't over like everyone thinks; it's just beginning."

Diamond Dream

JULY 12, 2003

WE HAD JUST SPENT A HOT MUGGY NIGHT at an Albuquerque motel where the air conditioning barely worked. We woke early this morning and were sitting in a small coffee shop, waiting for our breakfast to be served. I sipped my coffee and thought about what shops and galleries to take our jewelry to before the heat of the day descended on us again.

Dennison interrupted my contemplation saying, "Last night I dreamed about someone giving me a large diamond." "That would be nice," I replied. "What did you do with it, or do you remember?" He was quiet for a few moments, recalling the dream, then said, "I was inside a cave of some sort, and there was an opening somewhere above my head where light streamed in, illuminating the place where I was standing. I could see the floor of the cave was covered in red dirt. There was an old man sitting across form me, wearing old faded clothes. I thought he was an old prospector or a miner or something like that. I could see his hair was white, but I couldn't see his face, the light from above was in the way, like maybe it was too bright." At this point I paid closer attention. I suspected this was more than an ordinary dream. In many of his visions I've noticed that "teachers" or, as someone else noted, "masters" appear with light where their faces should be, so he is never able to see their faces, but their words have meaning. "This old miner told me to sit down, so I sat facing him. He said he wanted to show me something. He took a small canvas bag out of his pocket. I noticed it looked real old and dirty, like he'd had it for a while. There was a tie wrapped around and around the top. It took a while for him to loosen the knot and unwind the tie. I could see the string underneath was clean, like it hadn't been opened for a long time.

"After he opened it, he dumped it out on the red dirt in the patch of light between us. There was a bunch of different colored stones that scattered in front of me. He reached and picked up the largest one and held it out to me and asked, 'Do you know what this is?' It looked like a Herkimer Diamond in a matrix like it hadn't been cleaned up, still in the rough. I told him it looked like a Herkimer, but as the light hit it, it really sparkled so I looked closer. Somehow I knew it was a diamond in the rough. I handed it back to him and said, "I think it might be a diamond." He refused to take it and told me, 'I want you to keep it if you can use it. I've had it for a long time and it has brought me a lot of luck.' I told him I thought it might be valuable, but he still wouldn't take it back. He just said, 'see what you can do with it.'

We both wondered what it could mean, being given a diamond in the rough. I told Dennison that maybe he was the diamond in the rough.

JULY 21, 2003

IT WAS LATE WHEN WE MEDITATED THIS EVENING. After we had meditated for a short while Dennison began to snore lightly. I sat there listening to his breathing, letting him sleep for a time. I tried to meditate but couldn't concentrate with his snoring. Finally I stretched and added some sage to the coal. He took a deep breath and after a couple of minutes said, "I think I fell asleep." I laughed and said if his snores were any indication he surely had. He went on to say, "I was dreaming of a diamond mine." I thought this interesting since he had been dreaming of diamonds just a few nights ago. "There was a bunch of people working, putting these diamonds into small barrels, containers. There was a hole or cave in the side of a hill and all these Black people were working there. They were carrying these small barrels out on their shoulders and loading them into trucks. There was a bunch of guards or military, people in camouflage with rifles guarding them. That's all there was to it. I don't know if it means anything or not. I wonder why I keep dreaming of diamonds."

ID Cards

JULY 22, 2003

WE WERE ON OUR WAY TO A NEARBY TOWN when Dennison said, "Last night I was dreaming we were all being given these ID cards. Everybody had to get one and we had to carry them with us all the time. I felt like they had all our information in them, who we are, our health records, financial records, credit history, job history and so on. We had to use them in order to do any sort of business, like a debit card and ID card all in one. One side of the card had a design like half of a dollar bill."

Stockpiling Oil
AUGUST 11, 2003

A FAST MOVING THUNDERSTORM woke us up about 1:00 AM this morning. I got up and went to the bathroom while Dennison closed some windows. As we settled back down to sleep, he said, "I was just dreaming about barrels of oil being stored or hidden away. I saw these black barrels with white lids in what looked like some place underground. At first I wondered if it was toxic waste or something, but somehow I knew it was oil. I felt like it was secretly being hidden away or siphoned off or something, to affect the economy and drive prices up. You know, create a shortage somehow. The reason was to force people to accept something or allow something that they normally wouldn't.

Then I was dreaming of freight containers being moved on flatbed train cars. I looked and could see there were miles of them. The word "supplies" came to me, but I don't know what kind of supplies. I didn't see any military equipment or anything.

Diamonds Again
AUGUST 15, 2003

WE WERE DRIVING HOME FROM A DOCTOR'S APPOINTMENT. It was a long drive and we were lost in our own thoughts. Suddenly Dennison spoke up and said, "Last night I was dreaming about diamonds again. I dreamed I was trying to cut that diamond in the rough that I dreamed about a long time ago. I was going to cut and polish it, and then see if I could sell it. However I discovered it was too hard and I didn't have the right tools. Then someone said to me, 'Why do you want to cut it? Why not leave it natural like it is and just visualize what you want it to be and then that is what it will be. That way it can be anything you want it to be. If you want it to be money, then that is what it will be; if you want it to be a house or your health, just think about it, and it will be that."

Mandelbrot
AUGUST 16, 2003

Dennison had been in his shop cutting stones for a pendant order most of the afternoon. He came into the house, sat down and then asked, "What is a Mandelbrot?" It was such a strange question to ask, I couldn't imagine what he could be leading up to. I recalled a few years ago there was an unusual crop circle that was called the Mandelbrot. I had read up on what a Mandelbrot was, trying to figure out what the crop circle might be saying. Now I tried to recall the information and wondered how to explain something I didn't fully understand myself. I told him, "It's a math term for something called fractals. A group of fractals is a Mandelbrot set. It has something to do with dimensions or worlds within worlds, within worlds, and it has something to do with creating order from chaos." After my explanations he went on to explain that while he was cutting stones, the word "Mandelbrot" popped into his mind, then a voice was telling him the earth is coming into "Mandelbrot" energy. For a time it will create chaos, but in the end it will all balance out. It somehow has something to do with the destruction of male energy that dominates things now. It will bring in feminine energy to put things back into balance. They said something about natural disasters, fuel shortages, economic and social problems, all happening within a relatively short period of time.

Troubling Dreams
AUGUST 23, 2003

Dennison has been suffering from allergies, or a cold, the past couple of days. At night he feels miserable with his stuffy, runny nose. About 2:00 AM I woke up as he was getting up. I asked if he was okay, and he said, "Yeah, I just can't sleep." I got up with him and made us some tea and gave him some allergy medication. As we relaxed on the couch drinking our tea, he said,

"I've been having a bunch of weird dreams, half awake and half asleep. I saw a building exploding and a voice said, 'They've bombed a U.S. embassy. There were some important people inside, now some heads are going to roll. Then they said, 'The enemy who is in hiding is ready to strike. It will happen soon.' I don't know if it is Bin Laden or Saddam or if it could be someone else we don't expect.

"I saw two nuclear submarines. I've seen them several times in the past. I don't think anyone knows they are there. I don't know who it is, but they are ready to do something.

"Then I saw a black serpent again, except he was coiled up and ready to strike. I noticed it had a reddish/greenish triangle on its head. The triangle was iridescent like an opal and I wondered if the serpent represented the same person or country as the 'one in hiding and ready to strike.'

"I had the strong feeling the war was going to grow and just get bigger and bigger, like Viet Nam."

Oil Shortage
SEPTEMBER 3, 2003

EVEN THOUGH IT WAS LATE THIS EVENING we decided to meditate a little before going to bed. We prayed and then settled down for a short meditation. Dennison's back still hurts him and after a long day of making jewelry he often has a cramp there that won't relax. As we meditated, he kept shifting his position, trying to get comfortable. Because of this I was unable to get focused and finally gave up and added some more sage to the coal. Dennison opened his eyes and said,

"My back hurts too much tonight to concentrate. Let's just go to bed." We each smudged again and as we finished Dennison said, "I got a little bit while I was meditating. I saw a bunch of barrels on a boat dock. They were all on fire. People were standing around, just watching them burn. Someone was telling me our government is going to create an oil shortage. They also told me, 'The one who is in hiding will soon be brought forth.' I couldn't get whether it was Bin Laden or Saddam or even someone else."

Black Dragon
SEPTEMBER 22, 2003

WE DECIDED TO MEDITATE AGAIN TONIGHT, but once again the pain in Dennison's back cut it short. After a few minutes Dennison complained that his back was in such a cramp he couldn't concentrate. I asked if he'd gotten anything at all. He said,

"I only got a little bit. I saw a black dragon chained to a high tower. He was whipping and lashing his tail around, trying to hit the ones who had him chained up with the barbs. I could see where the shackles were cutting into his leg as he struggled against the chains."

I wondered again if the black dragon symbolized Saddam.

Bush
SEPTEMBER 23, 2003

WHEN WE WOKE UP THIS MORNING Dennison said,

"I was dreaming of President Bush. He was making a speech and then the audience began throwing fruit and stacks of paper at him. I felt like there is a lot of stuff about 9-11 and going to war with Iraq is going to come out soon. It will turn a lot of people against him."

The Earth's Grid
NOVEMBER 3, 2003

TODAY WAS DENNISON'S BIRTHDAY. A group of our friends wanted to take him out for dinner and we agreed to meet in a nearby town at a steak house that was renowned for its good food. It was an enjoyable evening with lots of laughter and everyone was in high spirits as we parted to go home. As we drove home, I mentioned an e-mail from my sister saying she had recently watched a program on NOVA about the magnetic poles weakening and the possibility of a magnetic pole shift happening. She said there was geologic evidence that this had happened several times in the history of the earth. The program went on to describe what might take place should such an event happen. She said she recalled Dennison saying something about a pole shift and wondered if it was the same thing they were talking about. Dennison agreed that it sounded a lot like some of the things he had seen before in his meditations.

Even though it was late when we arrived home, we both felt charged from the evening and weren't at all ready to go to bed. I suggested we say a little prayer, and then meditate. In particular I wanted him to see what he could get in regard to a pole shift…just see if he could get clarification on what he has received in the past.

When we finished meditating, I was astonished to see how much time had passed, more than an hour and a half! Dennison then asked me, "What exactly is the earth's grid?" I told him I didn't really know too much, but it was my understanding that it was like a web of energy that surrounded the earth. It sort of linked parts of the earth to other parts through lines of energy that intersect at certain points, like a grid. Those points of intersection are places of high energy or power spots. A lot of the ancient sacred sites are on these spots. It's sort of like acupuncture points on the human body…Mother Earth's acupuncture points. He digested this information for a few minutes, then said, "They were telling me that something is going to happen to the earth's grid. Somehow it has to do with the magnetic field that surrounds the earth. Something is going to happen that will affect the earth's grid. Before it happens, people will start to feel agitated and a lot will just go sort of crazy. If they are emotionally unstable, they will get worse. Animals will sense something is about to happen and they will start acting strange, like walking in to the downtown part of the cities or going right up to people. Birds and other animals that migrate will be most affected. They use the earth's magnetic field to migrate and sense direction. When the magnetic field gets messed up, they will lose their sense of direction and crash into buildings and trees and things like that. Whales and dolphins will beach themselves in record numbers. Others will be lost and confused.

"Things just start falling apart, and the social structure of the world will break down. Everyone will be afraid unless they are really strongly grounded spiritually.

"Then there is going to be a 'moment' of non-time, like the pause of a pendulum that has swung completely in one direction and then starts to come back the other way. At this same time there is like another world or dimension that is going to start coming in or we will be going into it. It's like the fingers of both hands inter-meshing with each other. I think we will somehow actually see both worlds or dimensions as they come together. So nothing seems real. As this happens, we will start to change our vibration rate and we will go into this other world. Things that are man-made just disappear, and only natural things and things made with natural things will go into this new vibration.

"It's like a miracle and we are transformed. We will be able to manifest anything we want because we know how to use our minds. Those who aren't progressed spiritually, that are grounded in greed and material things will remain in their old three-dimensional world to begin again.

"This happens every so many thousands of years and it's about to happen again. In the past mankind wasn't ready, but if enough have changed their thinking, we will be able to change when it comes this time. Somehow technology is stopping people from growing more spiritual. It has removed us from Nature and our connection to the earth. It has created more and more greed and desire for material things at the cost of turning our backs on our spiritual nourishment. It has created so many marvelous gadgets that it steals our minds, like the internet and television. It can be a wonderful thing, but when people are like addicted to them, they can't pull their minds away and they no longer have a desire for spiritual nourishment. We've made technology our god.

"Then at the end I saw numbers running backward. Remember those old gas pumps that used to have the numbers rolling one after another? I saw something kind of like that, but the numbers were going backward. I don't know what that meant."

Coliseum Collapse
DECEMBER 22, 2003

DENNISON WOKE UP THIS MORNING saying, "Last night I dreamed of something like a stadium or a coliseum, a place that had tiered seats. I saw it collapse like a building does when they demolish it with explosives. There were a lot of people inside."

More Scenarios
DECEMBER 31, 2003

Once again it was New Years' Eve. There was an annual Fire Department Auxiliary fund-raising dinner and dance at the Country Club, but I had no desire to go out in the cold and spend the evening in a smoky room, waiting to bring in the New Year. Instead we rented a movie and spent a cozy evening at home. Afterward we decided to meditate and try to see to what the future might hold.

Dennison lit the sage and we both prayed, giving thanks for my returning health, and all the many blessings we've received this past year. When we finished our prayer, we relaxed and meditated for a while. When we were through, Dennison said,

"I saw a bunch of kids, or students protesting.

"Next I saw a bunch of dead birds lying all over the place. After that I saw a city burning, the whole city was on fire. After that I saw a huge explosion at a power plant.

"I saw a scientist, a man in a lab coat holding a test tube full of a clear liquid. He said, 'This is going to help a lot of people. It can cure cancer and a lot of other diseases.'

"The last thing I saw was...it was like those movies about time machines, where it shows numbers going forward as they travel toward the future, except the numbers were going backward. Remember I saw something like that before? Anyway they were telling me 'Time can only go so far, then it stops and reverses itself, kind of like a pendulum.' And we're about there where this is going to happen."

I asked some questions about this last scene, trying to get clarification, but Dennison said that was all he could get.

Dennison then poured us a glass of champagne and we toasted the New Year early and went to bed.

This past year was much better for us. Our business picked up in the summer and I also finally began to show signs of healing. In some ways the past couple of years seem like a nightmare, but they have also made us stronger spiritually. I think we're finally back on track.

Personally I know I've grown. Anyone who has had a serious injury or illness knows how it often turns one inward. For me it has been a time of reflection and getting to know myself. It has brought home to me just how dear our friends are. More importantly I have learned to receive, which is a difficult lesson indeed. It has given me a new perspective on what is important in my life and a new empathy for others who are ill. It has also brought Dennison and me much closer together. I know now there is a place in the grand scheme of things for illness. It is a great and demanding teacher. I now look forward to the New Year, knowing each day I am growing stronger.

2004

A Series of Scenes
JANUARY 15, 2004

As we finished praying tonight Dennison leaned back and said, "I feel like we should meditate a little if you want to." Afterward Dennison related a series of scenes that came to him as he meditated.

"I saw a jet plane landing and catching fire somehow as it hits the runway. The side of it said "United States." This is the second time I've seen that.

"I watched two eagles fighting or sparring, like in a cock fight. Sitting beside them was a cup or chalice.

"I was shown a scene of a large herd of buffalo lying dead in the snow. There was steam rising up around them.

"I saw nine clay or stone tablets partially buried in the sand. The wind was blowing, exposing the tablets. There was writing of some sort on them and a staff or shepherd's crook beside them. The top of the staff was gold and around it was tied a golden cord. There was an ornate golden or brass container with a lid on it, kind of like something wine would be in.

"I didn't get any sense of what any of this might mean."

What Was That?
JANUARY 29, 2004

We were driving home after shopping and visiting with friends. It was late twilight, the time of night when you feel nostalgic and think of home fires burning. We drove without speaking, each of us lost in our own thoughts. Suddenly a large bright light appeared in the sky ahead and slightly above us, and just as suddenly it disappeared or blinked off. It was like a giant flashlight blinked on and then off. We both exclaimed together, "Did you see that?!" and I asked, "What on earth do suppose that was?" We searched the sky above us, trying to see it again or at least see what the source was. The sky was completely clear and there was still enough light that if there had been a plane or anything else we would have seen it, but we could see nothing but a few stars beginning to show themselves.

A little later in the evening Dennison remarked that he felt we should meditate. I told him I really would like him to see if he could get something regarding the earlier meditation where he saw the numbers going backward and was told that time reverses itself and we are at the end of time.

In this meditation he was told many things, which he tried to repeat to me exactly as he had heard it. The end result was confusing to me and I finally asked him to explain it in his own words as he understood it.

"Our minds evolve. The world's mind evolves (collective consciousness?). It's sort of like the rings of a tree. You know how you can count the rings from the center and tell how old it is. Our minds are sort of like that. From the beginning of man until now we've evolved and our minds have evolved, layer on layer. We were at first more like animals, using our minds to survive. Then we began to think creatively and we invented tools, and so on. In this way our minds evolved.

"We create time with our minds, with our collective mind, and right now we are nearing the end of our time; it's very close. Soon we will begin our next step in the evolution of our minds. They said we are on the edge of a miracle, if all of our minds can change; if we can all change our thinking.

We will all have to think in a different way, a more spiritual way, in order for this to happen. People who are now spiritual are seeds to help others learn and become more spiritual, so that this can happen. But there is so much to be overcome. The more spiritual we become, the easier it will be for this change to happen. If we don't become more spiritual in our thinking, we're going to destroy ourselves and we'll have to begin again.

"There are a lot of things happening, or are going to happen, to help us to change. For instance we will have to have wars, so people will begin to see more and more how horrible it is. And they will see the true reasons wars are brought into being. They will refuse to fight, and refuse to support wars, and it will change a little. It is already happening. Remember when the war with Iraq was gearing up and all the millions all over the world protested. And now there is so much about the greed behind it and how we were all manipulated by our government to go to war.

"There will be droughts, famine, wars and catastrophes happening more and more until it forces us to think differently. When we thirst, we will come to see how we did it to ourselves because of the way we have treated the earth. The same will be true when we are hungry. We will have to work together and share in order to survive. It will force us to think differently and become more spiritual. When enough people change their thinking, the collective consciousness, the mind energy, will suddenly overwhelm the other thinking and we will all change. As we change, this new world or dimension will be coming in to this reality.

"Another thing, for some reason technology is blocking our spiritual energy."

Bill of Rights
FEBRUARY 28, 2004

IT WAS LATE WHEN WE DECIDED TO MEDITATE THIS EVENING. After a few minutes we both fell asleep. Later Dennison woke up and in doing so woke me up. We both laughed and went to bed. A few minutes after we were snuggled in he said, "Oh yeah, just before I fell asleep I was seeing a scroll of paper. It was yellowed with age. Part of it was unrolled and had fancy writing on the top of the paper. It said, 'Bill of Rights', and lying on top of it was a bill, you know money. I noticed Jefferson's face was on the bill. Then as I looked at the money, it caught on fire and started burning the Bill of Rights."

More Visions
MARCH 12, 2004

THIS EVENING WE HAD BETTER LUCK with our meditation and neither of us fell asleep. After meditating some time Dennison yawned and stretched and added more sage to the coal. We smudged and fell silent for a few minutes. Dennison spoke saying,

"Tonight I saw an American flag, the blue area with the stars was torn and hanging down over the stripes.

"Next I saw a neon sign flashing the word ANTHRAX in red.

"Then I saw two white horses running, pulling a white chariot. There was no one in the chariot, no one to guide it.

"After this I saw a large crowd. They seemed to be protesting something and were yelling and chanting; some were carrying signs, but I couldn't see what the signs said. There was a long line of soldiers standing in front of them holding guns on them. Then the soldiers began firing into the crowd. I could see people falling and others running out of the crowd toward the soldiers, yelling until they too were shot.

"Remember those old fashioned gasoline pumps with the glass containers on top where you could see the gasoline? I saw one of those old pumps and two men in suits, like businessmen or politicians, were standing beside it. One man was holding the gasoline hose and the gas was just running in a stream all over the place. Off to one side was an Arab wearing their traditional robes and head covering. He was holding a thick wad of money and fanning it like he was counting it."

MAY 2, 2004

IT HAS BEEN A WHILE SINCE WE MEDITATED. Time somehow gets away and it's late before we finally wind up our day, and by then we're both too tired to meditate, so we've just been praying before going to bed. This evening we finally sat down early and prayed and then settled down to meditate. After our meditation I related my few impressions to Dennison and then he told me, "They said, watch your leader, he's about to show his other face; he's about to show his back.

"After this I saw the black dragon again. This time he was in a big puddle of oil. The oil was on fire and his tail was burning.

"Next I saw a group of Arabs, all were wearing white clothing and head coverings. They were all sitting together in a circle. Then an Arab dressed in black robes came up to them. He was holding a big bag of money. Then he opened the bag and dropped a bunch of cash in the middle of all the people in the circle, actually dumping it on them. The odd thing was the Arab in black had one side of his face painted black and the other side of his face was white.

"They were telling me John Kerry would be a weak President if he is elected. They said he would have the rug pulled out from under him. I felt somehow the economy would take a dive. But if Bush gets re-elected, things will get worse for everyone and we will continue to have war.

"They said the white serpent and the black serpent are fighting now, but the red serpent and the yellow serpent haven't yet shown themselves. About the same time our economy gets bad we'll be fighting the red and yellow serpents.

"There's also going to be a serious terrorist act here in the U.S.

"Global warming will be recognized all over within the next couple of years. We haven't seen anything yet. It is causing something in the oceans. The currents are changing somehow. It's like the ocean turns over; the cold water at the bottom heats up warmer than the water on the top. It causes terrible winds and tidal waves all over the earth.

"There's going to be at least six volcanoes erupting around the same time. At least one in California, two in Washington State, a couple in Mexico, one or two in the ocean and Hawaii or some place like that. Ash will be carried with the winds, filling the air and covering the skies. This is a sign the shift is near."

Dreams

JULY 5, 2004

WE WOKE EARLY THIS MORNING, just as darkness was beginning to fade and a few birds were welcoming the dawn, Dennison turned over to me and said,

"I was just dreaming about a black dragon again. It was getting up out of a pool of oil and then began walking away and a bunch of people in business suits were following after him."

I lay there sleepily, digesting the dream and wondering what it might symbolize. A few moments later he said,

"I was also dreaming about a cross, before the dragon dream. It was a really big cross, made out of stone or something like that. It was lying partly down in the sand, like in the desert. Part of it was still standing up and a chain was wrapped around the top of it. The wind was blowing and there was books, maybe Bibles or hymn books blowing around in the wind, pages flying all over. There was also a large heavy door lying there too. It had a stained glass window in it.

"Another thing I was dreaming about was a white horse galloping across the sand. There was no rider, but there was a red cloak draped over its haunches. You know how kings and generals used to drape those cloaks over the back end of the horse. The cloak had gold trim on it and the horse had fancy headgear that was red cloth with gold tassels. It was also wearing breast gear out of the same red cloth with gold tassels. There was a saddle on the horse with the stirrups tied up on the saddle horn.

"I was just wondering if they could mean anything."

The Buzzard and the Eagle
OCTOBER 4, 2004

WE WERE HAVING OUR MORNING COFFEE and watching the news when Dennison said,

"Last night I dreamed about a very large eagle and a buzzard fighting in a cage. The cage was made out of like chicken wire. The buzzard had these silver spurs, long pointed sharp tips on his feet, like they use in cockfights. He also had something like knives on his wing tips, on his long wing-tip feathers. He was beating the poor eagle up and it was broken and bloody and he looked tired. Even though the eagle was bigger than the buzzard, the buzzard was winning, because he wasn't fighting fair. The eagle couldn't get away; he was trapped in the cage."

More Dreams
OCTOBER 8, 2004

EARLIER THIS EVENING a friend called and asked for our prayers. This evening after we prayed we decided to meditate and, as Dennison put it, "see what's going on in the world." When we finished, Dennison said,

"I feel like Bush will get elected.

"I saw an earthquake in a large city. I saw bridges collapsing into the ocean and steam or smoke rising from large cracks in the earth.

"I saw a group of kids, mostly boys, hiding in a tunnel. They seemed frightened and I also heard gunfire and explosions nearby.

"I saw a very large grocery store; its shelves were nearly empty. People were fighting over what little food there was left.

"I saw semi-trucks lined up for miles, blocking the roadway. I think they were protesting high fuel prices or something. Cars were honking and couldn't get around them.

"I saw these ammunition boxes floating down a river and felt they had something to do with Bush.

"I saw groups of Arabs huddled together; suddenly they got up and scattered. When they ran away, I saw an effigy of Bush lying in a puddle of oil; one leg was soaked in the oil. It was wearing a shredded flag and a blindfold over the eyes.

"I saw business men on a balcony on top of a tall office building. One man removed his coat and threw it over the railing, and then he jumped after it. Then one by one the others followed. Money and assorted bills were falling through the air like confetti along with them.

"I saw Asians in Khaki uniforms marching shoulder to shoulder. A missile, covered with a camouflage net, followed them, like in a parade.

"I saw a fleet of aircraft carriers and smaller ships traveling together in the ocean.

"Last I saw rain. It was raining and people were holding their hands up to the sky, welcoming it. Then the clouds cleared and there was a beautiful rainbow."

North Korea Again
OCTOBER 18, 2004

I GOT UP THIS MORNING EARLY to go to the bathroom; when I got back in bed, Dennison was awake. As soon as I was snuggled in, he told me,

"I was just dreaming about two flags. One was an American flag and the other was that flag I've seen so many times before with a red star. What was strange was they were each folded in that triangle they fold flags into. Each was also partly wrapped with aluminum foil.

"They were lying in the center of a table, along with some stacks of money...you know, how they put that band around a bundle of bills. There were stacks and stacks of those along with stacks of gold coins.

"There was a group of people that looked like business men or politicians sitting around the table, playing cards like poker, and throwing dice like they were gambling."

We lay in bed speculating on the symbolism until it was time to get up. Our thoughts were the flags were the U.S. and North Korea. Perhaps being wrapped in foil symbolized maybe something "cooking" or something heating up. The poker could symbolize taking a gamble or taking a chance and the stakes are high.

Crop Circle Dream
NOVEMBER 7, 2004

EVEN THOUGH DENNISON'S BIRTHDAY was earlier this week, we waited until last night to celebrate. I invited several friends over and each brought a dish of food. I supplied the cake and ice cream. It was late when everyone went home. Often on his birthday, Dennison seems to have an interesting dream or experience, and this year was no exception. This morning he woke early and said,

"Last night I dreamed of crop circles. First I was seeing it from above, like I was flying over it. What I was seeing was a large oval 'circle' with three round circles inside. The top circle looked like the earth. Underneath were two circles side by side. The left circle had two flags crossed in it. One flag was a U.S. flag; the other flag had a line down the middle of it, with a crescent shape and a sword or knife across the crescent. The third circle was a skull and cross-bones.

"The outside of the oval had what looked like leaves of some kind around it, sort of like a wreath. On top of the oval was a ribbon tied and on top of the ribbon was a crown of thorns.

"The next thing I knew I was inside of the crop circle and for some reason it looked like a ring when you look at it from the side. It made me think of a Masonic ring for some reason.

"As I stood in the crop circle, a butterfly came up to me. It was large and it was colored black and orange and yellow. It flew up real close and said in my ear, 'This should be erased; it shouldn't be here.'"

The thing that stood out to me in Dennison's dream was the crown of thorns. I immediately knew there had to be a symbolic message in it somehow. When I got up later, I asked Dennison to draw the crop circle, then I looked up on the internet as many symbols as possible and came up with some interesting meanings.

I started with the "butterfly." It symbolizes change, metamorphosis, transformation, souls and death. The word "psyche" is the Greek word for soul as well as for butterfly.

The way Dennison drew the large crop circle with the leaves surrounding it, I thought it looked like a wreath.

Then I noticed the bow on the top of the "wreath." When Dennison drew it, the center knot looked like an acorn. So I asked him if it was, and he said "yes." It seemed so out of place that I knew it must have some significance. All I could come up with is that an acorn is a seed and from it grows a mighty tree...tree of life?

Of course the crown of thorns is readily associated with Christianity and Christ.

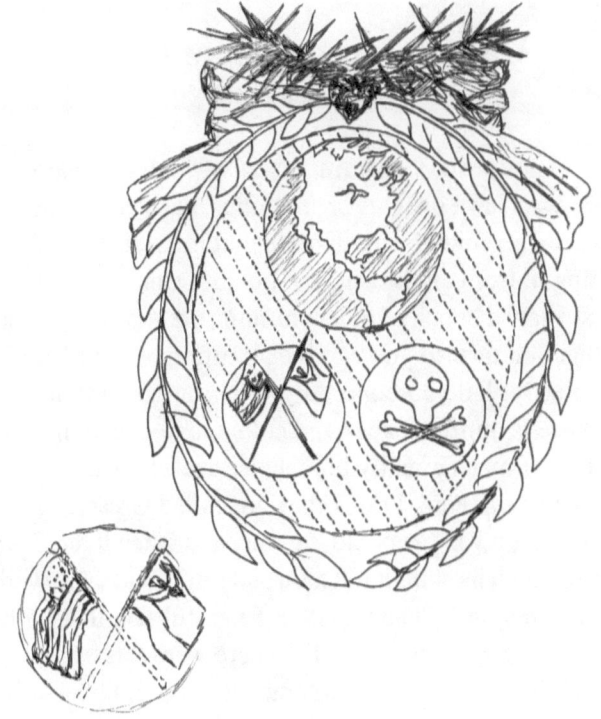

The full meaning eludes me at the moment; maybe time will tell.

~ On the Tip Edge of a Miracle ~

Black Limo Explosion
NOVEMBER 30, 2004

THE STRESS OF THE CHRISTMAS SEASON is on us and we are working long hours on a daily basis, trying to fill last-minute orders. Tonight we forced ourselves to relax and take time to pray and do a short meditation. In this meditation Dennison said,

"I saw the side of a mountain explode or maybe it was an earthquake. Something major made the side of a mountain slide down.

"I also saw a black limo explode. There were several limos traveling together and then one of them just exploded and people were running everywhere.

"The last thing I saw was a black dragon swinging its tail back and forth. The end of its tail looked like a spiked ball, you know a mace. There was a smaller white dragon and the mace at the end of the tail struck a solid blow and the white dragon went tumbling head over heals."

More Visions of Future Events
DECEMBER 2, 2004

DENNISON'S MEDITATIONS ALWAYS AMAZE ME. I try so hard to get to a place where I can have insights or see things, but seldom does it happen. I just can't keep my mind focused long enough and soon outside thoughts come drifting in from all directions. Tonight Dennison said,

"At first I saw a bunch of colors turning, you know, kind of like that kids' toy that you turn so you can see all different shapes and colors... what's it called? A kaleidoscope! Anyway I started hurtling down a tunnel of all these beautiful shapes and colors, and ended up in an ocean. A large whale, I mean a really big whale, one of those whales that are black with white on them, I think they are called Orcas.... Anyway this big whale swam up very, very close to me, and when it did, I was told to reach out and touch its skin. It felt hard and rough and there were patches of stuff like sores on it. Then I saw a beautiful fish that looked like a ribbon, swimming ever so gracefully. There were lots of other beautiful creatures and fish all around. Then someone was telling me, 'The oceans are getting warmer. Sun rays and warm water is harming them and they have no place to go. Without them the oceans will die.'

"Next I was shown a rain forest. There was a beautiful flowering plant growing on a tree. Someone told me, 'This plant can cure some forms of cancer.' I was shown other plants and some beautiful tropical birds. I was told, 'Many birds and animals use these plants to nourish from and clean their stomachs. These plants are now dying and the Rain Forest is being cut down. It is the Earth's lungs; without it the Earth will die. Everything was once in balance, but global warming and mankind is upsetting the balance.'

"After that the scenes changed to some type of motorcade going down a street. Two black limos are driving along and one explodes. I think I got that before, didn't I?

"Then I saw two elephants fighting. One was white and one was black. They were really beating the heck out of each other, but the white one was getting the worse beating and it finally went down. Just when the black elephant goes in for the final blows, an orange dragon with a red tail comes swooping down out of the sky and attacks the black elephant and drives him away. Then he tries to help the white elephant up, but he just lays there. Soon the dragon just flew off.

"I also saw a large army in tan and red uniforms marching in unison. Last thing I saw was Africans dancing, you know, like tribal dancing."

We discussed his meditation's images and I noted once again the black and white imagery. He said he sensed the elephants represented two powerful countries and the orange dragon is another unexpected country that enters the conflict. Neither of us had any clue what the African dancing could represent.

More Images
DECEMBER 4, 2004

I<small>T WAS AGAIN LATE</small> when we finished for the day. In spite of being tired we decided to pray and meditate before going to bed. I relaxed and began my meditation and that is the last thing I remember until Dennison asked, "Did you get anything?" Once again I had fallen asleep. However Dennison related the following information he got from his meditation.

"They asked me, 'What is Democracy?' Then they said that if the U.S. really practiced democracy, we'd have more people backing us, because we set an example for the rest of the world.

"Another thing they said was, before we have peace in the Middle East, a large sacrifice will be made.

"I saw that limo exploding again.

"I think something is going to happen to our food supply or to our resources for food imports.

"I saw two empty seats in the White House, like two factions or two leaders are fired or suddenly and unexpectedly quit. The reason they leave off-balances the government and people begin to see what's really happening. It's like eight pillars are holding up a roof and then two are taken away and the roof collapses.

Importance of Nutrition
DECEMBER 7, 2004

OUR WEATHER HAS TURNED EXTREMELY COLD this past week, breaking records for this time of year. It is our busy season, and Dennison has been working long hours; between that and the cold, his back has been in a cramp that can't be relieved. This evening when we sat down to meditate after our prayers he couldn't get comfortable and after a few minutes declared, "I just can't seem to relax enough to meditate." After a couple of minutes he got a kitchen chair to sit in and we tried again. I think the following teaching may have been because of his discomfort.

"They were telling me about energy tonight. We are energy, everything around us is energy; this is what is called life force energy and it permeates all things. Water is energy and food is energy and both are designed to nourish us. This is why it is so important to drink lots of water and eat the right foods. Most everyone needs to drink more water. Water increases our energies and even heals us, water IS THE MOST IMPORTANT thing we nourish from. You can also put energies from other things, like flowers, and crystals, into water and drink it.

"Different foods have different energies, and some are of a higher vibration than others. They told me we need to eat lots more vegetables and less meat. We should mostly eat foods that are in season, cook them to crisp tender, and whenever possible get them fresh grown and vine or tree ripened. Grocery store lights destroy the nutrients.

"Whole grains and whole rice are very nutritious; there's lots of vitamins and minerals in them. Mix rice with beans and you have a perfect protein. Spinach is very nutritious and can be eaten raw or cooked. Eat red potatoes instead of the others. Beets are very good for us and can also cleanse our blood. Cabbage, celery (cut on the diagonal so the vitamins stay in it), greens, beans both fresh and dried, turnips and even onions are all high vibration foods. Corn is a perfect food and so is wheat. You can soak whole wheat and use the water for high nutrition.

"Eat fresh fruit in season, and honey is better than sugar.

"Range-fed meat and wild meat is nutritious because the herbs and plants they eat are nutritious for humans. Eat cold water fish like salmon and trout."

The session ended because Dennison's back hurt so much he had to come out of meditation.

Energy
DECEMBER 8, 2004

TONIGHT DENNISON'S MEDITATION seemed to be a continuation of last night's. He said,

"They were telling me different foods have different energies and we should eat higher energy or vibration foods. We should stay away from low vibration foods such as processed foods and consume very little alcohol and coffee. They also said slow stretching exercise such as Tai Chi would help our aches and pains and so would learning how to breathe correctly.

"They said, when we get up in the morning, we should think of a butterfly and how it is reborn from a cocoon. We should see ourselves in the same way. We are born again each day with new cells and a new outlook. Each night we replenish our cells and cleanse our bodies of toxins and we should leave the problems of the day behind. In the future mankind will be like the butterfly and be reborn.

"All things in the universe are connected through energy. The Creator or God energy flows through all things. Everything we think, say and do affects everything else in the universe through this energy connection. And everything in the universe affects us in the same way. It's like throwing a pebble into a pond and the ripples it creates. The ripple of positive things and love moves instantaneously and negative things such as anger and hate vibrates very slowly, and that energy dissipates slowly. The stars' energies affect us, so does a solar flare, and the tides, and even war in a foreign country. Prayers, good thoughts and kind acts, they all affect everyone and everything. All is connected through Creator's energy.

"This multitude of vibrations creates a symphony throughout the universe…everything is in harmony. But when something or someone becomes too negative, it is like a sour note and it is disconnected from the Source.

"They were telling me also there are these pulses of energy that travel through the universe. It spreads through all things and it nourishes everyone and everything, including us, through our molecular structure. It is Creator's energy or Source energy, what we might call the life force that is in all things."

Blue Star and Flooding
DECEMBER 20, 2004

W<small>E HAVE BEEN IN THE MIDST</small> of our annual Christmas insanity. Almost everyone, including ourselves, seem to put off Christmas shopping until it's nearly Christmas. It works for some things, but when it comes to making custom jewelry pieces, it surely puts the pressure on us. For the past several weeks we've been working long, long hours, seven days a week, trying to get Christmas orders completed and mailed off in time to arrive before Christmas. Lately it's been after 1:00 AM before our heads hit the pillow. Finally today we have mailed off the last order and now look forward to a few days to recuperate and get our own lives back in order. It has been a while since we have taken the time to pray and meditate, so tonight, even though we're exhausted, we decide we need to do so.

The smell of the sage filled the air as Dennison lit the smudge and I felt all the tension of the past month dropping away as we prayed and settled our minds. However, meditating when you are so tired doesn't work too well, and I relaxed and got into my meditation and kept dozing off and waking myself up. When I heard Dennison begin to snore, I knew it was time to get up and call it a night.

Later as we were finally settling down in our wonderful bed, Dennison remarked,

"I saw a blue rainbow in my meditation. I wonder what it could mean...?" Over the years I've gotten fairly good at divining a lot of the symbolism he gets, but for the life of me I couldn't come up with even a good guess what it might mean. I told him it was probably a dream. He replied, "Well after that I saw a blue star coming toward the earth. Then I saw a huge flood happening, and this big wall of water coming. There was water as far as the eye could see. Someone said, 'You'll soon know that global warming is real.' After that I saw something happening to Florida, like part of it is sinking or breaking away. And another place, New Orleans, I think, is flooded. I think it's hit by a huge hurricane. That was all I got."

Tsunami
DECEMBER 22, 2004

TODAY WE DELIVERED SMALL CHRISTMAS GIFTS to friends and family who lived within driving distance. It was late when we returned home, but we felt happy and blessed after being with those we love. We decided to do a little prayer and meditation before going to bed. When we were finished, Dennison asked,

"What do they call those big tidal waves?" I replied, "Do you mean Tsunamis?" He said, "Yeah, that's it. I heard someone say, 'Tsunami!,' then I saw this big wall of water come crashing down on a coastal city and the whole area was completely demolished. Remember I saw that once before I think.

"After that I saw a bunch of bluebirds flying around, circling. I don't know what that means.

"Then I saw a very strange thing. I was inside of an old building of some sort. I think it was an old library. It was dim and smelled musty inside, like it hadn't been opened in a long time. The walls were lined with real old books. Some of them were really large. Some even had leather binding. I tried to look at one, but the pages just crumbled when I touched it. There was a table inside of a glass enclosure and on the table was a very large book lying open. I went over and looked through the glass to see what was so special about it. On the left page there was a picture at the top that looked like a cluster of crystals that came together like the fingers of two hands forming a pyramid. Between the crystals was a circle with a six-pointed star inside. Underneath was this fancy writing, like calligraphy, but I couldn't read it because it wasn't in English. On the other page was another picture of two ravens or crows. What was strange was that they were wearing clothes, old fashioned clothes, like a top hat, spats, vest, one eye glass, a cane and the like. I have no idea what that was supposed to be about."

Hopi and UFOs
DECEMBER 23, 2004

RECENTLY WE WATCHED A PBS PROGRAM entitled, "The Power of Intention" with Dr. Wayne Dyer. In it he talked about how to manifest what you want in your life. We decided to try some of his suggestions when we meditated tonight. When we finished, Dennison said,

"They said we should be more clear about what we want and why. We can't just say we intend 'abundance' because that can mean anything from food to shoes. If we want to manifest money, we should just say money and how much and why. We have to be very clear or we might just get what we ask for, not what we really want.

"Do the Hopi have a belief that in the hard times ahead they will be directed to go to a certain Kiva, which has an opening or tunnel that goes deep into the earth, and stay there until the worst is past?" I told him, "I'm not sure if they do or not, but their legends say they did something like that in the past when the earth was previously destroyed."

Dennison continued his questioning about the Hopi, "Do they believe aliens will come and take them away in UFOs in the end?" I told him, "I don't know about that either, but I vaguely remember many years ago some Hopi elders met with some people in Prescott who gathered to witness a UFO. I can't remember the details, but a newspaper reporter was there and said he saw one. They also have some rock writings that seem to depict a UFO; I remember seeing it on one of those UFO programs."

Dennison absorbed that, then continued, "I saw a large basket, a real finely and tightly woven basket. It was shaped sort of like a barrel. There was a wooden spigot or tap on the side, like a bamboo with a plug in it. It also had leather straps on the side, as if it could be carried like a backpack. Beside it was a large bowl or gourd that served as a cup. I decided to open the spigot and placed the cup under it. A very thin trickle of water came out. I waited a little while, but it was taking a long time for the cup to fill so I wondered if it might be empty or plugged up or something. I stood up and tried to look in the top, but couldn't quite see in; suddenly I noticed in back of it was a pipe. This pipe went on and on, as far as you could see, until it was lost in the darkness, like it went on forever.

"I think the water symbolized Creator energy coming from the Source. The spigot or tap was tapping into the Source. We can manifest anything we want. The pipeline goes to the source and the energy from it is limitless; it goes on forever and never stops. When I looked to see if it was empty, it was my doubt that Source is always there. I think the trickle meant my own connection to the Source isn't very strong. I'm not very open."

End of the Year Reflections
DECEMBER 31, 2004

WE WERE INVITED TO A NEW YEAR'S PARTY at a friend's house. Earlier it seemed it would be a nice way to bring in the New Year, celebrating with several of our friends. But as the evening drew nearer, we both realized we were tired and really didn't feel like going. Instead we opted to stay home and watch a movie and go to bed early. We looked forward to what has become our annual prayer and meditation to see what the future may hold for us.

As Dennison lit a candle and started his smudge, we talked about how quickly the year had passed and where we were now in comparison to where we had hoped to be at this time in our life. We also talked about the changes we hoped to make in our lives in the coming year, especially in regard to diet, exercise and renewing our focus on spiritual growth.

~ On the Tip Edge of a Miracle ~

We then talked about things we could do to increase our business and our income. We felt stuck and tired of spinning our wheels and getting nowhere. It was sobering to think we are nearly sixty and we have no back up or security for our old age. After all these years we are financially no farther ahead than we were when we made the decision for Dennison to quit his job at the pulp mill and to follow our dream. Then Dennison reminded me of all the stones, silver, tools, equipment and supplies we've invested in for his jewelry and art businesses; that was where a substantial amount of our money had gone. And he reminded me also of all the things we've experienced during those years, of all the adventures we've had and the many, many people we've met who touched our lives. We both agreed we wouldn't change a moment of it for all the security in the world. Indeed we have much to be thankful for, we are taken care of in so many ways, and we live in a beautiful place where we are free to follow our dreams. There are some who would call that a perfect life.

We each took a pinch of sage and cedar, and prayed for our loved ones, for our Mother Earth, for our leaders and for ourselves. Then we offered our bits of sage and cedar to the coal to carry our prayers. In the end we settled down and quieted our minds in meditation. It felt good to "let go and let God." When we finished, Dennison added more sage to the coal and we again smudged.

After a moment Dennison broke the silence saying,

"I think I saw our book tonight. The cover was gray and there was no picture or title on it, like it wasn't finalized yet. It was lying on its spine and partly opened. There was a spot-light shining on it from above. I felt like it wasn't finished yet, that it wasn't complete. I also saw a heart and sensed the book has something to do with the heart, like it should be from the heart or maybe it touches the heart.

"Another thing is that I feel like we're going to be traveling again. I saw us in an airport with bags slung over our shoulders. We were running like we were trying to catch a plane or make a connecting flight."

2005

We Are All Connected
JANUARY 1, 2005

IT HAD BEEN SNOWING LITTLE SPITS OF SNOW ALL DAY and, as evening approached, a howling wind whipped the snow into a blizzard. Although the thermostat said the house was warm, a chill crept into my bones. We had heated with wood for years, and now the forced air heat of a furnace just didn't seem to do the job. This evening Dennison built a cozy fire in our fireplace, and though it was more ornamental than functional, it seemed to help ward off the winter blast outside.

As we prepared to do our prayers and meditation, Dennison added a log to the fire and shoveled a few hot coals for use in our smudge. Soon the room filled with the fragrance of the sage and cedar and we turned off the lights and sat quietly listening to the snap and crackle of the fire and the howl of the wind. After our meditation Dennison said,

"They were telling me, 'We are all connected through "God" energy or "Source" energy. The only way for peace to happen would be if everyone could see how he/she is connected to everything else in the universe through this energy, which is the energy of creation.'

"In order to have peace we must find it within ourselves first. That is done by facing our fears and working to resolve them. The other side of fear is love. There are many reasons for war such as anger, greed, hate and prejudice, and these are really only aspects of fear.

"Our thoughts are energy and they affect everything in the universe through the energy that connects us. Right now that energy is high for war because there's not enough thoughts for peace. If there were enough peaceful thoughts in the collective consciousness, it would overpower the energies for war. We must learn to be mindful of our thoughts and realize how our thoughts affect the very world around us."

Vibrations and Energy
JANUARY 2, 2005

THE TEACHINGS ABOUT ENERGY seemed to continue with tonight's meditation. As we both finished meditating and stretched, Dennison said, "Everything in the universe is numbers or can somehow be translated as numbers. Numbers vibrate to certain sounds or key notes. Everything has its own sounds that it vibrates to; the whole universe is like a symphony.

"Words also vibrate to certain key notes and have numerical equivalents. (This made me think of the Hebrew alphabet.) There were certain words in the past that carried power and were used by magicians and sorcerers. The use of a word or combination of words of power could cause certain things to happen, like casting a spell or sealing an opening.

"Colors also have vibrations and correspond to key notes. Some colors have higher vibrations such as purple and blue, while others have lower vibrations like red and orange. Colors are healing and different colors heal different physical ailments. When one sends healing energy, it works best if they can send it as a color that heals that ailment. There are good books on this that we should read. They said this is why it's good to give flowers to people who are sick. Flowers are very healing, partly because of their color vibrations. Also they have other healing vibrations and can be soaked in water and the water then used for healing.

"Color affects moods. When we feel a desire to wear a certain color or surround our self with a particular color, it's because we need that vibration at the time. Colored light can be used for healing too.

"Another thing they were telling me is that our names have certain vibrations. The letters in them have numerical equivalents. If you know it, you can find your personal number. This can be good in games of chance like the lottery."

Solar Flares?
JANUARY 18, 2005

"I SAW SOMETHING EXPLODE IN OUTER SPACE, like a planet or a star or something, and debris flying out in all directions. A massive, huge, huge cloud of debris and dust remained. I sensed the earth is moving into this cloud of dust and debris and it will affect us in some way.

"Next I saw sun rays shining on a blue ball, then I saw what seemed like huge eruptions coming off the sun and hitting the blue ball. I wondered if the blue ball was a planet or something." I spoke up at this point and asked, "Do you think the blue ball could be Earth?" He agreed and continued to speculate the eruptions could be huge solar flares.

"Next thing I saw was an eagle pin, you know, like an eagle with its wings outstretched and its head turned sideways. In the center of the pin was a swastika. It was pinned onto the lapel of a uniform. Do you remember those old wooden clothes brushes with the black bristles? Anyway there was an old wooden clothes brush dusting off the pin and the uniform. It was like it was getting cleaned and ready for something. A voice said, 'Hitler is here to gather his angels, the Holy City will be wiped out.'"

The Blue Pearl
JANUARY 23, 2005

I WAS FEELING STRESSED over the lack of business and the abundance of bills when we began our meditation this evening, and found it difficult to relax enough to meditate. Dennison on the other hand had no problem.

"I was under the ocean...under the water like I was diving. Up ahead was something like an open clam shell, a very large clam shell. As I swam closer, I could see this beautiful large blue pearl. As I reached for it, suddenly I was looking at a Buddhist monk sitting under a tree meditating. This tree was sort of twisted and looking really neat, like a painting. The monk was sitting under the tree with his legs crossed and his hands resting on his knee, palms up, and his thumbs and fingers forming a circle. His head was bowed.

"As I watched him, the petals of a beautiful flower opened up behind his head. The flower was so beautiful and white with a little touch of pink on the petals. After this more and more white flowers began to cover the trunk, and then the limbs of the tree.

"A rainbow encircled the monk and, as I watched it, dissolved into sparkles that drifted down on the monk. As the sparkles touched him, he turned into a large white flower. Then the petals of this flower began to form a fan and became eagle feathers. The handle of the fan was a gnarled twisted piece of wood that had long roots hanging from the bottom like fringe, continuing into the earth.

"I don't really know what the symbolism is, but it made me feel as if we should be focusing less on the material and more on the spiritual, and therein lies the true wealth."

Stop Worrying
JANUARY 24, 2005

TODAY WE GOT FOUR ORDERS FOR JEWELRY! Two of them paid fully in advance and the other two paid half down. We also received final payment on some jewelry Dennison had finished last month and were waiting on the final payment. Indeed we are blessed.

FEBRUARY 3, 2005

AFTER TONIGHT'S MEDITATION DENNISON SAID, "They were telling me Israel and Palestine will sign a peace agreement; they are going to make peace with each other. When it happens, it will be a fulfillment of prophecy and it will be a sign to us that things are really moving quickly in a certain direction, as well as show how close we really are to the end.

"There is a large religious group that has a lot of power. They are trying to get control of all the world oil resources. It is part of what makes up the 'One World Government' that is trying to control the world."

We Are Being Pushed
FEBRUARY 22, 2005

THE DAYS SLIPPED AWAY QUICKLY and somehow we never seemed to find time to meditate, either being too tired or doing something else in the evening. I hate to have that happen because it gets easier and easier to get out of the habit. It felt good as we lit our candle, started the smudge and settled down to meditate and pray.

"Remember how the Hopi and other Native People believe the earth has been destroyed four times? Each time mankind changed and came back in a different way. We evolved layer on layer over the old. In a way this is getting ready to happen to mankind again. We are being pushed in a certain direction and into a certain way of thinking—through earth changes, economic failure, fuel shortages, diseases, epidemics, terrorism, wars, and corporate greed. The general breaking down of society is what will push us to a breaking point. We will reach a threshold or point that, if we go beyond it, we will change. We will no longer need to rape the earth and plunder its resources because we see what that has done. We will refuse war because we realize what it's all about and want no more. We will look into alternative fuels such as the sun, wind and water. We will seek things that are natural and won't harm the earth to sustain us. We will learn to grow healthful foods and live in harmony with the earth. Eventually the earth will renew herself."

More Information
FEBRUARY 23, 2005

SOMETIMES DENNISON GETS INFORMATION IN MEDITATION and then a day or two later it seems he gets a continuation or expansion of what he received. I don't know if he just gets tired and they come to him later with the rest (since there is no time where the information is coming from) or why that is. Tonight's meditation seems to be a continuation of what he received last night.

"As things happen more and more and we are forced to change our thinking, we ourselves will change. Our very DNA will actually change and we will become greater than we are now.

"There's going to be two more wars. One will be over fuel, over oil. Then the next one will be over who will rule the world. It will be the creation of the One World Government. He who controls the oil will rule the world.

"When the second war happens, there will be a separation of people: those who are caught up in the greed or the fear and those who are not.

"The government will seek to control through fear and through restrictions. Those who are spiritual will break away and form small self-sufficient communities. They will work together and support each other in order to survive. They will unite together in order to resist the governmental system. They will be a strong force. They will create other fuels, other ways to grow food and live in harmony with the earth and each other. As time goes by, more and more people will leave the old ways and join them.

"The next election will really be dirty, ugly, as those in power work to remain in control and the secret government will work to put their puppets into government positions.

"At the time of the separation of the people more and more will come to see what is really going on in the government. Even people within the governmental system will leave to join these communities. By working together we will be able to stand against the government and their control. There will even be two money systems. One will be based on some sort of exchange or barter for goods, the other will be our current system.

"Then our DNA changes. Our minds and bodies actually change. We become lighter and less dense or physical. Our old programming, our old baggage falls away. We will live a more simple and spiritual life. We are able to heal our selves. I think somehow the Watchers come back to interact with us again. They will show us new ways of living and help us rebuild our new world.

"There are somehow two worlds. Those who don't change will remain in the greed and fear world.

"I also saw a blue star or meteor coming toward the earth."

Blue Star Again
MARCH 6, 2005

"TONIGHT I SAW A BUNCH OF WHALES AND DOLPHINS beaching themselves, not just a few but a LOT of them, like their sense of direction was messed up or something. How do they sense where they are going anyway? Would a change in the magnetic energy of the earth affect that?

"I saw that blue star or whatever it is again. I don't really understand what it represents or why I keep seeing it.

"I also saw a crystal...it was a large green crystal; the top of it was faceted like a jewel, the rest was real long and ended in a point. As I looked at it closer, I noticed there was something hanging from the bottom of it. You know, how a cocoon looks, this thing looked a lot like a cocoon, I could see it twisting and turning, and the sides of it looked like something inside was trying to get out. At first I thought of an alien like in those weird alien movies, but as I watched, I could see these insect legs break through one by one. It continued to struggle until a wing appeared, and then the other wing appeared. It just hung there slowly flapping its wings like it was drying them off or something. It was a butterfly, the most beautiful butterfly I've ever seen!

"The color was very unusual, with the edges of its wings a purple with yellow and orange, while the rest of it was white. It finally turned loose and began to fly toward me real slow. As it got closer, it became an eagle gliding toward me with its wings out-stretched, gently flapping right toward me.

"When it was almost upon me, it became an ocean with lots of turbulence, but as I watched, it began to grow calm and peaceful, and as it did, so did I.

"Then there was something about the sun. It was a deep red-orange. I could see these eruptions coming off of it. I think they were solar flares.

"I saw a strange thing.... I was looking at a forest covering rolling hills, but what was strange was that the leaves on the trees were all turning in the same direction, toward the sun. Also the flowers and grass was the same way. The sun was covered with a sort of haze and you couldn't see it very well."

Fear Blocks Energy
MARCH 8, 2005

TONIGHT THEY WERE REMINDING ME that fear blocks energy. Fear actually blocks things from coming to us. They said, "You are like a plant. A plant can lose its leaves, but if it is firmly rooted, it will re-grow. We all must root ourselves in our spiritual beliefs and nothing can destroy us. Like the grass that is cut down and trampled, we will always be able to come back even stronger.

"I also saw that green crystal again with the butterfly hanging from it. I think maybe it represents mankind somehow."

Emotional Times
APRIL 2, 2005

THIS PAST MONTH OUR DEAR FRIEND IN CANADA, who wrote the introduction to our last book, passed away after a long battle with breast cancer. It was her dying wish to see us one more time before she passed away. Thankfully her family made it possible for us to travel up to be with her during her last hours, and to say our goodbyes.

The trip home was long and tiring and filled with sad memories. We left Edmonton at 2:00 AM and flew to Houston where we had to lay over for six hours before flying back to Albuquerque. From there it was another five hours to drive home. It was very late when we got home and we went right to bed. We had barely gotten to sleep when we got a call saying Dennison's mother was near death. We quickly dressed and drove another three hours to hopefully be there with her when she passed.

It was an emotional time for both of us, especially Dennison, losing a dear friend and his mother within a day of each other. Tonight is the first chance we've been able to settle our minds and emotions enough to meditate. Afterward Dennison asked,

"What exactly is the difference between a star and a planet? I saw two stars or two planets and somehow there was some kind of a starburst or big explosion. Anyway a lot of pieces broke off and there's lots of dust and debris. Somehow this is going to affect the earth.

"I saw the sun turn red again; I saw that before, didn't I? There was like a red haze around the sun. Maybe it's caused from the dust and debris of that planet they showed me.

"There's going to be a large earthquake off the coast of California, down by San Diego. I think I've gotten that before too. It's going to be a really big one. They were saying there's two plates that are pushing against each other. They are coming together edge to edge and the pressure is tremendous. I don't know when this is going to happen, but I feel like it is going to be soon.

"I keep seeing a star...." I interrupted and asked, "Is it that blue star you saw a couple of months ago or the star/planet you saw tonight? He shrugged and replied, "I don't know, just a star. Is there such a thing as the North Star? They were saying something about sea travelers and early ships used to travel by it, navigate by it. There's something about it we need to watch. It's going to move or something. It's not going to be there somehow!" (I speculated it could be from a polar shift where our north pole shifts.)

"I also saw a series of numbers, like years or dates that are significant somehow: 1939, 1946, 1961, 2001 and 2011. Then I saw an hour glass after the last year with sand almost run out of it; then I saw 2020 flashing on and off."

Portent of a Disaster
APRIL 4, 2005

IN TONIGHT'S MEDITATION Dennison was wanting to get some clarification on the North Star "moving." I'm not sure if this pertains to it or not.

"They were telling me the earth is heating up: the core of the earth, that 'ball' in the center of the earth that spins...you remember?...they showed me that before. Anyway somehow it creates an energy field, a gravitational field around the earth, and that somehow helps protect the earth from being hit with things from outer space. This shield is weakening, and when it's weak, it doesn't protect the earth as well. I saw a star or a large asteroid or something like that explode and there are three large pieces and lots of dust and debris. Some of it comes close to the earth or hits the earth and causes a shift."

A Teaching About Fear
APRIL 24, 2005

"LAST NIGHT I DREAMED I was in a large auditorium listening to someone give a lecture. I tried to see who it was, but a bright light like a spotlight was shining on him and I couldn't see his face. He was lecturing about fear though. He was talking about how animals use fear as a protection mechanism. If they become frightened, they will run or hide, but soon the fear will pass. However when something frightens a human, they become fearful and they can't let it go quickly. Fear blocks their thinking, and their mind doesn't function well. Humans, when kept in that state of fear, are easily manipulated."

Fear of the unknown and fear of change blocks us from going forward with our lives. When humans grow older, they often begin to feel vulnerable and become fearful of even small things. Once a person is afraid, it's very hard to let go of that fear, even if it is unjustified.

We are living in fearful times—gangs, freeway shootings, terrorists, job losses, large debt loads, and so on. All add to our fear level. Our government and others can use these fears and create more so they can control us and manipulate us to do things we would otherwise not do. We must learn not to buy into fear, because it will block us from receiving the guidance that is always there for us.

We Are Like Flowers
JULY 30, 2005

AS WE FINISHED MEDITATING, Dennison said,

"I got a teaching tonight. They said we are like flowers. A flower will turn any direction to get sunlight. It gets nourishment from it as well as from moisture in the air and minerals in the soil. Everything it needs to nourish from is there. All it has to do is be a flower. The Source supports it.

"We too are connected to the Source through our minds. Our bodies are designed to experience. Every part of our body down to the smallest hair is covered with a web of receptors that sense and processes everything around us. The Source also supports us the same as it does a flower.

"When something happens to us, it is supposed to pass through us. We are supposed to experience it and then let it go on through. They illustrated it to me by showing me a filter. The experience enters one side, passes through to the other side as an experience, and then the Universe or Source neutralizes it. Whether it is negative or positive, it doesn't matter, it's just turned into neutral energy. The only problem is that our ego steps in and it takes the experience apart, analyzes it and judges it, then hangs on to it and goes back again and again and repeats the process. The experience doesn't pass through us like it's supposed to; it just stays stuck until we finally let it go.

"If we wouldn't judge it and analyze it so much, if our ego didn't get involved, it would pass through and go on and no longer affect us. If we hang on to an experience and don't let it pass on through us, it will just keep repeating in our life until we finally learn to let it go.

"If we can live from our hearts and let everything that happens pass through us and experience it without judgment, we will discover we're being supported. Whatever direction we choose to move in that is heartfelt, the Source and all things around us will support that action. Opportunities, funding, connections, etc. all just seems to open up to us like a miracle."

A Dream of the Grandfathers
AUGUST 5, 2005

IT'S ONE OF THOSE PERFECT MOMENTS that you wish you could hold on to forever. The summer monsoons have worked their magic and everything is lush and green. The meadow by our house is filled with wildflowers and singing birds. The early morning air is slightly cool with perhaps a hint of autumn. We're sitting on our deck drinking our morning coffee, watching the hummingbirds and their babies suck down the sugar water in the feeders. I laugh at the babies, so small they are almost lost in the red plastic flowers of the feeders.

Dennison remarks, "I was dreaming I was sitting in a brush arbor, you know what I mean, those brush huts they used to build beside the hogans. Anyway I was sitting in one with four elders. In the center of the hut was a small fire. It was made of four logs laid in the four directions with a ring of stones around it.

"The grandfathers sat around the fire, each at the four directions. They were singing songs in the old language (there is a version of Navajo that is known as the "old language", much of which is no longer understood by most Navajos, and only used by certain elders and medicine people during ceremony).

"The first grandfather (a term used by the Navajo for any male elder) told me the songs were ancient, going back to the beginning of mankind. As they sang, he held up two flint knives; you could see they were both really old. He held a knife in each hand and in his left hand he also held a medicine bag. As they sang, he would strike the knives together. He said they symbolized how we can enter into another world. The clashing knives create an opening into another dimension.

"The second grandfather then held up a branch from an oak tree. He spoke and said the leaves nourish from the air as well as the minerals in the soil and the water. He said oak is sacred because it exists in both worlds. The leaves and branches reach up into the heavens, the roots go deep into the earth, joining the two realms. He told me the oak branch could be used to find water when it became scarce. He said there is a water source that can be tapped into by using it. He said with the right songs the branch can be used to manifest water when it was needed.

"The third grandfather stood and laid out four stones in the four directions. He then walked back and forth between the stones in each of the four directions. He told me we could balance ourselves by going back and forth between each stone four times, then sitting in the center and meditating. He said the stones were also used for healing. Each one represented an element—earth, wind, fire and water—and there was a song for each element when it was placed on a person.

"The fourth grandfather stood up and gave me a large skin bag. It wasn't a medicine bag; it was tied with a leather string wrapped around the end. There was a liquid inside. As I draped it over my shoulder, I had the impression it was filled with camel milk!"

I burst out laughing, "CAMEL MILK!? Why on earth would he give you camel milk?" With that Dennison too began to laugh at the absurdity of it. It was so far out of line with the rest of the dream. We both wondered why on earth he would get camel milk out of what was an otherwise reasonably coherent dream.

An Unbelievable Invitation
OCTOBER 18, 2005

I WAS SITTING IN THE VAN READING A BOOK while Dennison went into an auto parts store to buy some more acetylene for his jewelry torch when my cell phone rang. The voice on the other end identified himself as being from the Mayor's office in Tucson. My BS alert immediately kicked in: after all how often does one get a call from the Mayor's office, especially when you don't live even close to that city. The man proceeded to ask if he could speak to Dennison "Toasty" and I replied he wasn't available. He asked if we had a jewelry store and I told him we made jewelry and sold it through the internet. He then asked if I was familiar with the Sister City Programs and I told him, "Somewhat, at least I know what is meant by a sister city." He must have heard the frosty skepticism in my voice for he followed this by declaring, "This is not a joke, so please don't hang up." I waited for him to continue, expecting a solicitation at the very least or more likely some con game.

The man went on to explain that Tucson had a Sister City in Almaty Kazakhstan and asked if I'd heard of the country. I told him that I had and he seemed surprised. Then he asked if I knew where it was and I admitted I was a little vague on that, but thought it was near Russia. He really seemed impressed with that. Finally he got to the reason he was calling. "We have hosted a group of Kazakh artisans to come over to Tucson and participate in the Gem and Mineral Show for the past five years. Now they want to reciprocate by hosting an artisan to go over there and participate in some sort of a cultural arts show they are putting on. They have asked specifically for a Navajo silversmith. I guess they think they are somehow related to the Navajo, and are, at the very least, extremely interested in the culture, the jewelry, and the rug weaving.

"We had arrangements for a Navajo jeweler from Phoenix to fly over there next Monday, but he has backed out on us. Now we need to find someone else to take his place. Do you think your husband would be willing to go over there and participate in an art show? They will pay all of your expenses and give you a place to stay...you are welcome to sell anything you want; we won't take any part of whatever you make. You would need to stay for about three weeks.

"I know there's a lot of trouble in other Middle Eastern countries, but they aren't like that; you would be perfectly safe."

That thought had not even occurred to me! I sat in shock, blown away by this bolt out of the blue. I finally said I would discuss it with Dennison and call him back later.

When Dennison returned to the car, I told him about the phone call and he just sat and stared at me like I was insane. We bought groceries and on the way home talked about the unlikelihood of such a thing happening to anyone and wondered if this was something we needed to do for some reason. And we talked about the impossibility of doing such a thing, especially on such short notice.

That evening Dennison called the man back and they talked for some time. When he hung up, he had decided to see if we could get ourselves together enough to go. The man wanted us to take rugs, pottery, jewelry and any other Native American arts from Arizona that we could bring, even if it was not Dennison's work. We had almost none of those things.

The next day Dennison called an old friend of his who owned a trading post and gift shop and told them of our invitation and asked if they had anything they would trust him to take for display. Amazingly they agreed and told us to come to their store and load up on anything we wanted to take with us. Even more than that they offered us a percentage of anything we happened to sell. That seemed a confirmation that this adventure was something we should do.

We called the man in Tucson back, accepted the invitation and set everything in motion. The next day we drove to the traders and loaded up with as many beautiful examples of our Southwestern Native American crafts as we felt we could easily carry, ending up with more than $60,000.00 worth of goods.

The next few days were a flurry of getting passports and visas updated, and all the other necessary details arranged. The following Wednesday we were on our way!

I kept a journal of our trip, and the following pages are the highlights from it. I know this book is about our spiritual journey, but even though this seems unrelated in the grand scheme of things, everything is a part of that journey. Who knows what this trip may have accomplished on a higher level.

~ 2005 • I ~

You're Going Where?
OCTOBER 2005

I

WE ARE BLEARY-EYED AND SLIGHTLY DISORIENTED as we enter the Almaty airport after our very long but uneventful flight. It is slightly after 1:00 AM. I notice the room is filled with uniformed officials carrying side arms and I feel slightly intimidated. We, along with the rest of the passengers, are being herded into lines leading up to the customs agents. After being questioned in depth as to our reasons to be here, the length of our stay, and where we will be staying, we are fingerprinted and photographed.

It is 2:00 AM when we finally emerge into the waiting area. I see two people anxiously searching faces as we leave the baggage room. I smile and wave at them. They both hurry over and the woman asks in slightly accented English, "Are you from Tucson?" When I reply that we are, she smiles and says, "Welcome." They each give us a shy hug and a brief kiss on each cheek. The woman introduces herself and the man beside her, "I am Gulmira and this is Izturgan. We call him the Patron because he takes care of us." She pauses then adds, "You will be staying with me while you are here." I recall that Izturgan is the head of the artists association that is bringing us here. He takes some bags from Dennison and we head for the doors leading to the outside.

Suddenly another official approaches and stops us just as we reach the doors. Izturgan talks to him at length and then produces a document that presumably explains the purpose of our visit. He also gives him some money, which I assume will help grease the wheels to get us through the process more easily. The man pockets the money, then indicates a small office with a sweep of his arm. We obediently follow and Gulmira whispers to me, "Don't worry, he just wants us to feel his authority. It's okay, there's no problem."

The official asks for our passports and carefully examines them and asks us a question in Russian. Izturgan replies for us. Then the man says in perfect English, "May I look in your bags?" Dennison begins to unzip our luggage. The man stops him and points to Dennison's inlayed watchband, "Did you make it?" he asks. Dennison nods in the affirmative. The man then asks to see our jewelry. Dennison opens our carry-on bags; they have the jewelry and rugs packed inside. The official looks thru the plastic of a few of the zip locked bags of jewelry and marvels at the workmanship, and then he indicates we can zip up our bags. He says, "You can go now." As we leave, he adds, "Enjoy your visit and good luck at your art show." His face now beams with good will.

Cold damp air hits us as we leave the building and I wish I had taken my coat out of the luggage. The car is quite a distance away and I begin to cough as I breathe in the frosty air. Izturgan stops and says something to Gulmira, then leaves us and walks toward the parking lot, waving his arms and whistling. A battered aging van emerges from a parking space and chugs over to pick us up. We load our baggage and climb in, thankful for the warmth inside. Izturgan gives the man some money and explains where he wants to go.

We arrive at a high-rise apartment complex that looks like it should have been condemned years ago. We wheel our luggage through open doors into a foyer of sorts where a dim light wanly illuminates the room. A row of vandalized mailboxes hang open along one wall and the floor is littered with trash. Gulmira pushes a button to signal the elevator. You can hear it groaning and complaining as it descends. The elevator door opens into a small 4ft. x 4ft. cubicle, Gulmira sweeps her hand for us to enter, and Dennison and I get in. Gulmira squeezes in with us and says Isturgan will follow with our luggage. Dennison wants to stay behind and help, but they both insist Isturgan will handle it. The interior of the ancient elevator is lit by a single dirty light bulb that casts a dim yellow glow over us as we creak and groan our way slowly upward.

We arrive at the 7th floor and step out on to a long outdoor balcony. We walk to the apartment at the far end and, after unlocking three locks, Gulmira opens the door and says, "Welcome to my home." I notice shoes neatly lined up beside the entrance, so I stoop and pull mine off. Dennison follows my lead. We know this is customary in most of the countries we've visited. Gulmira protests saying, "No, no, you are my guests, be comfortable. You can leave your shoes on." But we pay no heed and continue to remove our shoes.

The apartment is tiny and cluttered. Gulmira shows us her bedroom and says this will be where we sleep. It is filled by a freestanding wardrobe, a bed, a dressing table and barely enough space to move between

~ 2005 • I ~

them. I wonder where we'll put our luggage; there is simply no room. We are shown a tiny toilet room, and a tiny room beside it housing a bathtub that also serves as a bathroom sink. The kitchen is equally small, the size of a large walk-in closet. There is a sink and stove and a tiny refrigerator along one wall with cupboards above. Along the other wall is a long narrow table covered with teapots, and odds and ends of food. The light in the living room is turned on and we enter. It is the largest room, and the floor is covered with a fine red handmade traditional Kazakh rug. There is a black loveseat on either side of the room and two chairs at one end. An old TV is perched on a small table that is also piled high with books. In the center of the room, between the two love seats, is a large coffee table laid out with dates, nuts, dried apricots, cookies, candies, slices of bread, cheese and teacups. At the other end of the room is a cluster of pitiful houseplants and behind them heavy red velvet drapes. Gulmira says, "When Izturgan comes, we'll have tea." I take the opportunity to try out the bathroom. There is a roll of toilet paper on the floor beside the toilet; it is crisp and crinkled reminding me of crepe paper, but it does the job better than a page from a Sears catalog.

The heat in the apartment is oppressive, and sweat trickles down my neck while we wait for Izturgan. He soon enters with our luggage and there is a discussion about where best to put it. We end up stacking it in front of the bedroom door. It's very inconvenient, but we can't complain, there is simply no other place.

Our teacups are actually small bowls that she fills with strong black tea. She shows us how to grip the cup by placing our index finger inside the rim and bracing it with our thumb and second finger. She offers milk and sugar, which I at first decline. After I taste the tea I opt for the milk. She dips it from a small wooden bowl with a wooden ladle, adding about ½ a cup. I taste it; it's creamy and rich. I ask if it's cream and she says, "No, it's camel's milk." I gulp a little and then try to put it out of my mind. Milk is milk. We nibble at the meal set before us and make small talk. At last Izturgan excuses himself and leaves. It's 5:30 AM by this time and we're exhausted.

Our next surprise is when we at last climb into bed. It's as hard as a board. I look under the sheet and find we are sleeping on a box spring with no mattress. The room is unbearably hot. Behind the headboard is a radiator. I set our travel alarm on the dressing table; it shows the temperature as well as the time. It is 110 degrees Fahrenheit! I decide to get up and ask Gulmira if there is a way to turn down the heater, but I already suspect it is centralized heating, so common in Europe. She confirms my suspicions and shows us how to open the small bedroom window a little, to let in the cool night air. She warns we will catch a cold though, if we do so.

We try to sleep, but between the jet lag and the uncomfortable sleeping arrangement we both lay there on top of the sheet, wide-awake. I wonder, not for the first time, what we are doing here. I remind myself to suspend judgment and to stay in the moment without expectations and see what life will bring our way.

II

SOMEHOW I FINALLY DOZE OFF TO SLEEP. I awake to the sound of Gulmira rattling dishes in the kitchen. I look at the travel clock; it is 11:30 AM. Dennison is snoring beside me. I sit up, trying not to disturb him, but he opens his eyes as soon as I stand up. Every bone in my body tells me I've slept on a board and I feel like I've been hit by a freight train. I rustle through our bags until I find some clean clothing and the towel I thankfully thought to bring.

I slip in to the bathing room to take a quick bath. Gulmira appears at my elbow and points to some boards lying across the back end of the tub. She indicates that I should just sit there and wipe myself down with a wet cloth or else stand in the tub and splash a little water on myself from the faucet, what we would call a "spit bath." When I turn on the faucet, I understand why. The water pressure is low and only a slow narrow stream leaks out. Gulmira has "breakfast" sitting on the coffee table when I emerge. It is the same fare as last night, with the addition of some sardines and some berry jam. I note a pillow and quilt in the middle of the floor and I realize Gulmira had slept there. I surely could not complain about my hard bed, because she sacrificed it for the floor.

Later we walk down town and Gulmira points out various buildings, telling their history or their function. We continue walking for some time, ending up at a museum with displays of the Kazakh's history. We are intrigued to find some artifacts from the past that look very similar to the Navajo. In particular a silver belt that looks like a concho belt, and a Yurt that looks very similar to a Hogan. We note the designs in their weavings and see many of the same designs that are in the Navajo rugs. We see artifacts that show the progress of their history, and discover they were the Scythians and the Huns of the past. And they are related to the Nomads of Mongolia and Russia. The Nomads still live in yurts, and herd sheep and goats. There are old photos that look for all the world as if they were taken on the Navajo reservation. At the end of our tour we look at a chart painted on the museum wall, showing the genetic linage of the Kazakhs and follow it from the Middle East thru China, across the Bering Straits to Alaska and then into Canada and down to the Navajo land in Arizona. Dennison is very excited and keeps saying how he wishes he could show this to his dad.

From there we walk to a botanical garden, and finally end up at an art museum. Gulmira's brother has some of his work on display here and she is very proud. We pause to admire it and I find I am enjoying myself very much. We walk, and walk and walk until I am so exhausted my knees are knocking.

The streets are jammed with cars of every make and age. The air is filled with smog that stings the eyes. There seems to be no traffic rules at all and I marvel that it all seems to work. Cars park any way they wish, no one stops at the red lights, two lanes of traffic swell into three or four improvised lanes, cars stop suddenly or squeeze between two others. Gulmira explains that she's afraid to drive. She says there never used to be so much traffic, until two years ago; she also says that two years ago banking came to Almaty, along with credit. Now everyone has a car, because they are cheap to buy from Russia and credit is easy to get too. I recall when we were in Japan, we learned they have to buy new cars every two years or else have a new engine installed. Their old cars are shipped to Russia on large barges. I surmise these are some of those cars. After a few hours she asks if I'm tired. I tell her I am, so she says she will get us a cab.

We then stand in the road, off the sidewalk and she sticks two fingers out. In no time a car pulls up, she opens the passenger door and asks him a question. He shakes his head no and speeds off. This happens a few more times until someone agrees to drive us. The car is dirty and reeks of smoke and gas fumes. We drive for a time, then Gulmira hands him some change and we pull to the side of the street and get out. She takes us into a building filled with shops, and we find a place that serves tea. We sit down and she orders some lamb kabobs, salad and tea. When we leave, we again repeat the process of flagging down a "cab." This time the car is in better shape, but the driver darts in and out of traffic barely avoiding other cars. I grip the edge of the seat in sheer terror. We arrive safely at her building and I ask if he was a licensed cab driver. She laughs and explains that a cab was just someone willing to take you where you want to go, for a small fee. They have no cabs. It is just a form of hitchhiking that is commonly practiced. She remarks they also have no driver's licenses! Only the cars are licensed.

We enter her steamy apartment and she says, "Be comfortable. Later we will go and meet Izturgan for dinner at a Mediterranean restaurant." I regret eating the kabobs; I can't imagine eating anything more.

It is nearly 8:00 PM when we prepare to walk to the restaurant. I ask her if we should dress up and she says, "Whatever is your pleasure; what you're wearing is fine." The night is damp and cold and it penetrates my coat. We walk past a bar and several men are loitering in front, drinking their bottles of beer. As we pass, one man approaches Dennison and says something in Russian. We hurry past, ignoring him, but a little farther along Gulmira stops and doubles up laughing. When she gets her breath, she tells Dennison, "That man wants to sell you his dog for 2,000 tenga." We don't see the humor. Then she explains, as if we're dense, "He wants you to make love with his dog! To use his dog for a little while!" We then got it, but it still didn't seem funny.

When we arrive at the restaurant, I realize we should have dressed better; both Dennison and I look like a couple of Arizona rednecks. Everyone is dressed in evening wear; they turn and stare at the curious strangers in their midst. Izturgan is at a table with several other people; they stand and greet us warmly. They are the group of artists that will be doing the exhibition with us. We are introduced all around and a young woman named Akmaral says she will act as our interpreter this evening. She has studied English at the University in Tucson, and she will soon work for the US Embassy; her English is flawless. Izturgan asks if we mind that he orders for us. He says he wants us to try some of their traditional dishes. We readily agree, not having a clue what we would order if we had to do so on our own. Wine arrives and he offers a toast of welcome. Small dishes of food arrive along with small salads; I assume they are appetizers. We nibble and get acquainted until finally the main course arrives. It is sliced meat on top of a platter of wide thick noodles; thin sliced onions and fresh dill grace the top. Izturgan serves us, filling our plates. Another round of wine and toasting and we begin to eat. The food is delicious, and I try to do justice to my plate. Just as I think I'm finally done, Izturgan heaps another load of the meat and noodles on to my plate. Akmaral casually asks, "Have you eaten horse meat before?" Suddenly I feel ill; I ask in a small voice, "Is this horse meat?" She says, "Yes, didn't they tell you? This is a traditional dish, served only on special occasions, because it's very expensive. Do you like it?" I had to admit it tasted okay, but I was not used to the thought, horses at home were thought of more as pets. She reminds me, "Your cows, chickens, and sheep are also looked at the same way, yet you eat them." She assures me the meat is clean. "You know horses don't get sick, so you won't get something like mad cow disease or avian flu. These horses are raised especially for food, like cattle are." I nod my understanding, but the thought of eating Trigger is more than I can handle. I remember reading somewhere that during the Great Depression they ate horse meat in the U.S. and that it was supposedly served to our soldiers in the military during WWII. A little voice says, "When in Rome, do as the Romans do" but still I can't continue with my meal. I politely move my noodles around on my plate and nibble at the delicious bread and salads. Talk continues until late in the evening; everyone wants to know about the Navajo and the life style of an Indian.

III

I WAKE UP ABOUT 3:00 AM, every part of me aches and I can't find a comfortable way to lie. I squirm for a while, and then get up to use the toilet, tripping over our luggage on the way. Dennison wakes up and turns on the light for me. Later we lay there wide-awake waiting for dawn. I can hear that it is raining outside.

At 6:00 AM I get up and take a "bath;" a sleepy Gulmira emerges from the living room as I exit the bathing room. She demands to know, "Why do you get up so early?" I explain we are still suffering jet lag and can't sleep. Without a word she goes into the kitchen and turns on the teakettle.

Breakfast is a repeat of the morning before. Gulmira announces that Izturgan and a couple of the artists will be here around 11:00 and we will drive to a canyon, if the rain stops. She says we will take a picnic since there are no places to eat out there. Before we go though, we need to go register with the U.S. Embassy to let them know we're here. Rain patters down with a steady beat that says it's here to stay for a while.

The three of us get ready, then thankfully manage to find a "cab" before we're too soaked. Within an hour we've finished our business and when we emerge from the embassy, we find the clouds have lifted and the sun is trying to break through. A picnic doesn't seem such a bad idea!

About noon Izturgan and Company arrive and we all bundle up and climb into two small cars. We stop along the way to buy a pizza, wine and fruit to add to the picnic. Then we make our way out of town. Within ten miles it's beautiful open fields, and rolling hills interspersed with lots of trees. Small roadside stands of fruit and melons pop up along the way. We enter a small village, with quaint cottages and picturesque people working in the fields and walking along the roadside. We see a donkey cart loaded high with hay. It is as if we've entered a time warp into the distant past, like something out of Hansel and Gretel. We continue speeding down the highway, entering and leaving village after village. I imagine myself living in one of them. The simple rustic way of life tugs at my heart. It is soooo good to be out of the smoggy city.

Finally we stop beside a large street market. Gulmira indicates a house across the street and says we will have tea there. Izturgan goes up and knocks on the door; a man answers and points to another door upstairs. He waves us up and we enter a small café. He orders tea and a meat pie for all of us. As we are eating, a girl arrives with bowls of steamy hot stew. I casually ask if it is horse meat. They all laugh at me and assure me it is mutton. The absurdity of my willingness to eat a cute little lamb, but not a horse is not lost on me as I eat.

When we finish, Gulmira asks me if I want to use the toilet. We leave the group and make our way behind the house. A boy is chopping wood and Gulmira asks where the toilet is. He indicates a place across the yard where some large pieces of corrugated tin lean against each other, forming an A. We duck inside and find a long ditch covered with two

~ 2005 • III ~

boards placed side-by-side and oval holes cut into them. We each squat over the holes and urine splatters all over my shoes as I pee. I fish some tissue out of my coat pocket and hand one to Gulmira and then I try to wipe my shoes with another one. Outside there is a metal basin with a can suspended above it. Gulmira pushes a lever on the can and a trickle of water falls into the basin. We wash with a dirty bar of soap and I again fish out more tissue and try to wash off my shoes.

We walk across the street to the open-air market; it is filled with every sort of fruit and vegetable imaginable. People in colorful traditional dress sit chatting as they watch over their wares. They smile hopefully as we approach. Gulmira stops and buys two melons and some apples. I see a woman shucking corn and indicate I would like to take her picture. She nods, smiles and goes on with her work.

We continue our trip and the villages give way to a vast expanse of flat land, jagged mountains rise in the distance. It reminds us of the Navajo reservation. There is nothing for miles, no cars, no trees, no hills, no rocks, just vast empty land. Out of the vastness emerges a dark square shape in the distance, and as we come closer, it becomes a jeep, with a man underneath trying to fix something. We stop and offer help, but he declines and we go on. Finally we turn off the highway on to a dirt track. It is deeply rutted and the going is slow. After a long time the flat land surprisingly opens up into a canyon. It looks very much like Canyon DeChelly on the reservation. We step out of the car to find it's bitterly cold and a wind is blowing. It doesn't take me long to peep over the side, then get back into the car. The men all decide to hike down into the canyon. Gulmira gladly joins me in the car and we talk about our lives as we wait. I find out she has a five-year-old child, who is staying at her mother's while we are visiting. I tell her we won't mind if she brings the little girl home, but she says her mother loves to care for her.

It's almost dark when the men return, and we decide it's much too cold to try to picnic. We drive for miles back toward the villages. There is a truck stop on the outskirts of the first village and we stop and go inside. They have no electricity and the sound of a generator chugs in the back. A single dim light does little to eliminate the gloom. We carry in our picnic and spread it out on a long wooden table. A young woman brings us hot camel milk tea, cups and plates. We eat and drink wine from plastic cups and celebrate our day.

When we finish, Gulmira again asks if I need the bathroom and then asks the girl where it is. The girl vaguely points out back. We stumble along the side of the building, in the darkness until we can no longer see the cars and the men. We stop and pee right there next to the building, since we have no clue where the bathroom is or what we will find if we got there. This is surely better than the last one!

After we climb back into the car, I lean my head against Dennison's shoulder and, as we drive home, I fall asleep like a child.

IV

On Wednesday we drag our luggage filled with jewelry and rugs out to the street and Gulmira flags a "taxi." We drive to the exhibition hall, a large more modern building with lots of windows. There are several people inside, arranging showcases and hanging pieces of wall art. We open our suitcases and everyone in the room gathers around to look. Izturgan takes our Navajo rugs and gives them to someone to hang as we begin to unwrap our jewelry and arrange it in a glass case. A Russian woman comes up and talks to Gulmira. She in turn explains to me there are no price tags allowed. I explain they are also inventory tags that correspond to a list and without them I won't be able to know what is what. But the woman insists they be removed, so I spend the next hour writing an elaborate descriptive price list and remove the tags. The Russian woman returns again, this time wanting my inventory list with the prices. Up to this point we had believed that we would be there to sell our own jewelry, but we discover there will be a staff there full time to sell the jewelry, and that they will be adding a 40% commission on to the cost of each piece. I'm also told after tomorrow's opening we won't be returning until the exhibition is over. I reluctantly surrender my list, which she takes to be translated into Russian.

We have discovered in our conversations that the average income here is about $200.00 per month in American dollars. We realize our jewelry is priced way beyond most people's ability to buy, especially now with the 40% commission added on top of it. We worry we won't sell anything. Again I tell myself to suspend expectations and simply live in the moment.

~ 2005 • IV ~

We arrive at the exhibition hall at 2:00 the next afternoon, dressed in our best duds. Everything is in place and the room is beautiful. Several women are busily filling long tables with plates of food, breads and fruits. A TV crew enters and begins to take photos, someone points out Dennison and they ask him for an interview. They ask him numerous questions about the jewelry, the rugs and their meanings and have him pretend to be arranging the jewelry as they photograph him.

Another TV crew enters, and yet another. The room fills with people and there is a tangle of reporters with cameras; all are trying to get an interview with Dennison. A woman with one group of reporters explains she is from Reuters and they want to do a special report on this rare and important event where a real Indian visits their country. She says she imagines it will be picked up by several news organizations like CNN to be broadcast all over the country. More reporters and curious bystanders surround him, like a rock star. He sends me a panicked look as he tries to escape. I later remark to him he just had his fifteen minutes of fame without having done a thing to deserve it.

Izturgan and Gulmira later pull him away and introduce him to a man named Moldaguk, who is an art professor at the University. He is also a "Shaman." After the opening ceremonies they want Dennison to put on a costume provided by Moldaguk. He will don a similar one and the two of them will then enact a pseudo-ceremony representing the meeting of two cultures, as they might have done in the past, with the Shamans sharing a cup of tea. Moldaguk explains they will make it up as they go. Dennison seems a little bewildered, but agrees to go along with whatever they want to do.

Suddenly the ceremonies are about to begin. The room is packed and we have a hard time

pushing to the front of the room where we are to be introduced. There are two interpreters there, one to translate the Russian for us and the other to translate our English for all the people there. Dennison realizes at this moment he is expected to give a speech. I can see he is panicked. I whisper some ideas to him of what to say, but he doesn't act like he hears me. A dignitary begins speaking, welcoming everyone to this important occasion. He calls it the meeting of the century. After a time he finishes and an anthropologist steps up to talk about their Native American brothers. He has written a book about his research into Native

American cultures, in particular the Navajo. He claims he has found over 200 words with the same pronunciation and meanings in both the Kazakh and the Navajo languages. He tells everyone to welcome their long lost brother. A murmur ripples through the group and everyone claps. Then it's Dennison's turn. He introduces himself and me, and then he thanks Izturgan and the artists association for inviting us. He goes on to say he also suspects there is a distant link between the Navajo and the Kazakhs, because of their rug designs, their yurt, their nomadic past and even their jewelry designs. Suddenly he's out of words and just says, "Thank you." After the speech he presents Izturgan and Akmaral with certificates from the Tucson/Almaty sister city committee. Everyone claps. A woman who is a poet reads a poem and welcomes us. Then Izturgan takes his turn at welcoming everyone to their exhibition and encourages them to take time to view everything, in particular Dennison's display. He then announces he has a special treat.

Dennison is whisked off into a back room to put on the costume. It is a brown velvet dress with fringes cut along the bottom and at the ends of the sleeves, making it look like buckskin. A drum shaped like an ironing board is tied to his back. Moldaguk puts on a similar dress, along with a feathered hat, and a similar drum. They walk out with Dennison carrying a musical instrument.

In the meantime someone has spread out a rug, and placed a heart-shaped bowl in the center and two cups on either end. Instead of tea, a bottle of coke and a bottle of plain soda water sits beside the bowl, representing I suppose the two different cultures. The crowd and the cameras are packed around the rug. Dennison and Moldaguk emerge singing and making lots of noise. They sit at each end of the rug and Moldaguk pours coke into one cup and soda into the other. They then each pour the contents of their cups into the heart shaped bowl; it is mixed together and Moldaguk pours some of the mixture from the bowl into Dennison's cup and the rest into his own. This symbolizes the joining of the two cultures. They clink cups in a toast and drink. They rise and Moldaguk embraces Dennison in a bear hug, and everyone claps. It's over and the crowd disperses into the room with all the food.

Gulmira pushes me after the rest of the crowd and fills a plate for me. I'm sure some of the sliced meat has to be horse meat, after all this is a special occasion. I decide not to eat any meat, and just nibble at a few of the other delights. Gulmira hands me a glass of what looks like buttermilk and tells me to try it. "It's our traditional drink, fermented camel's milk,: she declares. She stands over me as I take a tiny sip. She insists I drink more. It really doesn't taste bad; it is sort of like yogurt, but like the horse meat, I psychologically am not ready to like it. I hang on to the glass until an opportune moment and then put it in the garbage.

A woman is suddenly at my elbow laughing. Conspiratorially she whispers, "That's simply awful stuff!" She introduces herself as the U.S. Ambassador's wife. She goes on to say our rugs and jewelry are beautiful. She says she has been here two years and in several other countries before and it reminds her of home to see our familiar goods. She is from Wyoming and the Southwestern jewelry styles are her favorite. She talks a little about Kazakhstan and how they are just emerging after eighty years of Russian rule.

"They are now trying to re-discover their heritage and culture, and what it means to be Kazakh. The government here is for the most part the old communist government that was in place when the Soviet Union collapsed. It is corrupt as might be imagined. This new generation of Kazakhs is moving to get them out. The Kazakhs know very little about the outside world since they weren't allowed to leave the country for eighty years. What they learned of the U.S. was from books written from the communist point of view. In it we are the boogeyman. What you are doing is wonderful and very, very brave. I know it must be hard to go to a place you've probably never heard of, and stay with people you have never met.

"You are ambassadors, you know. The U.S. isn't well liked in the world today. Your coming here of your own free will, without the backing of the U.S. Government, is a wonderful thing. By your being here, living with the Kazakhs and sharing your culture, you are doing more for diplomatic relations than all the diplomats have done up to this time. Bravo for you, I salute you! This is indeed an historic event."

She then offers to tour us around the city and gives us her card, saying if we find we have some spare time during our visit, we should call her.

Dennison shows up at my elbow and interrupts saying, "Gulmira wants us in the back room." Someone has brought hot tea, and we are given chairs and again we are toasted. We both feel bewildered, caught up in something we don't begin to understand.

Later we all pile into her brother, Serzhan's car, and drive to his home for another late evening dinner. The table is piled high with food and the inevitable horse meat is served on noodles as the main dish. I surrender, knowing I can't escape eating it without offending. These people are very poor by our standards, and they have spent a lot of money on this meal to honor us.

When we are "home" and again snuggled into our hard bed, I tell Dennison what the Ambassador's wife said. He voices what I've felt all evening, "I don't understand what we did. What was this all about anyway? We didn't do anything but bring our stuff for an art show."

V

THE NEXT DAY WE ARE TAKEN TO A "SCHOOL FOR ARTISTS" where Dennison is to demonstrate how he does his craft. The building is ancient; the cement steps up to the front door are crumbling away and I think to myself, 'this is right out of Harry Potter'. The director and one of the teachers greet us and lead us to an auditorium of sorts. There are several blue plastic chairs and in front a dilapidated table. The only light comes from a line of small grimy windows high up the wall, next to the ceiling.

The director asks Dennison what he will need. We are totally unprepared for this. Our understanding was that all the other artists would be set up to demonstrate. But we are apparently the whole show. We had also assumed the school would be much like ours, with a place set up for him to work and good light to work by. He has only brought a saw and some silver. He was told they would provide a torch and anything else he needed, but there is nothing here. Dennison asks for a light. The director goes into the hall and calls to some kids. Soon they come racing in with a bare light bulb on the end of an extension cord and a three-legged pole to hang it from. I'm surprised to see they are small kids, ranging from about ten years and up. I was under the impression this was more like a college.

~ 2005 • V ~

As Dennison sets up what little he has to work with, his silver and saw, I lay out an old *Arizona Highways* magazine showing pages of Navajo jewelry, a book with step by step photos of an old Navajo silversmith making jewelry, and an album showing photos of Dennison's jewelry. The kids are called in. The room fills with eager and interested faces. They swarm around the table asking questions we could not understand, eagerly looking at the books. We have a new interpreter, but she speaks very poor English.

Dennison begins with a brief history of Navajo silver-smithing and how he first learned from his grandfather. The interpreter repeatedly stops him and asks for clarification. I notice the kids are beginning to lose interest so I prompt Dennison to quit talking and get on with his demonstration. He begins cutting out a design in the piece of silver and explains he's going to make a bracelet. He goes as far as he can, cutting out the design while I try to hold the table steady. Then he describes what the rest of the procedure would consist of, since there is no equipment or torch for him to work with to complete the demonstration. The kids become restless and many leave. Dennison opens up for questions, but very few have anything they now want to ask. We thank them and gather our things to go.

The director asks if we would like to return the following day and visit the classes. He explains these kids are mostly from the country. They live here and go to art school four days a week and do regular studies, like math and science the remaining three days. They are in 5th grade on up through high school. Each teacher has five students. When they master one art, they then can learn another. When they graduate, they will have mastered all the skills needed to follow a trade in any of the arts.

We are indeed interested and agree to return the next afternoon. Izturgan leads us out and back to the car.

The following day we are greeted once again by the director and two or three teachers. We go from one room to another. By comparison to our schools there is almost nothing for the kids to work with, few tables and chairs, bad lighting, and very basic equipment. But the kids are very, very talented and seem eager, happy and absorbed in what they are doing. We are impressed again and again at the level of skill they display. In one room they are doing clay sculpture using a live nude model. In another they are building beautiful violin-like instruments, beginning with hewing out large tree branches. The finished instruments are exquisite, having fine carvings and inlay on them. In another room they are doing beautiful weavings, in another painting, and in another felting and embroidery.

We finally are taken outside of the main building and led to a building in back. The schoolyard is littered with garbage spilling out of barrels, rusted wire, pieces of metal, broken chunks of cement and weeds. A cat greets us as we walk along toward the building and follows us inside. The building consists of two rooms and a forge; a lone man is hammering on a piece of silver. The rooms are freezing inside. The workspace is covered in dirt, scraps of silver and silver filings. And again there is no lighting. The teacher leads us to a small office and invites us to sit down on a couch that is against one wall. He sits behind his desk and pulls out boxes of antique jewelry, as well as jewelry that has been made by his students. He asks Dennison endless questions and eagerly wants to show him everything he can think of. He's very excited to have Dennison there, and is very proud of his shop. When we get ready to leave, he gives Dennison a medallion he made himself, as a gift.

As we walk back to the front of the building the teacher asks about our old Arizona Highway magazines with the Navajo jewelry pictures that we displayed the day before. He expresses how impressed he is by the work and how fascinated he is at the similarity of some of the Navajo designs to theirs. Dennison offers to give him the magazines and he is overwhelmed with the gift, thanking him again and again. We leave humbled, realizing how much we have and how little we appreciate it.

Later Dennison talks endlessly of all the things he wishes he could buy and send to the school. He is reminded somehow of the boarding school of his childhood and feels a strong connection to the kids here.

As we are eating dinner, Gulmira mentions their religious holiday of Ramadan will begin tomorrow. I recall they fast during the day and eat in the evening. She says she will cook for us anyway, and I protest saying I wouldn't think of eating while she watched us. But the next morning she has prepared tea for us along with breads and fruit. I again protest and firmly say we'll fast with her. She ends up saying at least we should eat some fruit if we get hungry. We both agree, but I can tell Dennison worries he will starve.

~ 2005 • V ~

That night Gulmira prepares a traditional bread, which turns out to be what the Native Americans call fry bread. She makes mutton stew and Dennison feels happily at home.

After the Grand Opening the days seem to drag on. We have seen the sights in the city they wanted us to see, and now the artists have returned to their normal lives. We try not to think of home and all the orders we left hanging while we went on our wild adventure. We walk to town on our own and do a little shopping, looking for souvenirs to bring our kids and grandkids. Our money is limited, but we find everything here is quite a bit less than at home. Dennison buys a couple of books on Kazakhstan and one on their antique jewelry.

Each night we visit an artist's home for dinner, as they each take turns hosting us. We are always served the inevitable horse meat and noodles with a variety of salads, breads, fruits and tea. They toast us with vodka and wine and ply us with gifts. We take our personal jewelry to give them gifts in return.

Each silversmith takes pride in showing Dennison his shop. Each time we marvel at what they can do with so little. The talent here is endless.

Finally the show is over and we return to the exhibition hall to retrieve our jewelry and rugs. We are amazed to find we've sold almost $1,000.00 worth of jewelry. It isn't much, but it is more than we expected. A woman takes me into a back room and takes each piece of remaining jewelry and compares it to the inventory list, to show me everything is there. I notice they've mixed up a few pieces of jewelry, selling it at the price intended for another. A $200.00 wide cuff bracelet is sold for $50.00, which was the price of a remaining narrow silver bracelet. I'm a little upset, but say nothing; it is out of my control. Later I reflect on it and find it's okay with me. I'm almost glad. Someone here got a wonderful bargain, but so did we. I treasure my experiences here.

Akmaral, who acted as interpreter the second evening we were there, has called Gulmira and invites us to attend a ballet with her. This time we do dress up for the event. Gulmira is distressed over my purple fleece jacket and insists I wear a long black wool coat she has produced from her wardrobe. It is elegant and fits me perfectly. I now feel ready for the evening. The theater is very ornate and beautiful with white marble floors, mirrored walls and a gilded ceiling. The ballet is Russian and Akmaral gave us a brief overview of the story before it begins. The music is beautiful and the dancing is excellent. When we leave, we stop at a restaurant for tea and pastries. At the end of this perfect evening Gulmira declares the coat belongs to me. She claims it doesn't fit her anymore and against my protests she insists I take it home with me.

    We are approaching the end of our time here and we are anxious to go home, yet there is a sadness that we will be leaving so soon. Gulmira wants to prepare a farewell party for us. Today she is taking us to a large market. When we arrive, we find it is packed with people. I hang on to Dennison for dear life, for fear we'll get separated. Gulmira leads the way and keeps looking back like a worried mother, to make sure we're still with her. The place is enormous and vendors of every imaginable thing line the streets. There are endless stalls of the most beautiful fruits and vegetables I've ever seen. The air is filled with the scent of fresh breads and grilled lamb. Sides of beef, mutton and horse hang at a stall selling meat. Gulmira orders some mutton and the man carves off a chunk with a sharp knife. He weighs it and hands her the meat, unwrapped. She has a plastic sack in her shopping bag, ready to wrap it in. We walk on. A Chinese or Korean woman shoves a sample of her noodle salad in my face and speaks rapidly, trying to urge me to buy some. Gulmira carefully selects the things she wants to prepare, bargains until she gets a good price and we move on. Finally we arrive back at her home, our arms laden with bags full of food. I remark to Dennison that if I lived here I'd become a complete vegetarian. I wish I had taken my camera, but it would have been nearly impossible to capture the market place. It's simply too large and too many people, all pushing and shoving.

VI

WE HAVE FEASTED AND TOASTED and now it's nearly time to leave for the airport. Our plane leaves at 4:00 AM. We feel the warmth and love of the artists and their wives. They now feel like old friends and tears are shed as we gather our bags and prepare to leave.

~ 2005 • VI ~

Our trip to the airport is quiet. We arrive and Izturgan and Sherzan, Gulmira's brother help us wheel our bags into the airport. We hug and kiss goodbye. Izturgan is already planning for our return.

Leaving the country is as complicated as when we arrived, and we are questioned and searched through three checkpoints before we're allowed to get on the plane.

Nine hours later we arrive in Amsterdam and the very first thing we do when we get off the plane is buy a cup of coffee, the first we've had since leaving the U.S. Dennison is feeling miserable with the beginnings of a head cold. We have eleven hours to kill, so we wander from one end of the terminal to the other. Finally we discover a meditation room, complete with reclining chairs. We lie down and sleep for a couple of hours.

After another nine-hour flight we land in Minneapolis, this time with a fifteen hour layover. It's 7:00 PM so we decide to catch a shuttle and rent a motel room. It seems like a good idea, but in the end Dennison is so miserable with his worsening cold neither of us ends up sleeping much.

I watch the brown desert speed by my window as we land in Tucson. It feels so good to be back! Our house sitter has informed us he needs to leave. He has a plane to catch the following day to go home for Thanksgiving. We decide to drive the five hours it takes to get home; we both want nothing more than our own bed.

I find I dream of Kazakhstan every night now. Somehow it has taken hold of me and a part of me misses being there. I ponder this because we spent most of our time in an ugly city. I realize it's the people. They took us in with open hearts and made us a part of their culture and their families. It was sincere, and heart to heart. They are dear friends and not just people we visited in a foreign country.

Kazakhstan is the 9th largest country in the world; it has vast resources of oil, petroleum and gas (the Caspian Sea). It has gold, copper, uranium, coal and many other natural resources. I can see this being exploited in the near future. The country will prosper and perhaps even become a player on the world stage. The thought saddens me in a way.

~ On the Tip Edge of a Miracle ~

NOVEMBER 2005

We arrived home exhausted but ever so thankful to be back in our mountains, and our tiny rural town, glad to see our dogs, and above all glad to again be sleeping in our own bed!

The next days were a reality check with our Christmas order season in full swing and a stack of jewelry orders waiting. The trip to Kazakhstan was already taking on a dream- like quality as we fall back into our old routines. From time to time we wonder why it came to us; it seems such an unlikely thing to have happen. But then so did our other trips to Japan, Canada, and Ecuador. As we sometimes have in the past, we again wonder if there could be a higher purpose to this trip.

To most Native Americans the number 4 is a sacred number; sacred things are done in fours and the four sacred directions are honored. In our case we had now traveled in the four directions. Each trip at the invitation of others, and paid for by others, with no solicitation from either of us to make it happen. To be sure the invitations came unexpectedly "out of the blue" each time. But we mortals are seldom privy to the workings of Creator, so I doubt we'll ever know.

DECEMBER 2005

This has been a good year for us financially, compared to years past. My health has improved and my last visit to the lung specialist in early October brought the news that my pulmonary function was almost normal for my age. Dennison's back still bothers him a lot, but he has been told little can be done, except strengthening exercises and changing the way he works on jewelry. Like most people in their 50's we are becoming keenly aware our bodies are aging and we begin to pay for the lack of regard we had for them when we were young.

2006

Shifting Gears
2006

THE NORMAL SLOW-DOWN IN JEWELRY ORDERS after Christmas barely happened this year and we found our days slipping away quickly as we worked to fill the demand. With Dennison's back pain, the trip to Kazakhstan, and then Christmas, we had easily fallen out of the habit of meditating regularly. Instead we simply opted for a quick smudge and prayer before going to bed.

Winter soon gave way to spring with its wet snows and endless wind. On one such day in early April I was just finishing up breakfast dishes when the dogs began barking hysterically and running for the front door. Our door bell doesn't work, but the dogs are all we need to know when someone is there. I was still in my pj's and looking pretty scary. I glanced at the clock and noted it wasn't yet 8:00 AM. Whomever would dare come unannounced at such an hour deserved the shock they were about to receive when I opened the door.

It took a moment to recognize it was Sandy, the owner of the new soap and candle shop in town. I had only been in her shop a couple of times and didn't know her on a social basis so I was quite surprised to see her standing there. I stood aside and told her to come in out of the wind then quickly closed the door behind her. She stood there looking a little embarrassed and slightly uncomfortable. I motioned for her to sit down while she apologized for stopping by so early, explaining she was on her way to open her shop and wanted to talk to me and Dennison before she had to go in to town.

She had come with an offer, to try and convince us to open a small jewelry/gift shop next door to her and the new espresso shop in the same building. There was a room coming available and the two women wanted someone who would compliment rather than compete with what they had to offer, as well as someone whom they felt they would be compatible with. We were the chosen.

~ On the Tip Edge of a Miracle ~

    At first we told her we were in no way prepared to take on such a challenge, but after much discussion, generous offers of help, and a few financial incentives, we slowly became convinced to give it a try. By mid May we had opened a small jewelry and gift gallery.

    Summer went by all too quickly and soon the cold winds of November blew all the tourists home and we hunkered down to survive the winter months ahead.

2007

Teaching and Selling
2007

ONE SNOWY JANUARY DAY as we all sat in the coffee shop passing the time and wishing for a customer of some sort, Sandy suggested that Dennison should teach a class on his healing techniques and energy work. She felt sure that many of the local people who already knew and respected Dennison for his healing work would jump at the chance to come. She felt we could charge a nominal fee for evening classes. It would bring a little extra money, and if we held the classes in the coffee shop it would possibly generate a little business there too.

At this time Sandy revealed she was a Reiki master herself as well as an expert in aroma-therapy. No wonder she made such wonderful soaps and candles! She would also offer a class or two.

We decided to put up a few signs and give it a try. To our amazement more than thirty people signed up within a couple of days and more wanted to be notified if we decided to teach another class.

The classes evolved over the next few weeks and soon we realized we had a close knit group of spiritual seekers. We would gather one evening a week to talk, share and explore various spiritual and healing practices, along with a generous side of nourishing love and laughter.

This was a very idyllic time for us, our business was growing, we loved the shop and interacting with the customers and we loved our group and our teaching. It was like a dream realized and we hoped within the next few years we could pay off our debts and begin to build a little security for our old age. A couple of old farts puttering around in their gift shop through their rocking chair years sounded just perfect to me.

Our former practice of meditating regularly though seemed a thing of the past. By the time we got home from work, cooked dinner, tended to household chores, our animals and the e-mail, it was time to go to bed. There was little time left for meditating and I must confess neither of us made a big effort to make time. Even when we did manage to do so, I was not motivated to take notes on any information he received. We

~ On the Tip Edge of a Miracle ~

were now on the same rat wheel most everyone else seemed to run on. I was thankful at least that we had our little group once a week!

2008

Dark Days
2008

I AM NOT TOO SURE HOW MUCH TRULY PERSONAL INFORMATION is appropriate to include in a journal about Dennison's meditations, but in the end I feel I must include it because it is so entangled in our spiritual journey. Our greatest lessons are often found in our darkest hours.

The onset of colder weather brought with it a return of my lung problems. At first I lived in denial, hoping each day that the next day I would see an improvement. By early January though I knew I really needed to see my doctor. Upon finding she had retired, I sought out another in a nearby town. This change threw new light on my condition.

After listening to my lungs the new doctor declared, "I really don't feel competent to handle your care; I'm just a country doctor; you need someone who knows about the lungs." He said he wanted me to see another lung specialist and get a current evaluation first. He had his nurse make a phone call and because of a cancellation she was able to set me up with an appointment for the following Thursday. The visit rocked our world.

It was late in the day when he finally called me in to the exam room. After a glance at my bundle of medical records I'd given him, he asked, "Why are you coming to see me?" I was a little taken aback by his question, but replied that my new doctor had sent me down to get a current evaluation. He sighed, while showing me the printouts of the lung function tests I'd just finished taking.

I looked at the printouts, not really understanding what the graphs meant, then sat quietly waiting for him to listen to my lungs and sum up his findings. He in turn just stood there and acted like he expected me to say or ask something. Finally, instead of listening to my lungs and performing an examination, he stood in front of me and rather harshly stated, "I still don't understand why you've come to me. I have nothing more to offer you. I can't tell you anything different than you've already been told."

Wondering what he was getting at I replied, "Okay...." Seeing my puzzlement he continued, "Maybe your doctor's haven't been up front with you; a lot of doctor's dance around the issue, but I'm not afraid to say it: YOU ARE DYING!"

I sat there dumb with shock; to be sure, there are no words to describe my feelings. He was so positive and so final I didn't even question his assessment. The thought flashed through my mind, *"Oh please, God, don't let it be true!"* Another part of me acknowledged the possibility because I knew I did have some serious problems.

I sat for what seemed an eternity, unable to breathe. Finally I was able to croak out a whispered, "How long do I have?" He softened his tone a little and said, "I don't mean to be crass, but I believe in calling a spade a spade; you don't have long. See where your tests are now? He showed me a graph with numbers going from one end to the other). Your last readings were here...it's only been 2 ½ years since the last test and now they are way down here; there's not much left past where you are now, so what do *you* think?"

I then asked, "Is there nothing that can be done?" This seemed to infuriate him and he shouted, "Who do you think I am...God?! What makes you think I can do something? You need to face facts and get your affairs in order!!"

I sat numbly, blinking back my tears. None of my doctors had ever indicated there was nothing more to be done or that I was dying! I felt intimidated, shocked and unsure. After all it had been a while since my last lung function tests. To be sure I had not had tests of any sort on my lungs since then; a lot could have changed, so I didn't try to correct his statement.

I pressed him again and asked, "What about a lung transplant?" He replied, "You're over 60; no one will do it for you at that age. The best you could do is move down to sea level, within 100 miles or so of the sea, so you can get the benefit of the salt air. With a little luck you could extend your time by a couple of years."

He sat on his stool and began to scribble a prescription for some different medication and asked why I wasn't using my oxygen. When I told him I was only using oxygen at night and that no one had ever prescribed it for me to use during the day, he jumped up from his stool, threw up both hands and shouted, "I don't believe this! No one has put you on oxygen?!!" With that he sat back down and furiously wrote again on his prescription pad, then he fairly threw the prescriptions at me and said, "You need to go down immediately and get started on some oxygen; if they are closed, there should be an emergency number on their door; call it and get them down there to set you up." He then excused himself saying he had another appointment to go to and left.

Dazed and in shock I turned and walked back to the waiting room and motioned to Dennison and headed for the door. As we walked to the car he asked, "What did the doctor say?" I could only shake my head "no" and continued to walk quickly ahead of him. As we got into the car, he continued to press, "What did he say?" but I just looked at him. I couldn't say anything. I couldn't get the words out.

As we drove away, he gently asked, "Would you like me to get you some coffee?" I shook my head in the affirmative and we drove in silence to Safeway where they had a Starbucks. I opted to stay in the car while he went inside to order.

We drove several miles in silence, with Dennison throwing me a puzzled glance now and then. I kept my head averted so he couldn't engage my eyes. I didn't know yet how to tell him what the doctor said. I knew if I told him now I would break down, and I wanted to be strong when I did tell him. Right now I just needed to sort out my thoughts and pull myself together.

Anger and outrage over how I had been treated began to creep in, as well as denial that what the doctor said could be correct. After all no one had, as he claimed, ever indicated in any way that I was dying. He barely had glanced at my medical records. Where were his supporting tests? Surely there were more tests available to back up his assessment. Wouldn't most physicians do more tests before saying such a thing? And too, I couldn't believe my other doctors would be less than honest with me if I was dying...or could they? I surely didn't feel like I was dying...but how would I know? I felt confused, angry, frightened and even abused; mostly though, I just felt numb.

Dennison finally interrupted my thoughts saying, "*Please,* Lovie, tell me what's going on." I took a deep breath and tears began to flow as I told him. He just stared at me stunned, then returned his attention to his driving. Finally he asked, "Why didn't someone call me in to be there with you? I'm your husband, don't I count for anything? They shouldn't give you news like that without me there; it's just wrong to do that." I had to agree, from the beginning the whole visit had been handled in a very unprofessional way.

After a few minutes he gently said, "Doctors don't know everything; they are just educated guessers. I don't sense you're going to die. I think I would know if you were." He had no idea what comfort those few words gave me.

When we got home, we smudged and prayed. We tried to meditate and seek answers, but both of us were too upset and scattered. That night he held me close while he slept, but there was no sleep for me as I lay beside him letting my tears silently fall. My mind replayed every moment of my doctor visit over and over, like a broken record. I reviewed my past years of illness and took them apart piece by piece, trying to make some sense of it all. Had I been kidding myself all along? I always believed I was going to get better. How could this be the end of the road for me? The shaking inside wouldn't stop, as if I were chilled. I felt so frightened for so many reasons, but mostly for what would happen to Dennison if I indeed did die.

We went to our shop on Friday, but our hearts weren't in it, and when we had no customers by noon, we closed up and went back home. Later in the afternoon I called my doctor's office and talked to his nurse to see if the lung doctor had faxed his diagnosis and instructions yet. She looked and said he hadn't, but sometimes it took a week or so before they did it. Then she asked how things went. I bluntly told her he said I was dying.

At 9:30 that evening my doctor called me at home and asked if it was too late to be calling. I told him we were just watching TV. He then asked to hear all about my visit to the specialist. When I finished, he said, "Don't sell the farm yet! We are going to get you a second opinion, and if need be a third, until we find one we like! I'm so sorry I sent you to that man! I don't know him; he was just the closest pulmonologist, the only others are in Phoenix or Tucson. Give me a chance to call and talk with him, maybe we're getting ahead of ourselves. Then let's get you back in here next week and see what we can do. Right now I want you to go to bed and get a good night's sleep and don't worry about anything for now. We're a LONG way from throwing in the towel."

Somehow I felt better after talking to him, even though nothing had really changed. At least he was kind enough to call and give me some encouragement. I felt I had someone on my side, willing to help me in any way he could.

The next morning we opened the shop as usual. It was snowing heavily and I doubted we would have any customers. I felt like a zombie going through the motions of a normal day. It was as if I had entered another reality: nothing seemed the same and yet it was. I went to work dusting the glass display shelves and buffing jewelry, anything to keep from thinking. Dennison cleaned up his work space and vacuumed the large rug we had in the center of the shop.

A man came in about 11:00 and looked around the shop, then remarked about the beautiful jewelry and at what a nice job we had done with fixing up everything. He went on to say, "The last time I was in here this was just a storage room full of junk." I replied that must have been a while ago because we'd been here about a year and a half; then I asked where he was from. He reached into his shirt pocket and pulled out a folded piece of letter-sized paper and handed it to me with a big grin, saying, "I'm from San Diego, and I just bought this place!" With some surprise I accepted his piece of paper, unfolded it and glanced at its contents. I was heartsick as I read and reread the brief paragraph. It was a letter saying we needed to vacate the premises within one month!

In total shock I turned and handed the paper to Dennison. The thought ran through my mind that we had surely come to an end of some sort, all our doors were slamming in our face. The man was rattling on about his plans to turn the building into a sports bar and restaurant, seemingly oblivious of the livelihoods he was destroying. A sports bar of all things! Just what a sleepy town of 300 needed.

He wandered out of the shop a short while later and began prowling around in the large storage room in the back of the building. I went next door to see how Carol and Sandy were taking the news. I found Sandy on the phone with the previous owner and she was furious. Carol had picked up her coat and purse and was headed toward the door. She turned to me and said, "F*** 'em!! I was sick of this place anyway." But the tears in her eyes belied the truth of her words.

I went back into the shop where Dennison was gathering up his tools. I got the cash out of the register and said, "Let's just get out of here. I need to go home and get my mind together; this is simply too much to handle all at once!"

As we drove home he said, "Maybe this is a sign it's time to move, get you off this mountain and down to where you can breathe again." I looked at him and shook my head no, "It sounds so easy, but where are we going to get the money?"

Our summer sales had been less than spectacular, the fall even worse. Winter was typically slow but this year sales were nonexistent. We had put back as much money as we could to carry us through the winter season, but it was dwindling away quickly. After the visit to the specialist we barely had enough left to pay the next month's bills and our income tax! What we didn't know was the "Great Recession" was just getting started.

"What are we going to do with all this stuff we have in the shop?" I wailed. "We won't have time to hold a going out of business sale, and who would come anyway…there's nobody left in town! We need to figure out what we're going to do with everything in the shop. Then we need to figure out where this is all going with my health."

I moved like a robot in the days that followed, just focusing on the immediate now, scrounging boxes and newspapers, sorting, labeling and packing up all of our inventory. We tried to rent a storage unit, but the only facility in town was full; and the next nearest storage facility was forty miles away, so Dennison loaded and hauled everything to our house and crammed it into the garage.

My illness made it difficult to bend or lift without going into coughing spasms, so I was fairly useless, except for wrapping and stuffing things into boxes to be moved. I was exhausted and at the end of my endurance. I know Dennison felt hopeless and without direction, but I had nothing to offer him. I was more lost even than he.

Over the next few days Dennison turned one of our spare bedrooms into a makeshift workshop and tried to rearrange the tangle of display cases and boxes in the garage. The weather was bitter cold and snowy and he finally gave up, saying he was going to leave everything as it was until spring when it would be easier to heat the garage.

In the meantime I kept my appointment with my doctor. I walked in hoping he would tell me it was all a mistake. Instead he told me he'd called the specialist who simply corroborated what I'd already explained, and promised to fax the test results up in the near future. He asked me to be patient for a little while and let him work on finding someone else to test me. He said he was trying to get a pulmonologist from Phoenix to come up monthly and hold a clinic for all of his lung patients.

While Dennison worked on jewelry, I worked opening an online store with Amazon. Then I went through our inventory, box by box, taking pictures of some of our things and uploading them into my new online store. It was a monumental task and my heart wasn't into doing it in the least! I was tired, sick and discouraged, but somehow we had to keep going. And it served to keep my mind occupied so I didn't dwell on myself.

Each night we prayed and asked for healing and guidance, and then meditated to listen for an answer. Dennison also took it upon himself to call various friends who lived along the west coast to see if any energies to move lay in that direction, however nothing opened up for us.

At this same time the cost of gasoline was climbing up and up, gold prices sky-rocketed dragging silver prices right along with it. Our costs of doing business were going out of sight while our orders barely trickled in. Road trips to sell jewelry now cost more than we were able to make in sales, and the same soon proved to be true with participating in craft shows.

Both of us strongly believed when it was time to do something different the way would present itself and the road would be open to do it, however this was becoming a real test of that belief. No other options seemed to open up for us, and we were financially unable to do anything but stay where we were, so we settled in to make the best of what life handed us.

The days melted away along with the snow. The inevitable springs winds followed and blew themselves out until finally summer's promise was on the horizon, bringing along with it new hope. The online store hadn't brought even an inquiry, and the website brought in just a trickle, so now the plan was to tackle the mess in the garage and try to turn it back into a workshop for Dennison, and a storefront of sorts for our goods.

While we were in the middle of creating our new store, I got a call from my doctor saying he had a lung specialist coming up from Phoenix; she would be setting up a one-day clinic in his office and wanted to set up an appointment for me to see her.

~ On the Tip Edge of a Miracle ~

It was with great fear and trepidation that I went to visit her for the first time. In the intervening months I had slipped into a sort of comfortable denial of my condition, and now I was being faced with it once again. Yet, I really needed to know if what I had been told was true, and if it was, I needed to face it.

The doctor was one of those rare people who radiates a dynamic energy when they enter a room and everyone turns to see who came in. She was about my age, short, plump, piercing blue eyes and smile that radiated warmth. I sat down and she smiled and said, "So, tell me what's going on." I briefly outlined my medical history, then I mentioned a little about my doctor visit and last diagnosis. I got the impression she had been told about it before I saw her. Her comment was, "Only a jackass would leave someone without any hope. I know him and he *is* an ego-driven jackass…but don't quote me on that," and then she giggled. She spent almost an hour with me, talking, questioning and most of all listening. In the end she ordered a battery of tests.

When I returned the following month, the tests showed I had severe unremitting asthma, COPD (though I've never smoked) and a chronic lung infection that would yield only to a specific type of antibiotic treatment. I also had a slightly enlarged heart.

She too highly recommended I move to a lower elevation. When I asked about moving to sea level, near the ocean, she laughed and said, "Yeah, if you can afford it; that would be just great! Otherwise you might want to look at Phoenix or Tucson. Just find some place 3000 ft or lower in altitude and you'll feel a lot better I think, and do a lot better too."

When I her asked about the diagnosis of dying soon, she shrugged. "Who knows, I sure don't! You seem basically healthy to me, except for your lungs. Believe me, I've seen people that I wondered how they were still standing. I expected them to drop dead on the spot and yet they just kept on keeping on. You have a long way before you get to that point. I believe life is what you make of it; it's not about dying, it's about living. "

I asked her what would happen to me if we stayed in the mountains and she said, "You can stay if you feel good up here and want to stay. But you will need oxygen up here. The winters will be harder and harder on you too. However, I understand, this is your home and if I had the choice to make, I'd be tempted to stay here myself. But you would probably feel better down lower. If you have the ability to move, you might want to consider it."

Following the treatment for the chronic lung infection and a tweaking of my medications, I began to improve dramatically. My energy returned and along with it my optimism. By fall the past several months seemed like a nightmare that I had finally awoken from.

Sales in our makeshift store weren't anything near what they had been in our shop in town, but considering that we were off the beaten path, we managed to do better than we'd ever anticipated. As summer came to a close, we slashed our prices to the point of just breaking even and sold as much of our store's inventory as we could. We decided to focus on jewelry alone, as we had in the past, and to close our makeshift store at the end of September.

One sunny afternoon a local business owner pulled into our driveway, pulling an almost new white enclosed utility trailer. We'd known him casually for several years and Dennison had made wedding bands for him and his wife. He proceeded to back the trailer into a spot on the side of the garage, and began to unhitch it. Puzzled, Dennison walked out of the shop and shouted, "Hey there Dave, what the heck's going on?" Dave smiled and said, "I'm just parking your trailer, would you rather I put it somewhere else?" Dennison's puzzlement increased, "My trailer? What do you *mean* 'my trailer'?" Dave's voice went a couple of octaves higher as he enjoyed Dennison's reaction. "I'm giving you this trailer; you can use it can't you?" Dennison agreed that he could surely use it, but protested, "I can't take that, it's a nice trailer, you could get quite a bit for it if you don't want it." Dave was really enjoying himself now and came over and clapped Dennison around his shoulders and said, "I can't think of anyone else I'd rather have it than you, that's why I'm giving it to you. I don't need it, you do, so there it is, it's yours. I'll get the title notarized and mail it to you." Bewildered, Dennison led him into the shop and in the end humbly accepted the generous gift.

A few days later we learned Dave had just found out he had pancreatic cancer and only had a short time to live. He'd been going all over town giving things like the trailer to selected people and "getting his affairs in order." Hearing this hit me deeply. I had very recently been in similar shoes and all I had done was feel sorry for myself and cower in terror. He was meeting his fate head on with a generous heart and arms wide open. Life is indeed what you make of it. A real lesson for all us mortals!

Summer gave way to the golden days of autumn with its crisp mornings, and its deliciously warm afternoons, caught between the promise of winter and the memory of summer. The trumpeting of a bull elk enticing a mate broke the silence as I sat on the front porch, gazing across the meadow at the lake and the mountains beyond. I so deeply loved this country; how could I ever leave it and this idyllic life we enjoyed? Silently I made up my mind to stay here and make the best of whatever life offered and live out my days, however long they lasted. But somewhere in the back of my mind, something whispered that we would go…we had to.

UFO
NOVEMBER 19, 2008

WE WERE FINALLY GETTING A FEW MUCH NEEDED ORDERS coming in for Christmas, so we got up early in the morning and headed for Gallup, NM, where we bought most of our jewelry supplies. We took a shortcut across the Zuni Reservation, as we normally did. There wasn't much traffic on this road and the scenery was beautiful.

After arriving in Gallup we purchased silver supplies then stopped for a late lunch/supper at a favorite cafe, and enjoyed our favorite meal of fry bread and green chili, before heading home. The days were noticeably shorter now and the sun was low in the sky and shining in our eyes when we left town. I lowered my eyes into a book I'd brought along and began to read as Dennison drove.

It was about 5:30 in the evening as we again drove thru the Zuni Reservation. I got tired of reading, so I closed the book, made a little small talk and lapsed into silence. By the time we turned heading south toward home, we were each lost in our own thoughts. To be sure, I was half asleep when a bright orange flash in the sky ahead of us caught my eye. It was dusk but not yet dark. I made note of the flash, then told myself it was probably an airplane with the sunset glinting off of it, or maybe even some sort of light or strobe at the power plant just ahead and lost interest as my mind wandered to other things.

~ 2008 • UFO ~

About forty-five minutes later as we had sped past a minimum security prison along the way, I saw the flash again and became mildly curious of what it could be. This time it looked more like it was southeast over the next town. It was quite a bit darker by now so I figured it was probably something at the airport there, like a search light or such.

Another fifteen minutes went by and we were just entering the town when I saw it again! This time it really had my full attention…what the heck was it? It was quite a ways ahead at the far end of town and low in the sky above the eastern horizon. There wasn't much of anything out in that direction, certainly nothing that could make that kind of a light. It was larger (or we were closer) than before, and the light was quite intense…bright and it seemed more amber…orange/amber. From where we were it seemed about the size of a headlight of an oncoming car, but it was such a brief moment that it shone, it was hard to get a sense what it really was. I couldn't imagine what would shine so intensely for just a moment and just shut off so definitely.

My curiosity aroused I began to search the sky, hoping to see it again and figure out what it could be. Quite suddenly it flashed again, this time it reappeared higher in the air, and in the very direction we were going to be traveling toward home.

During these sightings I hadn't said anything to Dennison, because until now it was just a flash, something to wonder about and relieve my boredom. But Dennison had noticed it too and he now spoke up and said, "What the heck is that orange light? I saw it way back there after we turned toward home, but figured it was a plane or the sunset glinting off a car windshield or something." I told him I didn't have a clue, but I didn't think it was an airplane. If it was, I'd never seen one do anything like that. He suggested it might be a weather balloon that was lighted inside or something. I wasn't so sure and longed to see it again and get a better look at it.

About ten minutes later, as we were winding through the hills going due east, it flashed again; this time it seemed much larger and closer, and it looked to be above the mountains ahead. I exclaimed to Dennison, "Did you see that? What the heck is it?" He murmured, "I don't know…"

We were entering a flat area just before the road began its ascent through the mountains when the light flashed again. This time it was way down in the tree line of the very mountains that we were about to climb toward home. I could see the silhouettes of the trees against the light as it flashed again, a large, intense amber light, suddenly there and then just as suddenly gone. It was nearing 8:00 PM by this time. I noted the time because we were expecting a phone call from a customer at our home around 8:30 PM and we were hurrying to get home in time. Neither of us felt fearful as we drove, just intensely curious, hoping for a better, longer look at whatever the light was.

We both began anxiously watching for the light as we climbed up the divide, speeding toward home. We had just passed a lodge near the outskirts of our town, when suddenly the light flashed on again! This time it was right in front of us, very low in the sky, below the tree tops, right in front and above our windshield flying over the top of us as it flashed. ON.....then OFF!

In that brief moment we could see what appeared to be a series of large bright amber lights, in sort of squared off V shape on the bottom of a craft. You could just make out the impression of a structure above the lights, and then it was gone.

Dennison stopped and got out of the car and looked up, but could see nothing darker in the night sky above us, such as a craft of any sort would make. For sure the sky was light enough from the ambient starlight that a solid object would appear as a dark shape in the sky. He stood for several minutes, looking all around, listening and hoping to get another glimpse of the mysterious light, but there was nothing out of the ordinary in fact, strikingly there was no sound at all, almost as if we were in a vacuum.

We slowly continued driving into town, looking all around as we went. Dennison pulled into the parking lot of the post office and turned the front of the car to face back toward where we had seen the lights. We sat and watched for several more minutes and finally drove on home to get our phone call.

After we were inside the house a few minutes, Dennison went back outside and watched the skies for quite a while. When he came in, he had me look out our kitchen window. He pointed out a long streak of orange glowing light just above the tree line in the distance toward where we'd last seen the light. It was a glow like a large light would make, but there was nothing at all in that direction that would make such a light.

He finally decided to drive back into town and see for sure where the light was coming from, hoping I suppose, to get a better look at it. I stayed at home waiting for our phone call which was overdue. As I waited, I stood and watched the glow out of our window for a few minutes, then decided to go put on my pajamas. When I returned a couple of minutes later, the light was gone.

In town Dennison once again parked at the post office looking for the orange glow, but it had disappeared. He watched for a few minutes, hoping it would show itself again, then he drove out to a dirt road that runs through the forest at the bottom of the ridge where he figured the light had been coming from and looked around for a while. Finally when he was convinced the light was gone, or at least wasn't going to show itself again, he returned home with no other sighting.

The following day we asked around if anyone had seen any strange lights in the sky, but no one had. We also watched the local newspaper for any reports, but found none. It was hunting season, so you would think a hunter would look up and see something, but we never heard of any other reports being mentioned.

That same night Dennison had a dream, likely because of, or maybe even prompted by the sighting of the amber light.

Strange Dreams
NOVEMBER 20, 2008

AS I WAS PREPARING COFFEE THIS MORNING Dennison asked, "What does the number 4 mean? Last night I was dreaming of four number 4's, you know like 4444."

I'm sort of a zombie in the mornings, until I get a cup or two of coffee into my system, so I stared at him blankly as I tried to pull a meaning or symbolism for the number 4 out of my sluggish brain. In the meantime he got tired of waiting for an answer and he continued,

"I had another dream right after that, or maybe it was part of the same dream…it was kind of like a UFO dream. I dreamed it was night and we were looking up at a bunch of lights in the sky. There were several other people there too and we were all watching these white lights moving around, and blinking off and on. People were saying things like, "Ooooh" and "Look, look, look at what they are doing now." It was kind of like watching fireworks.

"Then all of a sudden these lights all come together and formed the shape of a Star of David in the sky. And then the Star of David turned into a dragon, a white dragon. The dragon started moving its head from side to side just like a real dragon would. Then it opened its mouth and blew out a ball of fire. This fire ball just rolled over and over like a tumbleweed, traveling toward us like a meteor, going right over our heads heading eastward across the sky."

This didn't seem like an ordinary dream; who in the heck dreams of a Star of David and four 4's! So I decided to look up the symbolism of number 4 on the internet as well as the main symbols of his other dream:

I first found the number 4 symbolized the EARTH: 4 directions, 4 elements, 4 seasons, 4 parts of the day, 4 weeks in month, in other words the *physical, material world.*

I then discovered the Alchemical meaning of 4 is *time.*

When I discovered a webpage on the Jewish alphabet and its numerical equivalent, I found the number 4 corresponded with the letter "D" Daleth, meaning: Door; the cosmic womb; Creation; Manifest from the VOID (which pretty much confirms the earlier definition of the physical or material world; our physical world is created or manifested out of the VOID or the place where all potential lies).

I got out my book on Numerology and found what it had to say about the number 4. In order to fully understand it though, I went back to the number 1 which said in the beginning there was the Monad, symbolizing the ONE, THE FATHER, THE SOURCE, THE VOID FROM WHICH ALL THINGS ARE MADE MANIFEST.

The ONE decided to reach out and take form, and in order to do so it had to cast its own reflection. By so doing the ONE created the negative and positive—unity separating itself thus dividing Spirit and Matter. This became the Duad, or TWO, duality.

In order to manifest, the ONE and the TWO joined together. The union produced the Triad or triangle, which was the first figure symbol. And since it is first, it is perfect, so it represents God. The triangle is the first structure to give support to any physical thing. It is the supreme expression of love: two who seek each other not only to become three (man, woman, child), but also to become one. The Triad then represents the Trinity, the Father, Son and Holy Spirit. Mind, Body and Spirit.

The Tetrad is the square, the number 4, and is considered sacred because it represents the beginning of form. The Sacred Trinity spoke the WORD which set up a vibration that manifested form. The first act of the Triad was to Create. So the number 4 represents Creation. The tetrad is considered the root of all things.

In numerology number 4 is *foundation*.
Add $4 + 4 + 4 + 4 = 16$; $1+6 = 7$
Multiply $4 \times 4 \times 4 \times 4 = 256$ $2 + 5 +6 = 13$; $1 + 3 = 4$

I found quite a bit on dragons: in general in the East, the dragon is a lucky or good symbol. In Europe and in Christianity it is more symbolic of evil or negative things. The dragon also symbolized the Great Mother, Earth, Guardian, Chaos, Fire, Negative, Evil.

Surprisingly, perhaps because of its breath of fire, the dragon also represents the WORD which was in the beginning, and which created and now sustains all things (John 1:1-4).

Dragons and Serpents also represent the sun as well as the universe. Because this dragon in the dream belched out a ball of fire and sent it hurtling toward the earth, I would think it might represent the sun in this particular instance.

The Star of David: Hebrew word meaning "Divine," also known as the Shield of David, a magical symbol of protection used to ward off evil. King Solomon is said to have worn a signet ring with the symbol on it, thus it is known as the Seal of Solomon. It has long been associated with the House of David (ancestor of the Messiah) and was widely regarded as a Messianic symbol of the coming of the Messiah.

The two triangles symbolize the reconciliation of opposites: unity, the interpenetration of two realms, heaven and earth. (Recall in earlier writings Dennison spoke of two worlds, or dimensions, or energies, physical and material coming together; perhaps that is what the two triangles would symbolize.)

~ On the Tip Edge of a Miracle ~

After spending some time thinking about all the information, I feel this is a message about a coming event, a meteor or solar flare, but it is more than that. It is the coming together of Spirit and Matter, the coming of the Messiah, or Christ consciousness, whatever that may entail.

Another Strange Dream
DECEMBER 3, 2008

I WAS COOKING DINNER when Dennison said, "By the way I meant to tell you that last night I dreamed of the number 7, actually I dreamed of 7 sevens. What does the number 7 represent?"

I paused, surprised that he had dreamed of numbers again. Jokingly I said, "Maybe you're getting lottery numbers or something. Remember that dream you had about the number 4?"

He replied, "No, I don't think so." He went on to say, "I sensed it has something to do with the sun and fire and war and the President."

I asked, "Did you get anything else? It somehow must have to do with the number four...." He shrugged and told me he couldn't remember if he did or not, he just remembered the seven 7s.

Numbers again! I knew deep inside the first number dream of four 4's and this dream were somehow significant. I contemplated what it could mean and tried the numerology thing of adding up the 7s to see if I could find some correlation to the 4444s. I added $7+7+7+7+7+7+7 = 49$; $4 + 9 = 13$; $1 + 3 = 4$. Four! That got my attention because I recalled the 4 fours added up to 7 in his last dream! Now what in the heck could that mean?

I decided to try multiplying the 7s and came up with 5764801, which when added together equals 31. And $3 + 1 = 4$: hmmmmm…?

I went to my computer and began looking up information on the symbolism of the number 7. Try putting "meanings of the number 7" into the search engine of a computer and you will be astounded and overwhelmed with its meanings and significance, for example:

The patterns of the number 7 run through the Bible more abundantly than any other number. In fact so abundantly that it could be called God's seal or stamp of approval. It's biblical meaning is Perfection or Completion. The number 7 has always been regarded in the Jewish traditions as the number of completion.

Alchemical meaning is: Transmutation, man becomes conscious.

In Numerology the number 7 (Zayin) is the 7th letter in the Jewish alphabet and is equivalent to the letter Z

I looked up the word Zayin to try to get a clearer definition and found it also symbolizes "straight light from God to man or Returning light." And "the Crowned Man equipped with the Sword of the Holy Spirit." The Sword of Time.

Kabalistic and Coptic meanings: Ascension of the Soul, and the return of God

Days later I was again thinking about the dreams and playing with the dates, adding up the numbers as in numerology to see if I could find some more symbolism…. I noticed the first dream happened on 11-19-2008 when he dreamed of four 4s ($11+19=30$; $2+0+0+8 = 10 = 1$; $30 + 1 = 31$; $3 + 1 = 4$). He dreamed of the number 4 on a date that added up to 4…it was probably a coincidence and I was simply looking for meaning where there was none….

Then I added up Dec. 3, 2008, the night of the second dream.

$12 + 3 = 15$; $1 + 5 = 6$; $2008 = 10$; $1+0 = 1$; $6 + 1 = 7$. His second dream of the number 7 came on a date that adds up to 7. Coincidence??

I was beginning to feel like someone was playing with our minds and trying to get us to see something more than the obvious, but all I could come up with is the obvious:

If the number 4 means the Cosmic Door, Creation, the beginning of our physical world, and number 7 means Completion, transmutation, man becomes conscious, we have the beginning of the physical world and the end when man becomes conscious: the beginning and the completion.

Year-End Meditation
DECEMBER 31, 2008

WE WERE BOTH GLAD TO SEE THIS YEAR COME TO AN END. We had faced some very difficult challenges, our Christmas sales had been low, our pocket book was flat, and our bills were as usual piling up. It seemed the same every year as we stopped to assess what we'd accomplished in the year gone by. If anything, we were sliding back a few steps; we certainly weren't getting anywhere. But as we sat reflecting on past events and future hopes, we both agreed we were truly grateful for each and everything we **did** have. We lived the life we wanted, regardless of how difficult it was at times; we had a snug home with a modest rent, we had loving friends and family who loved and supported us through our greatest challenges. And we also had each other! Maybe the goals weren't so important; just maybe it was really all about loving and cherishing each moment to its fullest.

We lit a smudge and prayed, thanking Creator for all our blessings. We asked special blessings for our family and friends, and for our Nation. The recession was making itself felt and local businesses that depended on tourism were barely hanging on, so we prayed for them and the recovery of our economy. Finally we prayed for ourselves and for guidance in a new direction.

With that we settled back to meditate and seek guidance, and hopefully glimpse what the new year held in store. When Dennison began snoring, I opened my eyes and gently shook him awake. I asked if he'd gotten anything before he'd fallen asleep, he laughed and said, "Nooo, I went right to sleep." It was well after midnight and the New Year was under way, so we blew out the candle and went to bed.

2009

Dream of Martin Luther King
JANUARY 22, 2009

OUR MEDITATION PRACTICE had long ago gone by the wayside. Even though now we weren't so busy, and surely we needed the peace meditating would bring, we humans are funny creatures and we don't always do what we know will help us. Dennison did have another odd dream though.

As I was waking up this morning, Dennison remarked that he dreamed of Martin Luther King last night. Sleepily I said, "That's neat, it's probably because there was a lot said about him during the inaugur-...." Dennison interrupted me at this point saying, "I was listening to him speak, at least I think it was him, it sounded like him. I was in this crowd and there was like a loud speaker and I could just hear him giving a speech. He was saying something about a lion.... He was saying,

"The Lion, The Lion of Judah has come! The Lion spoken of in your prophecies is here. He's here to slay the dragons of the world. No more prejudice, no more slavery, so more starvation, no more suffering; the waters of the world will be made pure again...."

"I wonder what the lion symbolizes. What is a Lion of Judah anyway?"

Dennison was not raised in a Christian faith and knows very little about Christian teachings other than what he learned from a few Hollywood movies. However I vaguely remembered from my early church going years that the Lion of Judah symbolizes Christ when he returns. He first came as the Lamb of God to be sacrificed for our sins, and he will return as The Lion of God to make things right.

The words Dennison quoted from his dream sounded so much like something MLK might say, that after we got the morning started I went to the computer and looked up as many of his speeches as I could find. None had anything like that in them. I did find lots about the Lion of Judah. I also looked up the symbolism of water and found it was symbolic of Spirit, healing, cleansing, life, eternal life, symbol of salvation, God's word, and of course as cleansing one of sin.

It is interesting that Dennison, who was never a Christian and who was never really indoctrinated with Christian teachings, would receive such a Christian-oriented message.

The first weeks after Christmas are typically slow for us, but as weeks went by we began to realize the orders weren't picking up as they normally did. We were really beginning to feel the pinch of the slowing economy. I finally had to make a phone call to our landlord to say we couldn't pay our rent and asked if they would be willing to trade for jewelry or art. Thankfully they did so, and continued to do so for the next three months.

New Beginnings

IN EARLY APRIL WE GOT AN ORDER for a set of wedding rings. The woman placing the order lived in Phoenix, and when the rings were finished, she said she would drive up to get them. We offered to meet her with the rings in a town roughly half-way between our house and Phoenix, and she readily agreed. To make it easier we named a popular Mexican food restaurant as the meeting place, and offered to buy her lunch.

We chatted over lunch and after a time the conversation hit a lull that began to stretch into uncomfortable silence. Reaching for anything to say I asked, "Are you moving to New Mexico to live with your husband or is he moving to Phoenix?" She became very animated and in an anguished voice she said, "Oh, I don't know what I'm going to do! He has a nice home and is under a contract where he works so he can't move. Besides he loves it there and hates Phoenix. But I have a large, beautiful home on 1 ½ acres that I've put my heart and soul into and I can't even think of selling it, especially right now with the real estate market getting so shaky. There are also other complications with selling it, so that's out of the question. I have so much stuff and so does he. I don't know what I'd do with my stuff if I sold it. But I don't dare leave it empty and I can't rent it with all my stuff still in it. If I could just find someone trustworthy to live in it for a few months until I can decide what to do, I would let them stay there for free."

~ 2009 • New Beginnings ~

I sat there not believing my ears; was this was the very "sign" we'd been waiting for? With my heart pounding loudly I briefly told her of my illness and dilemma of living in the mountains while needing to move to a lower elevation, but being unable to afford to. I asked if she would consider letting us care-take her house for, say, six months, if we could give her references. She was thrilled with the idea and offered for us to come down the following weekend and spend the night, so we could see if we would really want to give it a try. Poor Dennison just sat there listening.

We surely didn't have the money to make such a move and in our hearts neither of us wanted to do it, but here was the opportunity we had been praying for; we could not ignore it. If it was right, it would work and we had nothing to lose if it didn't. The only real thing was our years of accumulation, which, besides our household, included Dennison's workshop with all his machines, tools, benches, and so on, along with the display cases from the store, and the left-over inventory.

She obviously wanted to leave most of her household goods in her house, and it would cost a mint to store all of our stuff for six months. I was sure our landlord wouldn't allow us to leave our things in the house and not continue paying rent, which we couldn't pay now as it was. But if this was the guidance we had sought, then somehow all would work out!

The following weekend we stayed with her and discussed how we could make it work. She really needed someone to be in her house so she was willing to compromise and agreed to move as much of her belongings into her three-car garage as she could manage, then move the rest to her new home, leaving most of the house itself empty. Her only request was that Dennison do the much needed yard work around the acreage, take care of all the shrubs and trees, and keep it all watered. Between her work and commuting to be with her fiancée, the grounds had become overgrown and were in need of a lot of work. He naively agreed, not knowing what an incredible task it would be and the hot summer months were almost here. Before we left, we drew up a contract and agreed to take her up on her offer. Now we just had to figure how to make the rest of it work.

The task of packing was monumental, but we managed to sell, throw away, donate, give away and pack over the next weeks and by the end of

~ On the Tip Edge of a Miracle ~

June we were ready to make the life-changing move. As the time grew near, Dennison's family all got together and paid for a large U-Haul truck and the gas to make the move. We even managed to sell all of our fixtures from the store, as well as the rest of our inventory (for way below wholesale price).

Two days before the big move the post office called to say we had an insured express mail envelope waiting for us. We weren't expecting anything, so with some curiosity Dennison drove down to retrieve the envelope. It was from an acquaintance I had been pen pals with, but never met. The envelope amazingly contained $800.00 in cash "to help with expenses" and a note that said, "Many blessings to you in your new adventure. If, in the future, the opportunity arises, and you feel so moved, pay it forward." We were overwhelmed and humbled with her generous gift. It would be well used and couldn't have come at a better time. Armed with a little bit of cash for deposits and getting started again, we set off to begin a new chapter in our lives, burning all bridges behind us.

The move itself was exhausting, even with plenty of help from family and friends, but finally we were settled in for our first night at the house. As we lay awake in bed, too tired and stressed to sleep, the realization of what we'd done began to soak in. I turned to Dennison and cried, "Oh my God, what have we done?"

In the days to follow we began to feel the full impact of this new city life. The first thing we noticed was the energies here felt like a physical assault. Poor Dennison had never lived in a city; in fact he had never lived out of the mountains of Arizona, or far from his family. And even though we were at the far edge of the city, bordering on the desert itself, the noise, the smells, the constant movement, and the indifference of the people, took its toll on our psyche.

A little more than three weeks had gone by and we were pretty much unpacked and settled in. We now needed to locate silver and stone suppliers, so one hot July morning we set out to visit a jewelers' supply shop that was located several miles from the house. After stopping at Starbucks, a real novelty for us, we continued happily on our way. Upon approaching a blinking yellow traffic light Dennison slowed our van, looked both ways, then proceeded into the intersection. Suddenly, out of the corner of my eye I saw a full sized SUV bearing down on us, heading straight for the front driver's side of our vehicle. The rest was like a slow motion movie as Dennison braked and swerved to avoid it, then came the sound of the impact, the air bags deploying and the air filling with a white choking dust. "SHEE-IT!!!" I turned to Dennison and asked if he was okay. He assured me he was and asked if I was. "Yes, I think I am," I replied as I tried to open my door. When it wouldn't budge, I tried my window, but our engine had stopped and it wouldn't roll down. I turned to Dennison again and urgently exclaimed, "I've got to get some air; this dust is shutting down my breathing!" Just then someone outside managed to wrench my door open and the hot outside air came in like a relief and I could breathe again.

Miraculously we both managed to sustain only bangs and bruises. The SUV claimed they had stopped before proceeding through their red light, but the speed was great enough that they totaled our midsized van. Because the traffic light was malfunctioning, the police wrote it up as a no-fault accident. A fire truck drove us home, dazed and shaken, but thankfully alive.

Fortunately we had a second vehicle, a 20-year old full-sized van with over 250,000 miles on it. The best thing one could say about it was that it was paid for.

Suddenly the reality of our aloneness descended upon us. Back home we always had family and friends who were there to be counted upon when needed. Here we had no one to call on, even to take us home from the accident. As Dennison observed, we could die in the house and no one would even miss us until one of our kids tried to call, and even then it might be days or perhaps weeks before they became concerned when we didn't answer.

Homesickness set in with a mighty force and we began to feel like strangers in a strange land. The accident cast a negative pall over our lives and we both fell into a sort of depression, longing for a way to return to our beloved mountains. The way the house was situated on the very edge of the desert, away from neighbors, only magnified the feeling. Added to that, the remorseless desert heat made it impossible to go outside for more than a few minutes. We, who were so connected to Nature and the outdoors, were stuck inside the house like cave dwellers, with shades drawn to help keep out the heat and save electricity costs.

Not surprisingly Dennison began complaining of being very tired and found it quite difficult to get motivated to go work. A $380.00 dollar electric bill served as a strong incentive though, as did the need to keep his promise and care for the yard. Each morning he would get up early, as soon as there was light in the sky, and he would go out and work in the yard until it got too hot to keep going. He repaired water lines, trimmed trees, dug out dead bushes, cacti, and grasses, and he hauled old boards, brambles of wire and accumulated old trash to the dump. He killed snakes and scorpions and set traps for pack rats, trying to wrestle the neglected acre-and-a-half yard back into an acceptable condition. He would come in about 10:00 AM, take a shower, and start making jewelry. At night he would fall asleep as soon as he sat down on the sofa, and I would have to wake him to go to bed.

Financially things didn't improve like we had expected. We were now in the big city, with the Scottsdale galleries and shops virtually at our doorstep, but soon we began to realize how really bad the economy had become as we heard shop owners' stories and saw more and more places close their doors. It was disheartening to be turned away again and again as we sought an outlet for our jewelry. At the same time our internet sales had all but stopped. To make matters worse the cost of gold and silver continued to climb. If it weren't for the fact we didn't have to pay rent, we would have been in very serious financial trouble. As it was, we barely skimped by.

One day in early September we walked into a small bead shop near our house, looking for clasps. As I made my small purchase, Dennison struck up a conversation with the owner and by the time we walked out he had arranged to offer silversmith classes during the fall and winter. It would thankfully prove to be the thing that got us through the winter months.

As September drew to a close, Dennison began to complain that his joints and neck felt painful and stiff. I at first attributed his complaints to the yard work and even to his feeling blue and homesick. When he began to cough and get chest congestion, we thought it was a cold or even H1N1 flu. Dennison had seldom been even slightly ill in the twenty years that we'd been together, and he was extremely reluctant to seek out a doctor. Then very early one morning I woke up and, even on my side of the bed, I could feel the heat of his fever radiating off of him like a stove. I woke him up and took his temperature. It was over 103 degrees! I had him take a cool shower, and while he did so, I got online and found an urgent care center only a few miles away. We were waiting at their door when they opened.

They swabbed his mouth to test for H1N1, did several diagnostic tests and a battery of blood work, as I mentally watched the $$$ signs rapidly adding up like the gauge on a gas pump. The doctor asked him when he had suffered the heart attack, and all thoughts of money suddenly evaporated. Seeing our obvious shock, she then asked if he'd been suffering any pains in his chest or jaw recently that he could recall. He told her he couldn't recall anything, but he had been under a lot of stress lately. She explained there was something called a silent heart attack, and he might be one who didn't feel anything while having one. She told him to find a cardiologist and get some more testing done immediately. She also diagnosed bacterial pneumonia and sent him home with a prescription and told him to find a doctor and see if he could get in within the next few days and, if not, to return there for a follow-up.

A few days later the doctor called us at home and told him some of his blood work had come back and informed him he had Valley Fever, a local name for Coccidioidomycosis. This is a illness caused from inhaling microscopic spores of a fungus that resides in the desert soil, especially in areas that haven't been disturbed in a long time (like the back yard of the house where he'd been working so hard). The inhaled spores take advantage of the dark warm environment of the lungs and multiply. In some cases, such as his, they become systemic and can even prove to be fatal. The treatment for it is extended bed rest and sometimes a fungicide which is very toxic to the liver and is not given except to the worst cases. He had to take the fungicide.

Within six weeks he had lost over sixty pounds. His appearance was heart-wrenching for me and I was sick with worry. A heart attack and this! No wonder he had been so tired all the time. I had leaned on him so much these past several years, it rocked me to my very core to have him so very weak and debilitated. It was staggering to think I might lose him and that I nearly had! How precious and fragile life was and how very dear he was to me. I prayed with all my heart and soul he would soon begin recovering.

Jewelry orders were few and far between, and with Dennison feeling so badly, fulfilling even those few seemed like monumental accomplishments. Somehow though, he kept us going by teaching a silversmith class now and then, making jewelry, and resting in between.

Suddenly December was upon us and it was time to start looking for another place to live, but our lack of resources and Dennison's extreme weakness now made it an all but impossible task. We asked for another month in the house, with rent if need be, because neither of us were in any condition to pack and move; she said she could give us a little extra time but she had her own plans in the works and we needed to be out before the 15th of January.

The weather was cold and wet, with record-breaking rains and flooding all over Phoenix. I worried about Dennison as we set out in the rain and cold to look for a place to live. We heard through friends and on the news about the record snows happening in the northern part of the state. The house where we used to live was now buried under seven feet of snow and the whole town had been without power for nearly a week. Our rain seemed minor by comparison; we'd be in some serious trouble had we still lived up there!!

We looked at house after house, and apartment after apartment; the places we felt we might barely afford were in scary parts of town, small, old, dirty and in disrepair. It was disheartening to think we had come to this, after taking the leap of faith we felt we had been offered by Creator.

Christmas slipped by almost unnoticed as we divided our time between working on jewelry, looking for a place to live and packing. As the year ended, it seemed our many prayers were going unanswered. It was very difficult to continue believing we were being guided. But even as we thought such thoughts, we were beginning to see in retrospect an unseen "hand" guiding events: the free rent for six months, the gift of money when we needed it most for our transition to our new home, even the loss of our vehicle. We weren't seriously hurt, and in the end it was paid off. If we still had to make payments, we would have lost it by now. The money simply wasn't there. And we were able to move to the warmer climate of Phoenix just before the worst winter in Arizona's history. Winters back home were hard to get through in the best of times, and as my lung condition worsened, I became more and more unable to tolerate the cold; I'm honestly not sure I could have survived the winter up there. Then there was Dennison's heart—what if he'd had a heart attack while dealing with all the snow! We had to believe somehow something would now show itself when the time was right.

We prayed on the eve of the New Year and thanked Creator for all of our many, many blessings. We prayed for those less fortunate than we, who had lost their homes to foreclosure and now had no place to live. And we prayed for guidance in the new year upon us, that we not be among them.

2010

A New Home
2010

OUR SEARCH FOR A HOME ended after my son stepped in and helped us with deposits and part of the rent until we could get back on our feet, allowing us to rent a modest home in a quiet neighborhood on the edge of the city.

Miraculously, help to finish packing and moving came with a phone call from a friend in Canada who called to ask for Dennison's help. Her son was having a personal life crisis and she felt Dennison could help him get his thinking straight. She asked if she could send him down to stay with us for a couple of weeks while Dennison worked with him. I explained any other time would be no problem, but we were in the middle of moving and Dennison couldn't devote much time to him until we were moved and settled. She laughed and said, "Right now he's working for a moving company, helping people pack and move! Maybe Dennison could help him and he can help you." In the end her son called and offered his services to help us with the move while Dennison worked with him. It was the godsend we needed! He was young, strong and more than willing to do anything that was asked of him. We honestly couldn't have done it without him!! I'd say we came out on the winning end of that deal!

Dennison continued to grow stronger with each passing month and by summer his lungs were clear of Valley Fever. With sporadic silversmith classes and a few jewelry orders trickling in we managed to barely keep going financially. Now that the dollar had lost so much value, people from Europe were beginning to place a few orders for jewelry, which was a true blessing indeed.

Our new house proved to be a true haven for us as we quickly settled in and made it a home. Perhaps part of our problem with the last house had been the knowledge we were only going to be there a short time. It was more like we were visiting someone else's house rather than creating a home for ourselves.

Moving also brought us to an area with neighbors, which we had missed while care-taking the house. One of our neighbors was a mechanic and he generously helped us keep our old van going, rescuing us from what would have otherwise been financial disasters if we'd had to rely on a garage for repairs. Several of our neighbors were struggling like we were, with job loss or having adult children return home without jobs. The hard times of the recession created a bond of sorts that might not have otherwise been there. It felt good to again be in an area where we could build connections.

Mayan Connection
AUGUST 2010

OVER THE SPRING AND SUMMER there had been several programs on TV regarding the Mayan prophecies of 2012 and a coming doomsday. We watched a few, but soon they all seemed to be saying pretty much the same thing. After one such program I remarked to Dennison that some of what was now being presented he had seen in his visions way back in 1988.

I reminded him of his first vision where he saw a crystal city; and how toward the end of it he had seen what at first he thought might be a circle of structures like houses as seen from high above; however, "something" told him it was a calendar, an ancient calendar. Quoting from our book,

"I'm seeing symbols, like numbers or something. They are coming at me and going into my forehead. I think it's like a history maybe.... Time passing. Lots of time.... I'm asking what the symbols mean, but 'they're' telling me it's not important right now, just experience it, let it happen.... They're so strange—like little triangles and lines and circles.... Nothing I've ever seen before."

"I see a dark brown planet with these rectangular shapes.... Maybe it is a circle of houses in some sort of pattern. Oh. Something tells me it's a calendar of some sort, an ancient calendar...."

I got out a copy of our book and flipped it to page 13 where there was a copy of a drawing he'd made of the calendar in his vision. It was a very rough sketch, an impression really, of what he saw, but it was

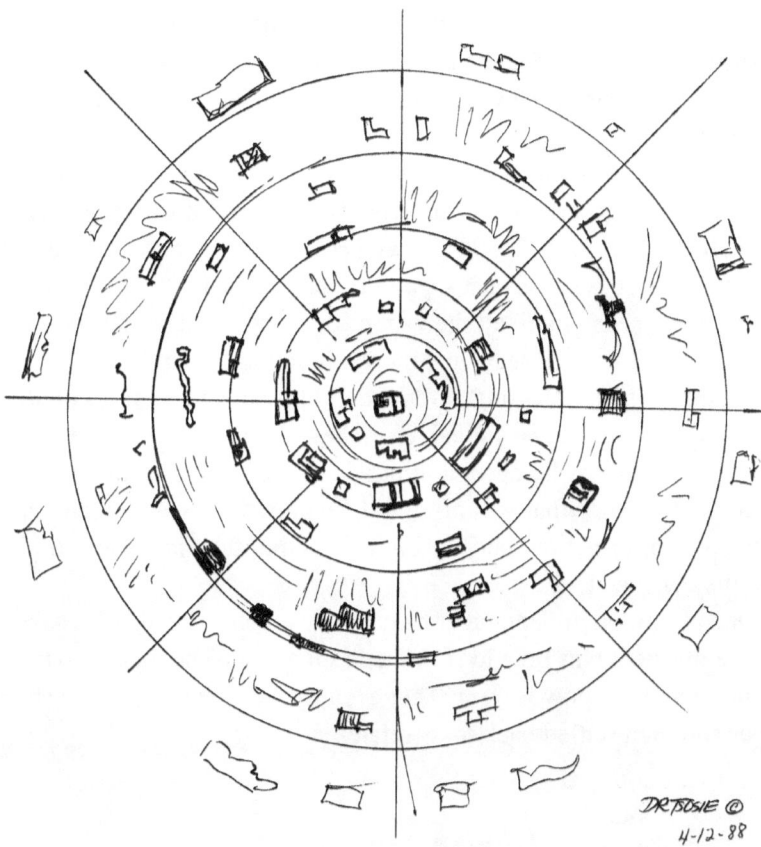

similar enough to make me wonder if this was the Mayan calendar that he was being shown long before it was such common knowledge. At the time neither of us associated it with the Mayan calendar; to be sure it was only as we were now discussing the program that it hit me what it possibly was.

I wondered if indeed December 21st of 2012 would be the end of the world as we know it. I believed something could happen then, but I was unclear what exactly: horrible disasters or instant transformation, maybe both and possibly neither. Maybe we'd wake up on December 22nd and just go forward into another year. There was so much confusing information and so many beliefs that it was hard to sort it all out.

Dennison has seen many visions of horrible disasters and he's been told mankind was going to be transformed, but when and how? He had been told it would be like the fingers of two hands coming together... negative and positive energy meeting and blending together as one... and the more positive we were, the easier it would be. But what really did that mean?

As we discussed it, I mentioned that I wished he would go back to meditating regularly again, because I felt we needed the guidance, especially if December 21, 2012 was THE DAY. He confessed he was reluctant to do so because he had gotten overwhelmed by all the negative things he had seen—with all the visions of death and devastation—and he really didn't want to see it any more. He felt knowing the future was more a curse than a blessing. I reminded him we had been told not to fear and that we would be guided when these times came, but how could we be guided unless he opened himself up through meditation and received the guidance that was offered. I suggested too that he could ask for happier information, but he laughed, saying they just showed him what they wanted to.

One afternoon in September he casually remarked that he was feeling like maybe it was time to start meditating again and agreed to try it that night and see how it went. That evening we smudged, said a short prayer and then settled back to meditate.

Hidden Knowledge
SEPTEMBER 16, 2010

"I SAW A PYRAMID and suddenly the next thing I knew I was inside. There were stairs going down into the earth, so I followed them down until I came upon some buildings, like a city inside the earth. A lot of the buildings were pyramid-shaped while others were different shapes.

"The whole place was lit up, but I couldn't tell where it was coming from. I saw rows and rows of flags hanging, sort of like prayer flags. Three beings came walking toward me through the flags wearing robes or shawls and a sort of head band. One headband had a circle in the center, one a square and one a triangle. They had their hands folded like in prayer, at chest level. Between their palms they each were holding crystals. They walked right through me and just disappeared.

"I saw an arched doorway with designs painted around the edges. As I got a closer look, I realized the designs were hands with the fingers entwined in different ways like our Buddhist friend used to do when he was doing ceremonies (mudras). I continued walking through the doorway and it was like I had entered an old church or monastery, or maybe a temple, some place where sacred things are stored. There was a long hallway that had shelves lining the walls. The shelves were filled with books, like some sort of library-something. The weird thing I couldn't understand was, these books weren't like books that we know. They were more like sheets, stacks of sheets of papers that had wood or leather covers on the front and back and were tied together with string or cloth or leather strips wrapped around them to hold these stacks of papers.

"I felt there was lots of knowledge and information that no one knows. This place actually exists today and the knowledge contained there will change the world; it is very important information. I think it will soon be discovered or revealed to the world.

"The next I saw was this huge, I mean *huge,* tree with branches that were thick and gnarled. Its roots went deep into the earth. The trunk was massive, so massive nothing could hurt it. The canopy overhead filled the sky. They said it was the tree of life. It represented mankind and it represented us as individuals. We need to see ourselves like the tree."

Out of Balance
SEPTEMBER 16, 2010

WE TRIED MEDITATING ALMOST EVERY EVENING in the days that followed, but if he received anything at all, it seemed less coherent and more like a nonsense dream. I often fell completely asleep or simply ran my current worries around and around in my mind. We were sorely out of practice with our meditating! Finally this evening he received something that seemed to make a little more sense.

"I saw an old-fashioned balance scale…you know what I mean…the kind that you added weights to on one side when you weighed something on the other. Anyway I saw this scale and a white dove sitting on the top of the scale. What was strange was it had something in its beak. When

I looked real close, I could see that it looked like a rolled up bill, like money rolled up. There was a big pile of money on one side of the scale, but no weights on the other side. I also noticed stacks and stacks of small boxes about the size of bricks stacked all around. Somehow I had the impression I was in a printing office, which doesn't make sense."

"I also saw grapes. Does a grape vine mean anything? I saw a vineyard with rows and rows of grapes growing. The grapes were winding along these wires, and all were loaded with grapes like it's harvest time."

We discussed the possible symbolism afterward. I worked in a bank at one time many years ago and his description of the stacks of small boxes the size of bricks reminded me of how new bills came in "bricks" when delivered to banks. I asked if the boxes he saw could have been bricks of money and he said he guessed it was possible, but he never knew it came in bricks. We also speculated the printing office could represent the U.S. Treasury and perhaps the scale meant out of balance.

The only thing I could find on the symbolism of grapes was abundance and prosperity, or maybe harvest time.

Another Crop Circle
OCTOBER 1, 2010

As Dennison came out of his meditation, he excitedly exclaimed, "I saw a crop circle being made! It seemed to be after a storm. It was either twilight or early morning and in the distance was a bank of dark clouds tinged with pink. Overhead were scattered clouds and everything seemed fresh and clean like it had just rained. Then I saw a beam of light come down and I could hear a slight electrical type of hummmm. The beam of light began tracing a huge circle in the field of wheat and I could see the wheat as it lay down, this way and that, like it was being woven.

"When the circle was complete, spokes began to appear, like a wagon wheel. Then in the center the light made what to me looked like the bottom of a round Indian basket; you know, like a basket lying face down in the center of the wheel.

"As I watched I saw a design appear on the basket. It really stood out to me like it was almost three-dimensional, making sure it drew my attention. You know that Navajo rug design that looks like a stylized tall corn stalk, with different colored birds sitting on each branch—that's how it looked, except without the birds (Navajo Tree of Life design).

"Then the crop circle seemed to lift up and revealed another mirror image of itself beneath. Then the mirror image also lifted up, and for a little while they sort of looked like two plates coming together. The two mirror images then began to slowly twirl around like a 3-D image of something on the computer will do, and as it went around, the spokes of the "wagon wheel" in each circle began to morph into fingers. Then slowly the whole circle morphed into two hands with the finger tips almost touching.

"As I watched, the finger tips of the two hands touched and then slowly began to interlace until finally the hands came together as though clasped. The hands turned toward me so I was looking at the thumb side, and where the thumbs met there was an opening and I could see a light glowing inside the hands.

"As I looked closer, I could see the hands were holding a clear ball inside and I had the sense the ball was made of water...like a water bubble with a light inside. As I looked even closer, I could see the light was coming from a cluster of crystals inside the bubble. It made me think of those glass balls with liquid in them and have a snow scene when you shake them (snow globe). As I was able to see even closer, I saw the crystals were a beautiful crystal city, like I saw in my very first vision a long time ago. The light I was seeing was coming from this city.

"As I was looking, the light became more like a laser beam which dissolved into a rainbow of light that filled the clear ball. Suddenly I realized the ball was the earth as seen from space. Brilliant blues, greens, browns and white. Pure and pristine. I felt it was cleansed and new again. I was so filled with joy I felt I wanted to cry; because I was so full, it overflowed.

"I really think I was being shown what is happening: two opposite energies are coming together and it's beginning to happen right now. The fingers are touching and beginning to come together."

Repeated Images
OCTOBER 8, 2010

Tonight I saw a cruise ship on its side. It had a large hole in it and I think it was sinking. I saw several military helicopters flying around it, so maybe it had been hit by a missile or something, or maybe they were just looking for survivors.

"There's a big weather changes coming up soon. Not like a hurricane or anything. I can't understand it really. Maybe just a general change in the weather caused from global warming or something, like more severe storms and droughts, and I sense it will be global.

"I saw a ball of light coming into the atmosphere. I didn't get a sense what it was.

"There is going to be a shake-up in the government coming soon, and no one expects it.

"I saw soldiers in special uniforms, maybe like special forces, except they were also in riot gear.

"Something happens to the Christian religion that nearly destroys it. Something is discovered or is brought out that makes what they teach all wrong, or incorrect.

"The last thing I saw was the number 2020 flashing: you know, how digital clocks flash when the power goes off and comes back on. I think the flashing means I should pay attention or that it's important, but I didn't get any sense what it represents."

2020
OCTOBER 12, 2010

It's a little frustrating when Dennison just sees scenes with no explanation; perhaps they are little teasers so we will pay attention, or perhaps they are like the headlines to the news, telling us to stay tuned. He says when he asks about a particular thing he's being shown, he seldom gets an answer. Tonight though, I urged him to see if he could get any more information about what the flashing numbers 2020 could represent in his last meditation, since they were calling attention to it.

~ 2010 • 2020 ~

"I asked about that 2020 and they said it's a date and it's when the earth is natural again. It is when mankind will be living in harmony with the earth. They showed me miles and miles of large windmills like they use to create power...wind generators.

"Next they showed me railroad tracks, but the train on them was more like the bullet train we rode in Japan, but not quite the same. This train was made of what looked like glass or some kind of a clear substance and it was very streamlined, like something out of a science fiction movie and it hovered above the rail bed. They told me 'new forms of energy are being used'.

"Then they showed me whole neighborhoods of these domed-looking houses. On the outside they were sort of silvery in color and you couldn't see inside, but on the inside the walls were transparent. On the top of the dome was some sort of machine with whirling blades and they said it was to generate power. The inside of the houses were very beautiful, with small gardens incorporated into the living areas and like a little stream running through and waterfalls, sort of like a greenhouse. There was air movement too, almost like you were outside. There wasn't really yards outside; it was more like one big park with walkways, flowers, waterways, benches, and play areas. Everything just flowed together and felt natural and relaxing.

"They told me, "Mankind's thinking has changed; everyone works together."

After he had related everything to me, I remarked, "2020 is just slightly over nine years from now. I can't imagine how we could get from where we are now to something like that unless something drastic happens between now and then.

(As I was entering my handwritten journal into the computer in preparation of this book, I noticed he also saw the flashing numbers 2020 on 4-02-2005; however he never followed up on asking what it could mean.)

Three Catastrophes
OCTOBER 17, 2010

When we again took time to meditate, I urged him to see if he could get any more information on 2020, to ask how we get from where we are now to the world he saw in his vision.

"When I asked how we could possibly get to that point that I saw in my last meditation by 2020, they told me, 'There will also be three world catastrophes before then that will bring the world to its knees.' They showed me two circles side by side, and then slowly one circle began to move into the other. Above the two circles was a real long oval shape…I don't know what that was. They went on to say, 'There are two dimensions coming together now. It's in progress and about one quarter of the way along. It's a very delicate process, somewhat like merging two crystal glasses without shattering them. It will be a very difficult time for the earth itself and many prayers are needed. It has only started and it will become more and more difficult for mankind as time progresses, for along with the disasters, the world economy will also break down. The year 2020 is when the whole process will be complete; then will come the Golden Age when man will live in harmony with Nature. The world you now know will be gone.'"

The Economy
OCTOBER 20, 2010

When Dennison went into meditation tonight, he asked about the three catastrophes that were supposed to happen in the future. This is what he received, but it is unclear if it is an answer to his question or just information.

"Something having to do with the economy is going to happen… something drops…? I don't understand what or how it works, but it is going to end up that everything is made equal. Right now you have the very rich and the poor, almost no middle class at all anymore. Whatever happens makes everything equal.

"The money movers, the big financial people on Wall Street are putting their money elsewhere; they aren't putting it back into our economy like they're supposed to. That and some other things happen that really hurts us on a global scale. Somehow people won't be able to pay their debts, banks collapse, money is worthless. There is like a mafia, a secret government that wants to rule the world. They will come in with a new money system and they will offer to bail countries out who agree to work with them, then they take over. This is when a new money system comes in. It seems for the good and everyone can live equally, but I don't think it really is.

"Then people begin to look for or begin to create small communities that are self-sufficient, off the grid, have their own resources and their own money or barter. People help each other to make it through hard times.

"Within the next year something will happen within the government. Something drastic and unexpected. I sense it's big, real big. I don't know if it has to do with the economy or not, or if this is something else.

"There's going to be an uprising. I don't think it's about the economy; I think it's a religion, people against people, people against their government. I think it's in another country and not here, but it's going to be pretty bad. Then they will make peace and come together and join forces...come together and create something stronger.

"I saw a city devastated. At first I thought it was something like a hurricane, but the more I watched, the more I felt it was a huge earthquake. Large skyscrapers and buildings just came down like they were being demolished by an explosion. I also saw liquefied dirt or mud flowing over a town.

"Another thing I saw was a swastika. I've seen it several times now... is there still a Nazi movement? I clearly saw a swastika hovering over the top of our American flag, not on the flag, but overshadowing it."

Purification
OCTOBER 24, 2010

THE SYMBOLISM OF THE FOLLOWING MEDITATION was at first very puzzling. I don't know why some of his meditations are so difficult to interpret, but suspect it is so we will research and find out even more than is given. Also the brain interprets through symbols or images (as in dreams) before it becomes words.

"I saw a star in the sky that looked like the Star of David. A voice said, 'The Lion and the Goliath are side by side.'

"I was trying to figure out what that meant when I saw this really bright blue star shining bright like the planet Venus does. As I looked at it, I noticed it was near the big dipper. I wondered if this could be the Blue Star that the Hopis speak of in their prophecies of the coming Purifier. While I was thinking about this, the star separated from the dipper and disappeared!

"What was that figure that was half horse and half human? Or like a horse with the head and body of a man? He was in the sky, you know, like the constellations. What constellation is he?" "Sagittarius?" I interjected. "Yeah, that's it. Anyway he was wearing a crown and holding a bow and arrow. The bow was fully drawn back and the arrow ready to fly.

"Then the man let the arrow fly and, as he did, his crown lit up as a bright gold light. Then he tilted his head and looked down toward the earth. As he did, a beam of golden light went down to the earth. On the earth there was a large gathering of people who were celebrating; everyone was happy and laughing and hugging each other and fireworks were going off like the 4th of July or New Year's."

Shortages and High Prices
OCTOBER 25, 2010

I WAS HOPING TONIGHT'S MEDITATION would bring more understanding of last night's images, but instead Dennison said, "They were telling me there's going to be some things that happen in the world that is going to cause food shortages and higher prices for food and other goods. There's going to be higher gas prices too. It's going to cause a real stress on the economy. I saw some riots, lots of people yelling and looting. I also saw some bad storms, lots of snow and flooding.

The Pressure Increases
OCTOBER 27, 2010

AFTER OUR MEDITATION Dennison asked me if I knew anything about the stratosphere. I told him I didn't know much, just that it was one of the layers surrounding the earth. He seemed to think about that a moment, then said, "They were explaining the earth is like a living organism; it breathes in and out, it adjusts itself and regulates itself through heating and cooling. They compared it to an eye with delicate membranes (layers of atmosphere) surrounding it. When something harmful comes toward it, like cosmic particles, it reacts like an eye blinking or closing, and the layers act like a shield.

"They said our galaxy was also like a membrane, sort of like a womb. The energies are feminine and it is surrounded by masculine energy. All galaxies are like that. Anyway something is happening that comes up only once in so many thousands of years. It's like a re-birth and the earth will be renewed. But right now there's an energy coming into the earth that will cause a pressure on mankind. It will cause people to feel stressed and they will lash out against that which oppresses them or is unfair. They will lash out against governments and against injustice and even against each other. Animals will feel it too and react in a lesser degree. Even the earth itself will react with more hurricanes, severe weather, earthquakes, volcanoes, etc. It will be a mess for a while, but in the end it will force change. Earth will eventually be made new again and so will mankind."

~ On the Tip Edge of a Miracle ~

A Spiritual Awakening Is Coming
OCTOBER 31, 2010

THIS HALLOWEEN WE SAT OUTSIDE in front of the house and delivered candy to the never-ending hordes of goblins and visited with our neighbors who were doing the same. It reminded me of the old days when my parents and the neighbors sat outside in the evenings and visited while all the neighborhood kids would play with each other in the gathering darkness. It felt good, and I briefly wondered why we seem to need a special occasion to do so now. When we finally went inside, we decided it would be nice to meditate a little before going to bed.

"They told me a cosmic spiritual awakening is about to happen. Mankind is going to be forced to awaken spiritually.

"I saw a bright flash of light; they said there's two forces or energies that come together, like two balls of light that come together or merge to become one light. I saw a light blue light coming down and covering the earth. They said it will be like we all go through a thin veil. As we go through, all of our beliefs will be challenged. We will emerge as one mind, one spiritual outlook under one light and one color. This is for the good of all mankind.

"Oh, there was another thing they told me, 'In order to receive your treasurers, your gifts and your blessings, you have to let go of control.'"

I pondered this last statement for a while. What were they trying to say…were we really trying to maintain control? Control of what? Our life, or our direction in life? Maybe.

The more I thought about it, the more I looked at how we lived and what we thought. Indeed we were always trying to steer our own ship, and not too well I might add. We were doing so because we were afraid of what would happen if we didn't. We didn't really trust Creator, even when we could look back and see how we had been taken care of in the past. Each new challenge in our lives raised new doubts. I realized we were trying to control things because we were distrustful, we were afraid.

We can't fully receive all that Creator offers unless we let go of fear. We're being asked to trust, to have true faith, to surrender control.

Let Go of Fear
NOVEMBER 7, 2010

This evening's meditation seemed to be an expansion of last week's meditation where they talked about letting go of control.

"Tonight they were telling me we are being faced with our fears, to force us to change and let go of those fears—rise above them and detach.

"They explained, 'It's in your DNA to feel fear when there is danger; you either run or you make a stand and fight. Right now the world is filled with fear. It is constantly coming from every direction, natural disasters, terrorist attacks, economic failure, corruption at the highest levels, greed, higher prices for food and gasoline, child molesters, identity theft, e-coli and salmonella in your food, and on and on. You can't run from it, and you can't take a stand and fight it.

"'Your minds are connected; you form a collective consciousness and fear feeds fear, so the more each fears, the more fear there is collectively. It's also in your DNA to access the Higher Power, but that has become dormant.'

"They showed me a flame and said, 'Each of you have within you an inner light, the spark of your Source. You begin life full of openness and trust, but with each hurt that life brings, you begin to build a shield or shell around your inner being, trying to protect yourself. However, when you do, your light grows dim and you can't get spiritual nourishment. When that happens, you begin to make wrong decisions and lose confidence, illness sets in and you lose your way, and you fear.

"'A small child is open and connected with its Source, its inner light burns bright, it accesses The Source through the openness and light. As they grow older and experience the hurts of life, you can see them change and they lose confidence and slowly grow afraid.

"'Even though your religions have a lot of truths within them, most also offer a lot of fear. It is a control mechanism. But fear blocks you from knowing the higher spiritual power that is within you. The only way you can access the higher spiritual power is to let go of fear, to face your fears and rise above them and detach from them. When you can do this, you will be able to be opened up and be guided.

~ On the Tip Edge of a Miracle ~

"'There is something miraculous happening behind the scenes that no one is aware of. In order for it to happen, you have to let go of your fears, have faith, open your minds. The more who do so, the more the collective conscious will change. If it can change enough, it will outweigh the fear and all will change and the miracle will happen.

"'There is a growing hunger within mankind for true spirituality. It is there to help you grow. The way you live now, the way you think, is based on greed. So many are only out for themselves. When you give to help another who is in need, you are the one who receives the blessing. When it is from the heart, you grow. Times are coming that will force you to give and share in order to survive. You Will Grow.

"'A miracle is happening! Only the thinnest of veils is separating you. LET GO OF FEAR, AND LOVE—LOVE YOURSELF, LOVE OTHERS!

"'You are being pushed to the next level through fear. Facing your fears and releasing them is how you grow.'"

This was powerful stuff. I had to keep slowing Dennison down as the words poured out of him, so I could be sure to get it all down. After we went to bed, I lay awake long into the night thinking of all the things we had gone through over the years. In many ways each year seemed harder than the one before. I knew we weren't the only ones who were struggling in one way or another; everyone seems to have private and not so private issues they have to deal with. So many have financial lack, have lost jobs, and/or homes, have health issues, lost sons and daughters to war, lost all of their life savings, and on and on.

I had spent many a long sleepless night worrying and wondering why so much was happening to us, wondering if we were being punished for some past misdeed and the law of karma had caught up with us; if there were negative forces at play; if we were creating our own problems with our thinking; if there was no god and we were fooling ourselves; or if we were being maybe tested for some unknown reason yet to be revealed. But it never occurred to me that we're being pushed to a higher level through being forced to face our fears…forced through fear itself, until we finally hit bottom and "let go and let God," as the saying goes. We are all being faced with our own particular fears until we're finally able to fully surrender and trust in our Creator as a child trusts; until we're able to find that tiny flame that has been snuffed almost completely out and rekindle it so we're able to reconnect and access that higher power within each of us.

God's Light
NOVEMBER 11, 2010

"Tonight I saw a veil...like a thin membrane. I could see the earth and it looked like it was slowly moving into the veil and going on through it. As I watched, I heard this music...it's hard to describe how beautiful this music was.... (Dennison paused for a long time as if he was still listening to it.) I heard this real beautiful music and I wanted to weep with joy. I could see the stars and planets and it seemed like they were celebrating too as they watched. I could see this light on the other side of the veil...God's Light."

As Dennison finished telling me his vision, I looked up from my writing and noticed he had tears streaming down his cheeks. It was a short and simple vision, but it profoundly touched him.

NOVEMBER 14, 2010

"Remember a meditation I had years ago where a 'Grandfather' asked me to choose between a new silver dollar and an eagle feather and I chose the eagle feather? *(The eagle feather symbolizes a bridge or connection to the spiritual plane, and is a sacred object to the Native American. The Grandfather pointed out to him the silver dollar had an eagle on it too, and asked him to choose between the two. The silver dollar of course represents the material world.)*

"Everyone is going to have to make that kind of choice soon. Those who have plenty will have to choose whether to share their wealth or not. I'm talking about big corporations, the wealthiest people, will need to share with those who don't have anything. If they choose not to, and hang on to their money instead, they will have a very hard time. They will have to learn to let go, willingly let go of what they have.

"They showed me a cross symbol. They said it also symbolized a cross-road. We have to choose whether we travel the material or the spiritual path. They said the cross is also a sword, the two-edged sword of TRUTH—it cuts both ways. The religions have taken the truth and corrupted it for their own purposes; that will soon be cut away and exposed. This is especially true of the Christian churches; they are greatly responsible for the shape the world is in now. They have become an important political power and have pushed through their own political agenda. They have come far away from the original Truth.

"Long ago something was written in stone, a guide how to live. It was hidden away because it was misused. It was taken apart and the teachings re-written in their own way, perverting the truth or losing it all together.

"They also showed me a sword with a crown hanging off of it. The crown was made of thorns, a reminder of the hurts and the pain Christ suffered. That pain and suffering is still in the world, and who but a few has tried to heal it? What is coming is to make mankind aware, each of us personally aware, of those who suffer, so it will be made right."

Solar Flare?
NOVEMBER 14, 2010

I<small>N TONIGHT'S MEDITATION</small> Dennison saw what I think might be the results of a massive solar flare.

"When do the Northern Lights come out?" I explained they mostly showed in the winter in the northern latitudes unless there was a solar flare that charged the ionosphere enough that they showed up farther south. That we normally don't see them down here, but a few times in the past we had seen them even here in Arizona.

He continued, "I think something is going to happen where people see something like the Northern Lights in places where they've never been seen before.

"I also saw what looked like mud coming down a mountainside and covering a town. At first I thought it was a volcano, but I'm sure it was mud and not lava.

"I saw a city in darkness. There were no lights at all, not even car lights.

"I saw miles and miles of cars stopped or stalled on a highway for some reason. People were in groups talking with each other. Some were setting up a sort of camp like they had been there a long time. Nothing was moving and no one seemed to be coming to help them."

The End of a Cycle
NOVEMBER 16, 2010

"We are coming to the end of a cycle. In the beginning there was an explosion that created outward, kind of like an ejaculation. Another explosion will happen that will begin our birth. We are going to be born! We are in a womb of sorts...the whole universe is a part of our womb. We're being pushed through a veil, a membrane, like infants, and we will emerge as new beings. We will be made new again in every way. No more illness, no more fear, no more selfishness, no greed and no insecurities. Family groups retain their connections, we retain our identities, but I don't know how our memories will be affected."

Aliens
NOVEMBER 18, 2010

"Years ago when I first was having these visions, I saw aliens coming to help mankind after some kind of a devastation. I was wondering what aliens really are and what role, if any, they will play. Will they help us and if so how?

"They were telling me those which we call aliens are cosmic beings. They are energy, light beings. They aren't "out there"—they are in other dimensions. They work for the Source and oversee mankind. They manifest bodies when needed. They navigate in and out of our three-dimensional world by using electromagnetic energy. Their vehicles are like time machines, or time boxes, and allow them to go into and out of our time-based dimension, our vibration. When the time is right, they will help us and guide us. There are some who are here now, who have human bodies and look like everyone else. They are to help and guide those who need it.

"We aren't ready to interact with them yet. There's a time coming soon where everyone will have to work together, and help each other."

I reminded him that when disasters hit, such as hurricane Katrina, there were plenty who took advantage of those less fortunate and plundered, robbed and took what they wanted, and even murdered. They were simply out for themselves.

He said, "Somehow that won't happen this time. The whole world pulls together; everyone pulls together. Just like during 911, only more so, much, much more so. There's an energy that will come in and change our minds, change our thinking and our way of looking at things. We will come together because we have to, in order to survive. The more we help each other and work together, the better we become and everyone changes.

"There's going to be something that happens, like what some call the Second Coming, except it won't be what we have been taught; it will be completely different."

A Miracle Is About to Happen!
NOVEMBER 20, 2010

LIKE A FEW OF HIS RECENT MEDITATIONS this evening's meditation seemed to be a continuation of the last one.

"We are about to experience a miracle! A miracle is about to happen again! At least there is a great potential for a miracle, but first we are in for a rude awakening that will, in the end, bring forth spirituality. We are going to be "pushed" with the four elements. The four poles of the Universe will be connected.

"They showed me two people hugging, hands joined behind each other. This creates an energy that brings healing to one another.

"There will be a strong uplifting and a desire to help one another, through suffering, hunger and thirst. Through this and with this, there will be a strong inner healing, creating strength and love within one's self.

"The Buddha used to call this 'the opening of the Lotus.' The way they showed me was the earth as a round ball in the center of a cross with two cross arms; one arm was white and one was yellow. A red serpent was intertwined around the cross, sort of like the emblem for the physician's staff (caduceus). It represents the negative and positive forces coming together. This is how the healing is represented as healing the world. When the serpents come together, there's a rebirth. Out of the emblem grew the tree of life. On the limbs I saw people, animals and birds, all life reborn. On the top of the tree I see a man and a woman coming out of it…like the two corns in Navajo legend, two people wrapped in a blanket, surrounded by a lotus flower.

"It's funny, the sound I heard was like a loud female voice making a wailing sound, like she would make while giving birth.

"No matter how dark or how tragic the event, there's always something new and pure that will come out of it and be reborn, like the phoenix.

"The other thing I heard was a voice saying, 'Different countries, different peoples, different races, different religions and status, each and all will reach out to help each other up. That's how mankind will come together as one, as you were meant to be from the beginning. There is always a doorway for a positive outcome, even in the most dire circumstances. There is an inner strength people will find to help each other. There's a healing that will come about in mankind.'

"The more spiritual we are, the more love we have, and the more we work together, the more we can avoid these terrible things and the more we'll be guided around it."

"'You must learn to let go of fear and trust Creator and the process, detach from what's happening and rise above it; don't be mired down in your own fears. Stop your negative and fearful thoughts and float like a feather above and over it. *Let go of control and you will receive your treasures, and your blessings.*'"

Rough sketch of the "Opening of the Lotus" symbolism given to Dennison

Numbers Have Power
NOVEMBER 21, 2010

"They were telling me that numbers have power; they vibrate at certain rates and correspond to certain notes or sounds. The right combinations have tremendous power. Our whole universe is based on numbers somehow."

In the past mankind was given certain numbers and certain sounds. Certain words were given for power and certain rules were given to abide by. Each civilization was meant to evolve in various ways, both mentally and physically, and each were taught certain technologies to help them evolve. Each gift was to be shared with the other in a loving way without greed. But rules were broken and power misused.

In our own civilization for instance we have made great scientific discoveries. But we have broken the rules. We were given charge of taking care of the earth; instead we have raped, plundered and polluted it to the point of destroying the planet for our own greed.

Each thing that happens breaks down the system a little, until we reach a point where we can't go on, and we self-destruct. We broke a law of Creation when we dropped the atomic bomb. We have been given much latitude, yet we continue. When rules are broken, something has to happen to stop it before we destroy completely all that has been given. It is now time to reap what has been sown.

There is still time to change the collective mind: if enough change, then the negative will be diminished.

Future Energies to Come
NOBEMBER 28, 2010

"THERE ARE CERTAIN ENERGIES that will be coming in waves over the next two years, increasing in frequency and intensity as time nears.

"The first energy is the energy for compassion, spiritual growth and self-empowerment. Each will experience it differently. Those who are spiritual will grow, those who are not spiritual, but are good-hearted will begin to look for something "more." Those of all religions will feel a pull for a more personal understanding and deeper spiritual connections.

Those who are stuck in materialism and greed-thinking will feel agitated and angry. The energy that is coming in now is going to destroy their materialistic way of thinking. They can feel it and it isn't comfortable. The change will be very hard for them."

Potential

DECEMBER 3, 2010

THIS EVENING'S MEDITATION proved to be another unusual one with rich imagery. I wish in some ways I could see and receive as he does, in other ways I think it's a blessing I can't.

"I saw a barbed wire fence with a wire gate…you know, how they make those old gates out of the barbed wire and fence posts. It had a wire loop that I had to slide up over the fence post in order to release the gate and open it.

"Anyway I was traveling along an old bumpy dirt track and up ahead was this fence with a gate across the road. On the gate was an old license plate. As I got closer, I could read the letters on the rusted old plate; it read: POTENTIAL.

"I stopped and got out to open the gate; as I approached, I hoped I could open it; it looked real sturdy and pulled extremely tight. I wrapped my arm around the post and leaned into it with all I had and pushed and wiggled until I was able to work the wire loop up. As it slipped over the post, there was a *whoooosh* sound of something vacuum-packed or sealed under pressure and at the same time the gate collapsed and I drug it open.

"I turned around and noticed there was a whole bunch of people behind me, like they were traveling with me and just waiting to see if I could do it or not, and when it opened, they all clapped and cheered and laughed.

"A voice said to me, 'When you release and let go, all potential is opened up to you.'

"Ahead, through the gate, was a huge field with row upon row of new corn plants, just coming up (corn symbolizes life to the Navajo). We all rushed through the gate and I reached down and caressed the little blades of the corn plants. They were wet with a little water trapped inside the leaves, and I put my wet fingers to my lips and drank it and blessed myself with it. The others watched me and started doing the same.

"Then I looked back where we came in from, thinking I'd better go close the gate, but strangely there was no fence and no gate, just fields and fields of growing things. When I turned back again, I saw all the corn had grown as high as my head and people were at work harvesting it.

"They showed me a word: INTEGRATED. What exactly does integrated mean?

"Anyway, they told me there are four Holy People from the four directions, representing the four races of man, who each have a word, like the Hopi have the pieces of the tablet. They are supposed to come together. The words will be the foundation of a new religion, a new spirituality."

He had been told about Holy People coming together from the four directions before, but this was the first time he had been told about each having a word. I'm not sure what the word "integrated" would mean in this context, unless perhaps the integration of the four races of man.

More Scenes of the Future
DECEMBER 7, 2010

AFTER THIS EVENING'S MEDITATION Dennison asked, "When is the winter solstice? There is going to be a wave of energy, a very, very powerful explosion of energy coming in then to bring in more spiritual thinking. It's very powerful and everyone will begin to feel it. Is there an alignment then? I think there is an alignment or something that takes place in the heavens then (there was a lunar eclipse).

"People are going to begin speaking out about how things are, about jobs, the economy, homelessness, etc. There is a group or organization that starts a movement for a more spiritual, peaceful way of living.

"Obama is going to have to step up. He will come into his power this next year. Something big is going to happen in the government... happen soon.

"There is a strong, very highly spiritual leader, who steps into the light and becomes known. He has a lot of followers. Somehow I don't think he is for the good.

"They were telling me this is a fragile time for the world leaders and for our nation. The Twelve Pillars of Freedom are weakening and some will soon collapse and the power within will spill over and some of it will be lost.

"The Liberty Bell will ring.

"It's time to begin gathering your resources!"

I looked on the internet to see if there was such a thing as the Twelve Pillars of Freedom, as it somehow sounded familiar. I was shocked to find it was a historical document dating back to the founding of America and was used as the foundation of the U.S. Constitution.

I also noted he said the Liberty Bell will ring. I recalled he was told something similar back before we went into Iraq. I found it again back on 1-23-02:

"Someone was telling me, 'The Liberty Bell has rung twice and it will ring again two more times.' They continued saying, 'The Flag has been waved, but then it should have been folded and put away in a drawer.' The last thing I remember is seeing an eagle silhouetted against a flag. He was carrying two arrows in his claws."

Again on 5-5-02 he dreamed someone said to him:

'The Liberty Bell will ring, and the sound will be heard around the world.'

I speculated at the time the Liberty bell rang once for WW I and again for WWII. And the mention of it ringing on 5-5-02 was a warning we were going to war with Iraq. I wonder if the mention of the Liberty Bell ringing in this latest meditation means we're going to enter another war—?

Rebirth of the Stars
DECEMBER 7, 2010

"They were telling me about an energy wave that causes the rebirth of the stars. It re-energizes the universe and it comes every so many thousands of years. They said it is about to happen again. This energy is electromagnetic and it comes in four waves. There will be a space of time between each wave. There will be like a shock wave, without any warning. The last wave will be the strongest.

"There are a lot of particles of matter, like dust particles, that come with the last wave, and the sun interacts with the particles in some way, maybe like a solar flare or something on that order, that's why it's the strongest wave. It is like the afterbirth.

"In times past it was called 'the Dragon's Breath' because that's what it will be like. It will also cause huge electrical storms and wipe out anything electric. It will cause searing heat and even forests will burn. It will cause earthquakes and tidal waves and then there will be extreme cold."

Birth
DECEMBER 12, 2010

OVER THE YEARS Dennison has heard beautiful music during some of his meditations. It seems to take him deeper and deeper into his meditative state. This evening's meditation was one of those times.

"The first thing I heard was someone saying, 'Gently reaching out in kindness pays in fulfillment.'

"Then I started hearing that beautiful music again like I've heard before. It seemed like it took me deeper into it.

"They showed me a worm in the Milky Way...a caterpillar. It was sort of superimposed over the Milky Way so I think it was meant to be a metaphor. Anyway the caterpillar was curved in a circle or a spiral, like the Milky Way is when you see it from the top. As it curled around head to tail, it went into a black hole in the center. Then I could see a butterfly coming out on the other side.

"They told me it is like a re-birth; the Universe, including us, is going through a birth process of some sort. We're becoming butterflies. We're being re-born as something different somehow. The center of the galaxy is like a womb where stars are born. When the caterpillar spins its cocoon, it transforms and then the cocoon bursts open, that's the 'big bang' and it's reborn as a butterfly...A MIRACLE!"

~ 2010 • Waves of Energy ~

Earthquake
DECEMBER 14, 2010

When Dennison first came out of meditation, he asked, "Where exactly is Costa Rica? Is it connected in some way to the San Andreas Fault?"

"When I first started meditating, a voice spoke and said, **'Time is of the essence'.** Then I started hearing that beautiful music again and went deeper and deeper.

"I saw a coast line and the ocean. There were high cliffs and tropical trees, like palm trees on them. Then I saw a big sign that said, 'Costa Rica'. Suddenly there was... (Dennison made motions with his hand and tried to find the words to describe what he was seeing)... there was this...like maybe a sound wave but no sound...there was some sort of force like a shock wave or something, followed by a *whoosh* and I could see the sign falling down, down, down as the side of the cliff crumbled away into the sea.

Next I saw the earth's crustal plates. I saw where two plates come together. They showed...it was like one plate was above the other; it lifted up and slammed down or dropped and a shock wave went out. I think a big earthquake happens. They said it's part of the San Andreas Fault and it affects the fault all the way to the North. Then there's a huge tidal wave that goes out across the ocean. What's on the other side of the ocean there? It's going to be caught unawares."

Waves of Energy
DECEMBER 17, 2010

We both had been wondering about the waves of energy Dennison was told about a few nights ago and if the last meditation had anything to do with the waves of energy.

"They said there will be several waves, with a space of time between each one. The first will be like a strong shock wave deep in the earth's crust. It will cause earthquakes, tidal waves and mostly affect the coastal areas.

"There's also an electromagnetic wave that affects the negative and positive energies at the North and South Poles. It will also affect air travel and ground airplanes. Being in coastal cities won't be good. There is some kind of an interaction with these electromagnetic energies and the ocean that creates like a shockwave.

"They didn't tell me about the next waves of energy, or maybe I just didn't really want to hear about them or see them."

Water
DECEMBER 20, 2010
(LUNAR ECLIPSE/WINTER SOLSTICE)

"THERE IS A WAVE OF ENERGY that is coming in now that is for water. It is also for feminine or female energy, to help balance all the male energy in the world. It will strongly bring in spiritual energy too because that is also feminine energy.

"This energy will make a lot of people feel real uncomfortable, especially men or people with lots of male energy. It creates a pressure inside because it is in conflict with what they now believe. Many will become frustrated, angry and even aggressive because of it. But it will force change, and eventually there will be balance.

"It will also deal with emotions, because water is associated with emotions and so are feminine energies. It's not about how one thinks, it's about how one feels inside. Many will become more sensitive.

"It also deals with water. There will be lots of rain, flooding, heavy snows, high tides, and so on. It will deal with washing things to the surface to be looked at and cleaned up; what is hidden will wash to the surface and be cleansed."

Forgive One Another
DECEMBER 23, 2010

"WHEN I FIRST WENT INTO MEDITATION, I heard the word 'AGGRESSION.' As the energy that is coming in now increases, we will see more and more aggression on every level. There will be small wars that suddenly break out. Families will get angry at each other over nothing; couples will argue and fight, etc. There is a pressure building on many levels. Those who aren't spiritual will feel it especially and will react accordingly.

"Did we talk about a time belt before? They were talking about a time belt; you know, how a tree has rings that show how old it is, it grows layer on layer as the tree ages...somehow there's something like that around the universe or the earth. I guess I don't really understand what they are trying to say....

"Another thing they said, 'There is often love that fades to comfort. That in turn progresses to frustration and anger. When anger is spent, there is exhaustion and finally that becomes forgiveness; in forgiveness there is love. Forgive one another, love one another.'"

Another Earthquake
DECEMBER 27, 2010

TONIGHT DENNISON SAW THE COAST OF NORTH AMERICA as seen from above.

"I saw a large area out in the ocean just off the coast of California, near the Mexico border. They showed me the coastline from the air and a red circle ringed by larger circles, reminding me of a target. It covered a large area, partly out in the ocean and part of it was up on the land.

"Something is happening deep in the earth that has to do with pressure building up from two plates pushing against each other and it causes a huge earthquake and tidal wave. I saw the ocean looked like it was boiling where the red spot was and the word 'IMMINENT' appeared in bold flashing letters."

Later we looked at the atlas and he showed where the area was. He said he also saw a "point of land" and some islands a little farther up the coast. He searched the map in the atlas until he suddenly spotted the place he had seen in his meditation. It was near Los Angeles and included Point Conception and Catalina Island and extended all the way to the Mexico border near Baja.

More Earthquakes
DECEMBER 28, 2010

This evening's meditation seemed to be a continuation of last night's. "I saw a large red circle in Alaska. It was close to a long finger of land that goes out in the ocean. There's a city called Anchorage that is where the center is. I saw the word "Anchorage" appear when I wondered where it was. It's not as imminent as the one in California.

"I also saw another red spot off the coast of Oregon, near where a big river empties into the sea. The red spot is not as large as the other ones."

See Through the Illusion
DECEMBER 31, 2010

Tonight we finished the year with a meditation to see if we could get a glimpse of what to expect in the year to come. As we finished, Dennison took a deep breath and said,

"I saw some words in large letters that said, 'SHED YOUR BELIEFS, LAYER BY LAYER, UNTIL YOU SEE THROUGH THE ILLUSION.'

"After that I saw a huge gnarled tree with huge roots running in all directions and finally down into the earth. You were walking with me across a meadow to go look at the tree and sit in its shade. There was a sort of ridge or shelf of stone that ran under the branches and I helped you up on it. As we were sitting there looking down at the valley below, I noticed notches carved into the stone. I stood up to take a better look. As I walked around it, I realized it was like a clock...a sun dial! The tree is growing up through it! Someone was saying to me, 'This is the tree of life.'

"Suddenly it was like we were watching a movie in high speed as scenes of the valley in front of us began to quickly change...sunrise, sunset, night, clouds, rain, snow, flowers, a lake appeared, iced over and melted, a town and then a city sprang up as the decades passed. Then it all stopped and I took your hand and helped you off the sundial and started walking away. For some reason I looked back and all these people that I never noticed before were getting off behind us. An endless sea of people coming. I wondered what the heck?? A voice said, 'Time is at an end.... Man will begin anew.'

2011

Riots

THE NEW YEAR STARTED OFF with more visions of possibilities to come:

JANUARY 15, 2011

"I SAW A RIOT IN A CITY. I couldn't see any other catastrophe, just a bunch of people running through the streets during the day throwing things, breaking windows, bashing up cars and shooting guns. It doesn't seem like it's in the U.S....

"I saw a bunch of soldiers fighting; they were wearing camouflage that's yellow and tan like they would wear in the desert. They are shooting at a bunch of people; they look like just regular people, but they are dressed like Middle Eastern. I don't think it's our soldiers. There's some other people fighting too. I think they are fighting the soldiers but they don't stand a chance. Somehow I think we get involved.

"Next I saw a city being flooded, and water is just seeping up the streets and rising higher and higher. It's a huge flood that is carrying cars away right off the road and even houses are floating...out to the ocean or something. There is a bunch of people huddled together on a hill just watching everything."

Revolution

FEBRUARY 22, 2011

THIS EVENING'S MEDITATION brought the following images. It took quite a while before I had an idea what they might symbolize.

"I saw two ships forming a blockade out in a harbor. There was another ship near a dock with a bunch of men throwing boxes of something over the side. There were soldiers on the ships in the blockade, but they were dressed in old-fashioned clothes with white stockings, like George Washington. They were firing into a crowd of people yelling.

"The next scene was of a mountain, sort of expanding and contracting, almost like a cartoon. I don't know what that could mean, unless a volcano. There was steam coming out, but no lava or smoke.

"The last scene I saw was oil fields on fire, like during the gulf war."

As I thought about his images, the only thing I could think of for the first scene was the obvious "Boston Tea Party," maybe symbolizing revolution or protest.

The second scene reminds me of a pressure cooker about to let off steam or blow its top. Perhaps this symbolizes just that, something or group of people letting off steam or about to blow up into a full-fledged protest.

The last scene of course sets the place where this is beginning to happen now, in the Middle East.

More Earthquakes
FEBRUARY 27, 2011

TONIGHT'S MEDITATION seems to be an elaboration on a meditation received last December.

"Remember the red spot I saw in the ocean near San Diego a while back? I saw it again, only this time it was bigger.

"I also saw a zigzag symbol, you know kind of like lightning, flashing on a map of the West Coast. I think it was flashing to call my attention to it. It's out in the ocean near where the border of Washington and Oregon meet...is there something out there like a fault line or something? Remember I saw something before about a river that empties into the ocean there?

"They also showed me a bad earthquake happening—it was really bad! There was devastation everywhere...a big tidal wave flowing in and taking everything with it, cars, houses, people, everything. Did I see that before? I don't know if it's in Washington and Oregon or somewhere else....

"I saw a rainbow at night....

"I saw that big river that goes from the top of the U.S. to the bottom, what is it...? the Mississippi...I saw it split into two rivers above Louisiana....

Blue Star Again
MARCH 7, 2011

AGAIN THIS EVENING'S MEDITATION seems to be related to a meditation he received last fall.

"I saw a constellation of a lion and one of a giant holding a spear in one hand. He had a round shield slung on his back and a metal arm band around his bicep.

"The lion looked like he was getting ready to attack the giant, and the giant had his spear ready to fight. Someone was saying, "The lion and the Goliath are about to engage."

"Next I saw a bright star with an intense blue beam coming down from it toward the earth. It was a real intense blue, like from my acetylene torch. There was another beam from an unknown light source intersecting it so that it formed a + . I don't have any idea what that could mean."

I looked up the symbolism for blue flame and found the following: A blue flame is the most intense and hottest part of the flame and thus a prophetic symbol of divine revelation. It also symbolizes Purity and Purification.

Japan Earthquake
MARCH 10, 2011

WE HAD JUST TURNED OUT THE LIGHTS and were drifting into sleep when the phone rang. It was a friend calling to say Japan had just suffered a huge earthquake, something like a 9.0 in magnitude! At the moment there was a huge tsunami seeping in on the land and carrying away everything in its path. We turned on the TV and watched horrified as the wave swept cars and people off the roadways and into the sea!

~ On the Tip Edge of a Miracle ~

We got up and Dennison lit some sage and prayed for the people of Japan. That they might have the strength to get through whatever was happening and whatever else would come. We thought of our many friends there from years' past and prayed that they were all safe and nowhere near where this devastation was taking place.

Suddenly these end-time scenarios Dennison has been seeing over the years seemed so real and so possible. When you see the devastation and anguish that follows along with it, it is horrifying...these are real lives, real human beings who love and feel just as we do who are being affected!

I'm reminded again that the more we grow spiritually, and collectively raise our consciousness, the less these things will happen: we can change it by changing ourselves and our thinking!

Hard Times Are Coming
DECEMBER 31, 2011

This year has slipped by quickly and once again our meditations have gone by the wayside. In late spring Dennison accepted a commission to paint several paintings for a new medical center. It seemed to be a good way to supplement our slow jewelry income; however it has proved to be a real challenge on many levels as well. One being that by the end of a day of painting, he has little desire to do much more than relax. And winter has brought the return of my lung issues, so once again more and more household chores now fall to him.

On the eve of the much awaited year of 2012 it feels a good thing to finally take time to reflect, pray, give thanks, and to meditate.

"I saw a thick book, like a Bible...it had a purple ribbon marker lying in the crack of the open pages. Next to it on the same table I saw an Egyptian staff or cane, a feather pen and a sort of dark mirror. A dragon fly appeared and circled the book, then landed on one of the pages, as if to call attention to it, so I went over and looked at it.

"On top of the page was written XXIII. Below it I could make out these words:

"'The hard times of the past that were spoken of in the ancient Sanskrit writings are now being bestowed upon mankind.'

2011 • Hard Times Are Coming

"That scene went by, then I saw two Arabian horses running side by side across the desert. One was black and one was white. I noticed their nostrils were flared and I could tell they were winded from running for a long time. Suddenly they separated and ran off in opposite directions."

Neither of us could figure the symbolism...perhaps they symbolize the U.S. and Iraq now that we are set to get out.

2012

Dragons Fighting Again
APRIL 3, 2012

ONCE AGAIN we have simply slipped into a habit of a quick smudge and prayer before going to bed. Dennison maintains he's too tired by the end of the day to do justice to a meditation and will just fall to sleep. This evening I was able to convince him we should try a meditation.

"Remember I used to see dragons fighting in some of my meditations back when we were first going to war with Saddam? Tonight I saw dragons again; one was black and one was white. They were circling each other like they were sizing each other up, getting ready to fight. The funny thing was, they were standing on a big disk of some sort...more like a manhole cover I guess. It was covered with dirt, but I could see part of what looked to be a red star. I kind of felt it had to do with North Korea. Anyway as the dragons were making moves at each other like they were going to fight, suddenly the disk thing they were standing on shot up between them and, as it did, it let off a bunch of steam, hissing as the steam came out of it. The two dragons separated, backed off and went in opposite directions.

Kim Jong Un
APRIL 28, 2012

AS WE WERE EATING BREAKFAST, Dennison said,

"When I woke up this morning, a voice said, 'Watch out for the baby-faced leader. He's about to show his true colors. He's trying to make his mark.'"

Finish Your Book!
AUGUST 24, 2012

OUR JEWELRY BUSINESS continues to sputter along. In meditation Dennison asked for guidance, a direction to go in.

"They showed me a door, so I walked up to it and opened it. When I opened the door, it became a book cover, with the numeral II on it. I opened the cover and saw a bright light. Then a man wearing a white robe stepped out of the light and held out his hand to me. I could see there was something in his palm, so I went a little closer and saw it was a carved fetish of a dolphin! I reached over and took it and it turned into a key."

Obviously this is in reference to finishing our book. I have been procrastinating with getting my journal entries copied into the computer and finishing the book for much too long.

Melting of the Poles
OCTOBER 31, 2012

ANOTHER HALLOWEEN IS HERE. This time I'm too ill to sit outside and dispense candy, so Dennison dressed up in costume and took care of it by himself. We live in a young area and before 7:30 PM the little goblins had cleaned us out of some four pounds of candies! Even after coming in and turning off all lights, our door bell continued to ring.

After things settled down, Dennison suggested we do a prayer and asked if I was up to doing a little meditation before going to bed.

"I saw a piece of paper or calendar hanging on the wall. There was a big roman numeral X at the top of the paper. Below it was a picture of the planet earth showing snow on both the north and south poles. As I was looking at the picture wondering what was significant about it, I saw an intense blue flame, like my torch flame...didn't I see something like that here while back? Anyway this flame started burning the paper. As it burned the paper, it burned over the north and south poles, but it didn't burn up the rest of the earth. I just saw the snow disappearing from the poles, leaving the earth intact.

"At the end I heard someone saying, 'Don't spread fear, and don't take fear unto yourselves. There is no need to fear, for you have the Golden Key within.'"

At first I thought the Golden Key might be love, but after looking it up I found lots of different meanings such as, power, knowledge, wisdom, eternal life and immortality to name a few.

The number 10 symbolizes the full course of life; totality; the end of a cycle.

The End of the Cycle Is Near
NOVEMBER 19, 2012

I'VE BEEN NAGGING DENNISON TO MEDITATE. Since December 21 is on the horizon, we should try to see if something is really going to happen. He maintains he doesn't really want to know; however tonight as we finished our prayers, he said, "Do you want to meditate a little?"...

"The Mayan Calendar is like a time keeping machine. It is actually four calendars in one...one of the calendars marks long cycles of time, and it's coming to the end of one of the cycles on December 21st.

"Mankind is also at the end of a cycle. This happens every several thousand years. The energies for this are already happening; the process is already underway.

"There are two energies, negative and positive...material and spiritual that will merge and become one. As they merge, we will be caught in between. It is sort of like a balloon being squeezed between two hands until it pops. We are being squeezed between the energies until we either come apart or reach out to each other. The more spiritual we are, the easier it will be for us.

"There will be changes both outside, in the form of earth changes, and inside ourselves, in part caused by the outside changes. There will be more natural disasters, failed governments, failed money systems, economic collapse, wars, food shortages, job losses, and so forth. These will continue to increase over the next seven years until 2020.

"Mankind is being brought to his knees. We are being pushed to make us grow. We are being faced with our fears and our wrong thinking. When enough minds change, we collectively will change.

~ On the Tip Edge of a Miracle ~

"In the end, if we grow spiritually and reach out to one another, a miracle will take place...it is something beyond our comprehension...and the birth will be complete."

Epilogue

As I finish typing the last entry, I pause to reflect on what a journey it has been! For us it all began some twenty-five years ago with Dennison's vision of a crystal city, then bit by bit, vision by vision we were spoon-fed a different way of thinking and believing. For me the process has been nothing less than magical, filled with many unexpected adventures, travels, and miracles.

The message is—despite all the scenarios of economic collapse, disasters and war—one of hope. Mankind collectively is on the threshold of a miracle! The opportunity comes but once every few thousand years, and it's here again. Perhaps this time it will happen!

We are told we need to be prepared on a spiritual level because the more spiritual we are, the easier the transformation will be. We're being pushed to evaluate our lives and our impact on the earth. We are urged to turn away from greed and materialism and reach out to each other with love and compassion. If enough of us can do this, the energies will change and the miracle will happen. If not, we will continue on as we are until we self-destruct.

We're being asked to let go of fear and all the ills that are born from it: i.e. hate, greed, anger, selfishness, prejudice, judgment, revenge.... We need only to love, love ourselves and love others. If we can truly love, the rest will follow naturally.

You may wonder if the visions and information within these pages are real or just someone's dreams and delusions? I believe they are real because I have been experiencing them through Dennison as he receives them, but even if we are deluded, I ask you, what harm is there in living in a more spiritual and loving manner? We each are connected to the other, and to everything else in the cosmos on an energetic level. Our collective thoughts and actions affect our reality. Change our collective consciousness and we change.

~ On the Tip Edge of a Miracle ~

It is my hope some of you will feel the urgency of this message, look inside yourselves to feel its worth, then reach out to others and share it.

WE ARE ON THE TIP EDGE OF A MIRACLE!!!

Together we can make it happen!

About the Authors

DENNISON TSOSIE, a traditional Navajo silversmith and artist, did not ask to be a prophet. Neither did he think he would be a Healer or Shaman—yet that is where his life path has led him. With a humble and pure heart, Dennison's prayers and presence are like balm to those who are sick or in need. He prays in his native tongue and lets the healing energy and words from the ancient ones flow through him. Dennison says, "It's not me; I'm just a tool for Creator."

Dennison and his wife, Teddi, live a normal life in a small town in the White Mountains of Arizona where there is firewood to chop and chores to do. They make their living by selling their artwork—well-known, beautifully crafted jewelry and visionary paintings.

Their first book—*Spirit Visions: The Old Ones Speak*—at first photocopied and given out to friends and family—has a life of its own which has taken Dennison and Teddi to meet and pray with spiritual leaders in Ecuador, Canada, and Japan.

We welcome any comments or insights the reader might wish to share. Please send a self-addressed stamped envelope to:
Dennison & Teddi Tsosie
c/o Blue Dolphin Publishing, Inc.
P.O. Box 8
Nevada City, CA 95959-0008

or e-mail to: bdolphin@bluedolphinpublishing.com

**To see Dennison Tsosie's handmade jewelry and artwork please view their website
www.navajosilversmith.com**

Spirit Visions
The Old Ones Speak
Dennison & Teddi Tsosie
ISBN: 978-1-57733-002-8, 384 pp.,
6 x 9, paperback, $19.95

Dennison Tsosie, a traditional Navajo silversmith and artist, began receiving spontaneous dreams and visions in 1986. It all began when Dennison's wife, Teddi, placed a special crystal under their pillow. Quite dramatically, Dennison was guided into a visionary world of prophetic teachings which shed light on missing pieces of history—from a multitude of past cultures—and on our potential future.

An unsophisticated man who wasn't interested in world events, Dennison was mystified over messages warning of earth changes, political upheavals and possibilities of war, alien abductions, and secret government cover-ups. He was even more puzzled by references to the Holy Grail, the Mayans, the Order of Knights Templar, Goethe, and the Star Nations. He had never heard of these names, but Teddi had, and she wrote down the amazing visions Dennison described "in case they would be important later."

Spirit Visions: The Old Ones Speak, complete with sketches of places Dennison "visited in vision," will take you on a grand adventure up and down the time-track of past, present, and future ... through our own Earth history ... and the Star Nations of other universes.

Dennison Tsosie's visions and messages are universal ... and speak to the hearts of all of us. They hold urgent warnings about the careless exploitation of Mother Earth, but also hope and excitement about the "window" that is open right now for rapid spiritual acceleration ... and the opportunity to play a part in changing a negative prophesy into a positive one.

The message is short: The universe is teeming with conscious, intelligent life, and we are all connected—*together* we can create peace and open our hearts to universal love.

Available from Blue Dolphin Publishing
1-800-643-0765 or www.bluedolphinpublishing.com